DANGEROUS
Normal People

Understanding Casanova Psychopaths & The Narcissistic Virus

L.W Hawksby

Grosvenor House
Publishing Limited

This book is published by
Grosvenor House Publishing Ltd
Link House
140 The Broadway, Tolworth, Surrey, KT6 7HT.
www.grosvenorhousepublishing.co.uk

A CIP record for this book
is available from the British Library

ISBN 978-1-78623-601-2

Foreword

This book is a work of "Creative Fiction". Creative Fiction is a common literary term used by memoir writers in particular. This label refers to the fact that this book is my own truthful version of events and where relevant I have altered names, locations and defining characteristics to protect people's anonymity. I have also omitted some people and some events to further protect the characters involved.

I've written it to educate the readers on classic Narc Abuse Behaviours in romantic relationships just like the ones I've had.

This book is not intended to hurt or harm any individuals' reputations or feelings. It is simply my story, described in stark reality, of what happened and how I felt. I've written it to educate the readers on classic Narc Abuse Behaviours in romantic relationships just like the ones I've had.

I've chosen a song for the end of each chapter which you may or may not choose to listen to. Music can be even more emotive than words and I hope for your learning experience to be as multi-sensory as possible. When I left my 2nd Narc, it took me almost 7 months to be able to listen to music that triggered any thoughts about him or how I felt when with him—so this is my celebration of sound as well as survival.

No matter how painful parts of the book are, I've tried to show that in time, we can be healed enough to find music enjoyable and I hope that sometimes my "choon" choices make you think... smile or even...laugh.

LWH, July 2019

Contents

Prologue - April 1st, 2016

I'm chatting casually to two dishy police officers standing side by side at the entrance to the riot van I'm in. The same police officers who, twenty minutes ago, read me my rights in my ex-partner's bedroom then removed me from his flat.

The creature who has us all here, unwanted guests at a really shit party, is otherwise engaged- storming back and forth, kicking things and ranting like a rabid bear in the living room in his flat across the road. A third officer is keeping him in his flat and away from me. Stretching a little, I can see up to the flat through the windows I recently cleaned to watch my ex strut back and forth.

His teeth will be gritted and he'll have one eye-pupil larger than the other. If I squint, I can just about see him rubbing his stubbled chin in false fear. He's doing it deliberately- taunting me. He knows I'm only outside. I know him like he knows me. Oil knowing fire.

The officers who arrived were unmistakably surprised that the significant hole in my ex's front door was caused by the size 5 Converse trainers, now on my knee in a clear plastic evidence bag. My slim feet not quite touching the floor of the van are cold. I shiver not from the temperature but with the realisation that not only is this the end of us, but the beginning of a long road to recovering who I used to be.

Tired suddenly, I look away from the flat and lock eyes with the officers stood in front of me. They look at me with a mixture of interest and concern. Both are quiet too now, and I realise they are standing together in the doorway of the van to keep me inside. Drawn faced and oddly calm, I unnerve them. I can feel it.

They expected a wild-eyed junkie with booze breath. They got a sober, petite blonde with a Highlands accent. The domestic incident was phoned in by his alcoholic mother nearly an hour ago now. Oh ho, ho, ho! Of course he phoned her! This clever little tactic allowed him to create a witness. She can now claim she heard me screaming and shouting and in particular, begging to be with him. Her wonderful ex-convict, cheating, drug addicted son. As has become the norm, he's drunk, unkempt and grassy. A researcher fresh from a fucking BBC Springwatch wrap party.

The flat is dark, untidy and smelling of a bizarre mix of fags and e-cig oil. Overnight, terribly distressed at the respectful ending of our perfect relationship, he's been on yet another binge he'll blame on me. The poor soul's exhausted, broken-hearted and desperate for peace from the crazed harpy sitting here now.

The door to the living room was open when they arrested me. Firm hands over my wrists, I was walked out into the hall and could hear him bellowing as clear as fresh ice. "She's just a slut from AA. I've been trying to help her! I don't even know her!". I looked up at the officer beside me and pulled the "I told you so" face.

Two minutes ago, the same (rather gorgeous) officer had held open my backpack. Wide-eyed and jaw twitching, he watched me gather hairpins from a bookshelf, walk back from the bathroom with toiletries, struggle to pull the second of two red high heels from under the bed and zip it up. Attached to the zip, a keyring with a picture of myself and the man I used to love. Faces close to the camera, in flattering black and white, we look happy, content and young.

As the officer and I stepped out into the stairwell, he nudged me and raised an eyebrow at the repeated slurred shouts of "I don't even know her!". In trying to bark a short laugh, it catches and I half gag.

"Yeah, that's me! I'm a no-one. Just some psycho- just like all the others, love".

He doesn't reply but the way he relaxes his grasp on my wrists and is more gentle walking me down the stairs tells me all I need to know. He believes me and I thank God for that.

What the Hell Happened?

I'm one of millions of people across the world who've engaged with people with personality disorders. Not all people with psychological challenges hurt others, of course not, however there are a cluster of disorders, further along the psychopathy spectrum, that are emotionally and sometimes physically dangerous to others.

All survivors of harm are strong, but the strongest strengthen themselves with knowledge and create an armour of intelligence to break the chain. I want to help as many people as possible avoid and safely leave NPD Abuse relationships.

I've spent the last 3 years in deep research mode, learning how to spot these unpleasant characters. I wanted to write down my story to help others be their own heroes. Join me in learning about the red flags of toxic people and help yourself in ways I couldn't.

Most of you won't like me, I'm not a very likeable person. I have many Narc characteristics and although I'm told I don't have a personality disorder, my anxiety disorder and bouts of depression can occasionally manifest in some socially challenging ways.

7.7% of men and 4.8% of women are thought to have Narcissistic Personality Disorder. Many victims believe this statistic to be grossly underestimated. Why? Because they are among the best actors and manipulators on the planet. They rarely volunteer for diagnosis or treatment and can have such huge egos they think that actually their behaviours are right, and the world around them is wrong.

My psychotherapist said to me in 2017 "if you are worried you're a narcissist, then you aren't one"- an interesting point.

Who lies next to you in bed while you read this? Who sits on the sofa opposite? Who do you share a desk with or who do you wave at in the school playground? We don't know narcissists and sociopaths until they show us, because they want to keep that side hidden.

What we can look out for are the patterns of behaviour that distinguish them from the perfectly normal weirdos, loners and oddballs who actually don't have it in them to hurt anyone on purpose.

Look past the homeless guy talking to the letterbox who makes you jump when he waves his arms about and shouts about lizards- look past him to the smiling, polished mother pushing a pram across the road, or maybe have a closer look at the good-looking guy she is holding hands tightly with.

The worst lesson is, victims of Narcs often attract more Narcs because once we are broken, Narcs know it and we attract them over and over again. Sharks circling bloodied water. Vultures growing in number as more and more land and peck at a corpse. Casanova Psychopath is a well-used and dare I say, clever term for people who have Narcissistic Personality Disorder (NPD) and who cruise through romantic (or simply sexual) relationships causing harm with the Narc traits deeply embedded in their souls.

When you reach the end of this book, you will know what a Casanova Psychopath really looks, acts and sounds like. You will have an insight into who they collect around them, especially malignant co-dependents. You will also have a greater understanding around the almost mythical Narcissistic Virus and how it manifests in the partners and ex-partners of true Narcissists featured here in my own story.

PART 1.
The Love Bombing

November 2013

My anxiety's been bad recently. I've started thinking about my eating again. Picking away at that old scab. Unveiling the vulnerable, delicate skin beneath. Wondering how I can hide a binge or purge now I live with a man.

When I start thinking about it, I'm usually heading for relapse, although to date I've been clean of it for several years. I can't understand why I still feel so uncomfortable in my own skin.

The restless dark feelings of something being wrong rise and fall like waves, often getting so big I feel like I'm drowning. It hasn't been this bad for almost a decade! Insecurity and tension nag away at me and my sleep is disturbed almost every night now. "Things will get better. They always do" I whisper to myself, marching round the park burning calories, worrying about money and trying to forget the cruel words my husband said last night.

On impulse, I've closed my laptop and packed a bag for a swim at a fancy hotel and spa near home and I already feel guilty. My husband and business partner, Niall, will be annoyed I split the day up and went on a "skive". Later I'll be called selfish and reminded he did a 10-hour working day while I "messed about".

Walking towards the unfamiliar changing rooms, alone and nervous I desperately want to go home. I've no idea why I thought this was a good idea. We are far too busy at work for me to bugger off in the middle of the day to mess about in a bikini.

Awkwardly re-tightening my ponytail, I stop dead at the entrance to the changing area. A woman walks into my back, forcing me forwards. "Sorry! Sorry! Sorry!" My fault! Sorry!" I babble at her. Suddenly the doors open and warm, moist chlorine thick air hits me. Closing my eyes, I can't help but inhale.

It reminds me of when I was little and my dad used to take me and my brothers to the swimming pool on the mainland. I'd go up and down the flume for hours, screeching with joy at the speed and rush of it.

I was always a water baby who loved water in any form. I wonder where she went? That carefree child unafraid of freezing cold water.

Snorkelling off Calgary Bay in windy Novembers. Jumping off the ferry pier in the summer holidays with the local boys. The only girl who dared do it.

I let the door slap closed behind me and keep going.

I swim six splashy laps and later, sit in the Jacuzzi absolutely shattered. Jeez, I thought I was fit?!

The thrill of this new experience falls away as fast as my skin cools. Starting to dread home and the stretching, tense demands of being a working mum and new wife, my heart flutters out of beat a little.

Shampooing my hair quickly and leaning backwards out of the jets, I can just about see the clock above the poolside. "Shit. Shit. Shitty shit"45 minutes to get dried, dressed and up the road before he's home. Shit, shit, shit.

Squeezing the water out of my long blonde hair I spin round looking for the towel I left aside. Wrapping it round my body and grabbing at shampoo and conditioner bottles, I get in a panic and drop one. It spins away from me back towards the pool. "Fuck sakes!" I hiss too loudly. A mother showering her young daughter nearby scowls at me. "Sorry- bit stressed," I say to her and she turns away.

Not watching where I'm going, I stumble a little on the slippery floor and have to pull the towel tight against my chest but with only 1 free and, can't tie it.

A blur of blue and red suddenly appears and in a heartbeat, I feel someone grab me. It's a lifeguard. I recognise the red & blue uniform. Pulling me into a full bear hug against his chest, I smell chlorine, Lynx and something else.

He lets go after almost 10 seconds. Looking up I'm drawn into this strange dark stare so intense I can't help but stare back. "You have beautiful eyes! are they green?!" Deep voice. Gravelly. Not quite pure Glasgow. He's smiling. Wide, full lips, 24-hour stubble and some acne. Oddly, just reaching his chest with my forehead, I note he's the same height as my husband Niall. No, he's a touch shorter.

"Erm....yeah. They change colour depending on my mood". This feels weird. Soaking wet and with a fluttering hand, I quickly pull my towel shut again. He steps back and squats easily to reach the escaped bottle. Handing it to me, I realise he hasn't taken his eyes off me yet.

My teeth start to chatter with the cold so I quickly take the bottle from him. "My husband says they go almost lime green.... like a lizard when I cry". Why am I telling this man that I even cry around my husband? Why mention such a personal thing? I'm annoyed at myself and feel a bit blind-sided. I'm never stuck for words—ever.

He steps back and now there's 3 feet between us. A space that should have been there 30 seconds ago.

He takes in my diamond engagement and wedding rings and the smile falters. This feels strange. I can't quite put my finger on why he feels like a memory.

In a heartbeat, the air moves and the shimmer of familiarity is gone. "I'll let you escape then," he says and smiles. He walks backwards, still gazing at me. A bit risky on a wet poolside, but he's assured in his steps. He's worked here a while and is confident. "I'll see you again though, won't I?" with a thumbs up and a wide smile. He even has the cheek to wink at me before turning and sauntering away back to high five another lifeguard I realise has been watching us.

Its Sonny's birthday today- 10 years old. My long-lost little Buddha now has gangly legs, a mop of curly blonde hair and brown doe eyes. He's becoming rangy but his pins aren't quite ready yet for sports. He just laughs insanely when he falls and gets hurt. A sweet balance of risk and fun like me. I'm glad.

I told Niall about the creepy lifeguard being over-familiar a few minutes ago and he gave me that flat, expressionless face with the cold fish eyes. It only leads on to the angry face with twisted mouth and some sort of catty comment aimed at my figure, clothing or personality. He likes to make me feel less than him when his own insecurities are bobbing on the surface.

"You need to make a complaint. That guy's a creep," he says, swearing and grunting, as he harshly pushes red trainers onto my middle son's feet. "Fuck sakes Charlie, bend your toes and push." Niall's face is red and Charlie looks panicked. I've pissed him off.

I shouldn't have told him what happened at the pool. I could kick myself.

"You go close the windows and put the lights off." I'm upset at how strained I sound. I wish he had more patience. It's a special day and already Niall's off on one and taking it out on my middle son as usual. "I'll make a complaint about the lifeguard if he does something weird again, ok?"

Standing in the doorway to the living room now, I watch his broad back jolt back and forth as he yanks blinds aside, searching aggressively for the window latches. "Whatever," he says to the glass and shrugs.

The Following Day

Half-crawling, half-frogging back and forth in the pool, I keep catching the lifeguard watching me. Maybe he's just especially focused on me because I'm new and he's concerned for my safety.

Later at home, Niall makes a point of asking if the lifeguard was "pervy" again. "He didn't even speak to me, Niall," I say with a sigh. "I told you I told HIM that I'm married and he saw my rings so that's that. Please be cool about this," I wheedle and reach out to touch his shoulder.

He stares at me for a few more seconds, trying to decide if I'm telling the truth and then bored with this micro power game, looks away.

His face in profile, I can see he's grinding his teeth. "Ok- fine. Do what you want," and walks out of the room. "I need dinner early because I've a client sit at 7 in Renfrew. It's a big one."

Deciding it's best to make more of an effort to appease him, I walk into the bathroom and plaster a smile on. "Look love, this guy is a bit chunky, he has loads of daft fake tan and I think it's false teeth he has. He's nothing on you." Niall starts to soap up and still hasn't spoken. "He even has a bit of a bald patch!"- Still not turning round, my husband finally speaks. "No problem. Can you shut the door, there's a draught"?

Chopping up salad ingredients 5 minutes later, I examine that the lifeguard is nice and tall yes, dark yes, and withstanding the belly, I can see he goes to the gym. Strangely enough, if he was better looking, he'd be my type I realise with a start. I get a creeping unease and chop harder and faster.

Niall, on the other hand, is a striking and proud academic man. Slim but not muscular, he wears clothes extremely well. He is vain and self-conscious. In fact, almost too vain as he never quite relaxes. I used to love his tautness & preening- now it makes me uneasy.

I've now swam 3 times this week and can feel my confidence coming back a little which is exactly why I started in the first place. Yes! This was a good idea!

Sitting, eyes closed, in the jacuzzi today, that lifeguard came up behind me and pulled my ponytail. As he wanted, I jumped in shock and turned round, so we chatted a little.

In banter I took the piss out of his unusually terracotta complexion "I've bad skin so I get free sunbed sessions at a hospital," he says sternly. Standing up straight, he then moves away from the side of the jacuzzi.

To break the tension, I try to appease him. "Och, chill your jets, I'm just kidding! I enjoy a sunbed myself every now and again. I reckon I get that seasonal affective disorder," I babbled. "Me too!" he said, eager like a child.

Crouching at the side of the jacuzzi again he asked me why I started swimming. "Anxiety and just some me-time I suppose," I said. "Oh! I have anxiety too!" he declares.

We spent another 10 minutes chatting until he took my hand and helped me get out.

Listen to: Taylor Swift: "I Knew You Were Trouble"

Red Flags:

- *"The stare"*. *Long, unfaltering and hunter-like. Many victims mention this when they explain the first time they engaged with their abuser. You may also, as many others do, feel uncomfortable and even feel that on this first impression you don't like the Narc. Listen to your instincts...*

6

- *Lack of humour around jokes targeted at them or about them. You may see a fleeting anger if you make the mistake of criticising or mocking a Narc, but the mask will be replaced quickly enough for you to wonder if it that reaction ever even happened.*

- *Lack of awareness of physical boundaries. This happens in particular with Casanova Psychopaths. It is their version of flirting. It's way beyond normal "chat". They have an innate confidence that they can touch you and enter your boundaries-even if it's inappropriate. In this instance I'm sure you don't need reminded I was in a swimming pool alone, barely clothed and had never spoken nor met The Lifeguard and yet before words were even exchanged, he hugged me.*

- *Mirroring. Narcs like to share past experiences, hobbies and tastes with you so in your earliest times engaging with them you will have huge amounts in common. It will be flattering, exciting and comforting to feel such an intense connection with this relative stranger.*

December 2013

I've made our family recipe Christmas cake with the traditional 1- month recipe of faffing about turning it, feeding it with booze, re-wrapping it and repeating the process every few days. You can't legally drive a car after just one slice.

It sits high up on a shelf in the hall cupboard, decorated with white icing and scattered with little edible penguins all in various snowy activities-fishing, skiing, crawling out of an igloo. One is even head-first in a little blue ice hole. The kids, especially my youngest, Rufus love it. Just looking at it makes me smile.

Quite a few times I've poked my head into the cupboard just to secretly glory in the damn thing!

On reflection, avoiding that lifeguard is a good idea. Something 's off with how I feel every time we speak. I have to accept he has a wee thing for me and at the end of the day, it's not cool having made it clear I'm married. He gives off this eagerness. It's like an almost needy air. Like he's lonely and it's me he wants to fix that. I hardly know him but feel almost guilty for not being single.

I've successfully avoided him around half the times I've been in the spa although when he is working, he still watches me. True, he has tried to talk to me a few times but feigning being late for the kids, or too busy trying to beat my swim times, means I can avoid too much interaction.

Kicking my legs out and holding onto the side of the pool, I'm taking a few breaths before finishing my swim with another dozen laps. Not really listening to the lifeguard rambling- I'm focused on trying to catch my breath.

"So yeah, I attract psychos and both mums are saying I can't see my kids this Christmas. It was the same last year. I just get on with it, to be honest." My ears prick up.

He's got my attention now- my ex, the father to my two older boys can be awkward about access. My, my, parenting issues! Another thing we have in common. "My eldest son is to someone I was with nearly 10 years, but my younger one, Dan, is to a one weekend-stand sort a thing. Someone I went with when I was in a bad place. She took advantage. Wanted a kid like all the women I meet. She lets me see Dan sometimes but really, I'm just a taxi driver when she can't get out of bed to get him to school."

How awful! I feel so bad for him. "Does your partner not help you with it?" I don't know what else to say.

"Nah. I've not got a girlfriend. There's someone I've been with once, no, twice now...but nothing important. I'm just lonely so when she comes to my door all rain-spattered and crying about some guy in her work she's shaggin'.... I just let it happen. That's what she did last week actually." He laughs and leans back. He brushes my arm so lightly I wonder if it was a mistake.

A strange bolt of something like surprise shoots through me at his words about the woman. He doesn't seem the type to be single. He's way too confident. "I want to settle down but it's just not happened for me yet. Maybe it never will." He holds my gaze for a few seconds before standing up and walking away. "See you tomorrow!" I shout before I can stop myself. He smiles widely like he's just received a surprise gift. It feels Nice.

15 minutes later, I'm standing in the locker area, shivering and trying to get the little key off my bikini bottoms. I can't get a grip of the pin because I'm juddering with the cold.

Feeling a presence behind me, I turn around. "Let me help." Before I can reply the lifeguard's bending over me. It takes him just 5 seconds to release the key and deftly open my locker. Blushing, I start to gather my things.

"Oh yeah. That woman I've seen a bit- you know, the one from last week! has just told me she's pregnant! Not exactly my plan but hey ho, it is what it is. Must have been last month, the first time I went with her I hit bullseye"

Glad to have my back to him, I wince, unable to hide the shock. I turn around. "Oh! that's great news! No?" He doesn't seem happy......"Yeah well, these things happen. She just wanted a kid. One of those psychos. You know the type," he looks sad.

"I'm sorry. That's shit for you. You just need to put your foot down when the baby arrives. Get legal advice and do what needs to be done."

He's looking at the top of my towel where the pressure of me holding it is pushing my cleavage up. I re-tie it higher so I'm better covered. "Very silly at your age...." I chastise and wag a finger at him. I can't help but feel a bit angry that he's chasing me and yet has just got some woman pregnant.

"Yeah... well... it's not my fault. Like I say, what will be, will be," he says. I'm surprised he's so laid back about it. "Well, I'm impressed you're handling it so well. Good for you."

Leaving later, I stop to watch him walk over to lift a struggling child out of the strong current in the wave pool. I wonder what sort of person deliberately gets pregnant. How can they have such a hunger for a child that they don't respect the man's wishes? I feel quite sorry for her, but more sorry for him.

Listen to: The Pogues: "Fairytale In New York"

Red Flags:

> *Confused instincts. First instincts are important self-preservation methods but Narcs will confuse them. We will have a feeling that something is off or not right, but the things they say and how they act contradict it. There is a theory that when we meet a Narc, a deep-seated animalistic sense that they are dangerous does exist.*

> *The Pity Party. You may find yourself seeing the Narc as a poor, hindered victim when you actually have no evidence of it. They will use sob stories and support-gathering early on because they want you to like them, feel like you need to help or look after them and most of all, see other people in their life as "the bad guy". This is early training you for later, when you are supposed to hate the "bad guys" and ignore any hint of wrong-doing by your Narc. They are also testing your empathy levels and ability to believe the crap they spout.*

January 2014

I learned to swim on a holiday to Crete when I was 7. My dad spent hours each day teaching me the crawl and "the frog". We sunburned our backs while our bellies stayed white. Dad was so thrilled when I eventually swam the ultimate goal- 10 strokes with no going under. It wasn't pretty, but it was proper swimming.

My mum read her Jilly Cooper books, sometimes watching us quietly under dark Ray-Ban sunglasses, skinny legs all bitten by mozzies and covered in Germolene.

My two younger brothers would play at digging big, deep, cold sandy holes nearby their blond heads as close as Siamese twins.

I've decided that the lifeguard, whose name is still a mystery to me, isn't creepy. Just sad. He's told me he had a rubbish Christmas worrying about this new baby and most importantly how he'll pay for it. In fact, he wasn't as cool and collected today. Not at all.

"She caught me on purpose. She did this deliberately," he wails and looks almost tearful. I feel a spurt of anger at this woman, whoever she is!

"Why do I keep meeting all these nutters?" he sighs & leans against the tiled wall with his eyes closed in stress. Uneasily I look over to see if anyone can see how upset he is. "I just want to meet a nice girl. Someone like you." Suddenly cheeky again, he smiles and gives me a gentle shove in the shoulder as though we are old buddies.

"Hah! You need to stop shagging about then. Casual sex? And with another psycho?!" I back away and waggle my fingers at him. "I know how to pick 'em!" he calls after me then wanders off out of view.

Sliding into the water and taking a breath at how cold it is today, I can't help but feel pleased he confides in me. I feel useful and warm knowing he trusts me to share his troubles.

He's just a nice, easy-going, sensitive guy. I like the way he makes time for the older members of the pool and how he jokes around with the children. A real shame he's having a shitty time.

Listen to: Heart: "Barracuda"

Red Flags:

- *Narcissists will have a trail of psycho friends or psycho ex-partners behind them. You may notice they don't say what they did wrong, only in what those "nutters" did wrong. It runs alongside the Pity Party work they do with you. The Narc makes you feel valued & useful to their own well-being. It feeds your ego and natural desire to help others. In fact, a Narcs favourite food is The Empath. So, watch out if you are one!*
- *Signs of Selfishness. At the start, these are quite discreet, for example here the lifeguard makes no mention of concern for anyone else other than himself and oddly is focused on the monetary challenges instead the pregnant woman or new life about to enter the world.*

February 2014

Something's up with Niall. I feel a twitch of worry in my chest and keep flicking my eyes away from the kids to watch him. Like a sniper he's scanning the hotel spa reception area from where we are seated in the bar- café. "Eat the last bit, Charlie," I say, and hand my little boy the last bit of cake stuck to the wrapper. "It's bloody expensive in here." I wink at him and he smiles a big crummy, chocolate smile.

I ruffle his mop of brown hair and pass my youngest, a napkin at the same time- he's got lemon buttercream on his nose. "Lick it off Rufus. Don't waste it," I say to him and tap it gently. "More cake," he says & rubs greasy, sweet sponge in his hair with both hands.

I swipe his little nose with my finger and lick the cream myself, smiling at my little boy. Looking up to share the joke with my husband, I see only an empty chair. My mouth goes dry.

Spinning round left then right, I stop to catch Niall stood a few yards away with his back to me. He's almost touching the glass with his face and staring out at the pool. Quickly pushing my chair back, I walk over to give him a cuddle from behind. Placing my hands on his chest I rest my chin on the back of his left shoulder. I can feel how tense he is.

"He's not in today, Niall ....."- It's true, I haven't seen him.

"I think you should stop coming here," he grunts, brushing past me. I watch as he lifts Rufus from his high chair and walks fast out to the car park. I feel something close to fear spread through me.

Roughly undressing and quietly crying, I'm getting ready for a swim. Its early evening and an unusual time for me to be here but I had to get out of that house and escape.

What a fucking nightmare. Quite possibly the most embarrassing work thing ever happened today!

Half-way through the judging for a business competition I entered us in, Niall started interrupting my presentation! Panic, then embarrassment spread through me as, red in the face, he started to argue with both my points and the questions the competition judges had. I was doing really well and started to pick up on the judges smiling and nodding to each other. My confidence grew and the flow just got better and better...then Niall kicked off.

It was like he was on drugs or hated me or something- as he watched me he gradually went all flat-faced until both eyebrows knitted together in one solid, bushy line.

I think he swore a few times too. Struck dumb, I gave in and just stood there in my little pink shift dress, mouth agape while he completely sabotaged it.

Walking out into the car park, the shouting match started. "You're not as good as you think you are"; "you're stupid"; "I'm degree educated- I'm the fucking expert"; "no one likes you anyway"; "you have no friends."

Over and over he rants as we get in the car and pull away. "That's it. This is a fucking stupid idea. I can't work with you. Your ideas are stupid. We need to make money, not do competitions or work with charities, you stupid bitch!" he said as we pull too fast out onto the motorway. Over and over, mile after mile, he raged at me and it feels like he will never stop.

I cried most of the way, but then near home, he stopped the car and we sat in the silent, seething atmosphere together. The usual pattern; his rage replaced by embarrassment and silence and later no apology. As soon as we unlocked the door to the flat, I grabbed my swim bag and left.

I didn't have anywhere else to go.

"I'm mortified. I don't understand why he did that!" I sob 5 minutes later as the lifeguard walks me over to the side of the pool, away from prying eyes. I tried brave-facing it but as soon as I saw a friendly face, fell apart.

"What a total dickhead," he says. I can't help but laugh at his bluntness. Sniffling, I wipe my nose on the blue paper towel he's handed me. "Niall is a good man really. Well, sometimes he is. I don't know! He just does this sometimes. Goes way over the top. Says the most horrendous things and then later expects me to just.... forget it and move on." There it is again, that shooting pain of knowing this just isn't right. My marriage quite frankly is not right.

Burying my face in the paper towel, I feel a gentle squeeze as the lifeguard takes my arm in comfort. "Come on, let's go and sit away from everyone else in the disabled changing room."

"He's an ugly bastard anyway," the lifeguard says as we sit down side by side. I'm ashamed seconds after I let the giggle escape. "Give over, don't say that. He's my husband!"

But... I like this. I like someone comforting me. Someone on my side. Feeling like I'm special. I've stopped crying now and admittedly, do feel much calmer.

"I'm due on my break now anyway. Let's sit here and talk for a bit. You don't want your boys seeing you this upset, do you? Not over an arsehole like him!" This time I don't correct him.

Over the next few weeks, we get closer- he confides that the pregnant ex is not letting him attend any maternity appointments and is making noises that he may not get to see the baby when it arrives. He looks so sad telling me this. "Just give her space and wait it out," I say with a gentle smile.

I still don't know his name but he knows mine. He must've overheard me telling another customer or lifeguard. I've begun swimming with a lady called Roz. She's in her 50s & is some sort of medical professional. I chat to other regular swimmers in the jacuzzi about my boys, but to her, I share the growing flirtation between the lifeguard and I. "Enjoy it!" she says. "Don't end up like me- married all these years and getting my fun online from some photographer friend in Dundee!" It makes me smile. This feels like permission.

Him chasing me has gone from feeling mostly odd and out of place, to mostly flattering and pleasant. I like it but know I shouldn't.

Listen to: Fleetwood Mac: "Little Lies"

Red Flags:

- _Manipulation._ Narcs have a special attraction that often comes from how well they seem to know how to be around you, what to say and how to come across in different

14

circumstances. This makes you feel calm and safe and makes them appear consistent. It is subtle but it works and you won't recognise its fraudulent until it's too late.
- *Coercing you into verbally betraying people you care about. They want to know how loyal you are to the people they want out of your life. They like to feel that you see them as better than a current partner or friend. They will tempt you into criticising or moaning about whatever it is that they see as competition or a barrier to them getting you in their clutches.*

March 2014

"That's the best bum I've ever seen!" comes his distinctive voice out of nowhere. Spinning round, I find him slightly to my right. Fixated on getting warm in the Jacuzzi, I've accidentally ignored him.

Blurting this apparent compliment to get my attention, I'm a little shocked at him. His colleague, Steven, looks embarrassed, then I see him nudge his friend. Smiling a little awkwardly, I turn away and continue walking. I overhear Steven's harsh whisper "You need to apologise. She might make a complaint". Feeling a bit uncomfortable & unsure, I swerve the Jacuzzi in favour of a quick shower and home.

As I reach the showers, he taps my shoulder and starts to apologise before I even turn to face him. "I'm sorry. That was out of order. Please accept my apology."

I don't want him to be embarrassed, and for sure, it's not the first time he's over-stepped. "It's okay- honestly. It's been said before and will be said again." We laugh together and relaxed now at my ease with his mistake, he walks away. I wave at Steven & watch as they high five each Other then make X signs with their arms & laugh.

A yell and a splash catch my attention as I reach the wall at the end of the pool. Turning around, I hold onto the side to see what the ruckus is.

The lifeguard has childishly leapt in and is now swiftly swimming towards me. This feels intimate. He's no longer in

uniform and I am as usual in a two piece. Swimming together?
No, that's not right.

Swiftly lifting myself out of the pool, I poke my feet into
poolside sliders and grab my towel. Even with my back to him, I
hear clearly "Oh dear, something I said!" in an exaggerated,
affronted tone. I then hear him laughing and can tell he is right
below me in the water. Wrapping myself in my towel I turn
around. He's less than a foot away, bobbing below me and
smiling. He could lick my feet if he reached out. Stepping back,
I hold the towel tighter.

"No. I have to get up the road for the kids, I'm finished my
swim." I look pointedly at the smart brass clock on the wall
behind him & to my relief, it is indeed just after 2. He's finished
his morning shift and immediately got in the pool- to see me.

At my rejection, something flashes in his face. All jokes over,
I see annoyance in the set of his jaw and darkening of his eyes. For
a heartbeat, I feel bad for him. He's crushing all over me and I've
embarrassed him. "Look, today's too late for me. Maybe another
time." There I've said it before even I wanted to.

"Good. I'll look forward to it," he says, swimming backwards.
Now he looks easy-going and comfortable again. He turns in the
water and easily cuts through it away from me like a shark.

One minute I like him, the next I don't like myself. Things are
slipping and not in a good direction. He put me on the spot. No,
I wanted him to ask me! Oh fuck, I don't know.

It's harmless. I've plenty of male friends online- some ex's too!
It's fine. It's no big deal. Today the lifeguard just came out with
"Oh are you on Facebook?" like that's a perfectly normal thing to
ask a woman in a bikini in your place of work. Well, it is normal!
We are friends, kind of now?! That's how people make friends-
through the gym or some other hobby? I know he fancies me,
fucking Stevie Wonder could see it, but it's fine, I can handle this.
It's just harmless fun that isn't even really flirting on my part. Less
than 30 minutes later, the friend request buzzes in my pocket.

Sitting in the bus shelter a few metres down from my flat, I
open the notification. An extremely camp selfie in what looks like
his living room opens up. Gross...a red leather sofa?! Accepting

the request with the message "Are you sure you aren't gay?!" and laughing emojis to soften the cheek, my heart thuds with the thrill of this new excitement and a new friend, called Jonathan.

Having a nosey and cruising through his page I skim read stupid blokey chat streams with what looks like mostly other guys from his work and to be honest, I'm almost bored. He sounds chavvy, almost immature and I'm slightly surprised. Different online to how he is with me in the pool.

The boredom is replaced by a judder of anger when I see that he has "engaged" as his relationship status. He's charged round that pool making me feel special and important for the last 4 months! "Your Facebook profile says you're engaged. What's that about?!" seems the only thing to type in my second message to him today. Sitting at my laptop, jiggling bare feet in annoyance, I can't help but feel pissed off.

His fucking friends and colleagues have watched him chase me for months! Impatient, I storm into the kitchen. Niall's at a client meeting and the boys are playing Xbox next door.

At the sink, I wash 2 already clean glasses and a plate. Walking back into the living room, I can see the message has been read in the short time since I sent it. The messenger app dots are flickering. He's typing something. This better be good!

Four laughing emojis come through first and I want to slap the screen.

"Yeah. I just seen it myself. That's that pregnant psycho one I told you about. She's hacked my computer. It's sorted now". More laughing emojis and several kisses.

The surge of relief is distinct but uncomfortable. It shouldn't matter to me but it does. "Jesus- you sure do pick em! How the hell did she manage to get in your page and do that?!" Admittedly, a little jittery, I wait for his reply.

"My password's easy. She knows enough about me to guess it was one of my kids' names and then all she had to do was put my email or mobile in. I'm fucking changing it all and blocking her, again! She's crazy."

I check, and he is telling the truth. Status now: single. We chat a bit more and he tells me my picture is "stunning". I haven't been

17

called stunning in years and it feels good! It's been a long time since I felt good or I felt someone liked me, just for me.

Listen to: Clean Bandit: "Symphony"

Red Flags:

- *Things feel out of your control. When you are engaging with a Casanova psychopath (in particular) you will find you feel like something significant is happening. It can be a bit like a runaway train and you don't know where it's going or what led to it but you are swept along and often in a direction you know you shouldn't go.*
- *The Chase. Natural hunters, greedy and persistent, the chase is all part of the fun. They love harder targets like very attractive people, married people or really anyone who seems to stubbornly remain dismissive or neutral to their charms. Narcs need us to be trusting and naïve too...it's awful that these traits make us vulnerable isn't it?*
- *Different Personalities in different contexts. Narcs have no real true self so often mirror other people's accents or behaviours to "fit in" and stay "in the gang". They may even use different language and accents. They will behave around you the way they believe YOU want them to behave. Narcs will be subtly different to how they speak and act with friends, family, colleagues and so on. In Narc terminology we call this "wearing a Mask".*
- *No empathy or respect for your moral boundaries. With a Casanova psychopath, a wedding ring, young children at home or workplace rules will not stop them from pursuing you. Beware anyone who seems to need more than simply "I'm not single" or "I'm married" or "I'm not looking for a relationship" to simply leave you alone. *One day you will be at home and the Narc will be pursuing another target. He will chase her just as he chased you.*
- *Inconsistencies. Strange little things like this "engaged status" story will keep happening, maybe getting worse. You might*

find out they don't really work where they say or perhaps a deceased family member really isn't dead! They will have an unusual cover story or excuse when caught out on these lies to appease you & keep you on side.

April 2014

Fearing Jonathan had lied to me the duration of our friendship, for only those few minutes, unsettled me to quite an extreme level & I didn't like how I felt. This last few days; I've realised an emotional boundary has been crossed. Yes, I'm glad he is after all single, but I still want to pull back. I've decided to stop swimming for a bit and get my mess of a head together.

"I've missed you" comes a message while I run a bath. "Are we okay?" Jonathan asks with little sad emoji faces. "Still friends?"

"I'm just busy at home with Niall and the kids- you need to refocus! Go get that female sorted with that baby!" Trying to sound like I don't care, I follow up with laughing emojis and a punching fist.

"Lucy! Where's my blue shirt?! The one with the horse logo thing on it!" Niall shouts from the bedroom. I've only just sunk into the blissfully hot soapy water.

Sighing, I stand to get out of the bath & pad through to the bedroom. "It's already been ironed. I hung it on a hanger on the dryer in the boys' room so it doesn't get creased in the wardrobe, Niall," "Oh- good. Cheers," he says and brushes past me. "I think I might wear the pink one anyway. Can you heat the iron up?"

It's after 10 pm and I'm on Facebook reading other people's news and fielding referendum-based character attacks. Niall 's snoring next to me, facing the wall.

Ping. Message! It is a picture of a penis. The lifeguard's! I recognise the red shorts he swims in and the tattoo on his hand holding himself. Proud & unashamedly aroused, the penis has also sent a message! "missing you" and heart-eyed emojis. Trying to breathe properly, I keep opening and closing my eyes and trying to focus. It's right there. A willy. Another man's willy.

Jolting backwards I glance at Niall, then back to the laptop. Yep, still there. I slap the laptop shut and wince- that could be a sore one! I giggle. then place my hands over my mouth then fully over my face. Fuck, fuck, fuck. What the hell am I supposed to do now?!

I've never had a kinky picture sent to me, which seems a little sad since apparently, everyone does it! Niall's never sent me anything vaguely sexy and frankly, I never trusted anyone enough to do it myself. It's never been my thing and I never thought it would be but here, now.... I feel that long- gone flicker and warmth in my lower tummy that hints at passion and excitement.

At this point, I know I am on the edge (at the very least) of a cyber affair. This guy just seems to know what buttons to push. No man has ever focused on me so intently, in so many varied ways or for so long.

Distant warning bells are going off. They get closer & louder hour by hour and I lie there sleepless all night.

The chemistry between us is so obvious, colleagues are commenting on it now. I've not returned anything sexual online and I'm trying my best to manage this situation but, by God, it is addictive.

The attention is undeniably feeding the gaping hole in my confidence that's slowly opened up over the last few years. I'm weak and becoming more entranced.

Jonathan's Facebook has little to no comments or pictures of "the" ex or any other ex's: Insanely pleased by this, I relax further.

He's started to send me links to songs in the dozens of messages he favours me with across each day and long into the night. It feels strangely old-fashioned and romantic.

Sometimes he films himself in his car or kitchen, singing along to the songs. Almost cringing at how self-absorbed it is, I soften when I realise he's doing it for me. Embarrassing himself to make me feel good.

"Have you ever done this before? The pictures? The songs?" It's taken me 3 days to pluck up the courage to ask him about this. He's just so good at seducing me! I desperately want for this to be a unique experience between us. I wouldn't be lying to my husband if I thought it was any less.

"Never," he replies, assured and plain. That one-word message makes my heart lift. "You're different. I've never met anyone like you. I want You." Oh shit. I'm falling hook, line and sinker for this passionate, intense man.

A year later I find out this "musical wooing" is one of his favourite techniques to get females on-side. I'm not his first or his last.

Niall and I are getting dressed up to head out socially for the first time in months. We've been invited to a charity fundraising night in town. Having chosen a turquoise lace dress with a plunging neckline, and I impulsively send Jonathan a selfie. This is the first kind of sexy picture I've sent him. Emboldened by pre-departure drinks, I just went and did it.

He immediately replies with "Wow!" and asks where we are going. There are no kisses or emojis this time from him and I can almost taste the bitterness of his jealousy.

"A night out," I type and sign off. I'm determined to stay in control.

"How was your fancy night out then?" Jonathan is leaning on the metal railings at the side of the children's pool, pretending to be on guard. He hasn't made eye contact with me yet. In fact, he seems a little unsettled.

I've never seen him so...brittle. I'm a little hungover from the thing last night & could do with some friendly chat.

"Och it was a charity thing in town. Somewhere near Central Station. It was Roz from in here who mentioned it actually. She came too.

It wasn't just Niall and me." He stiffens and slowly turns to look at me. Omg, he's furious! I feel a surge of fear. "What's the matter? Are you ok?"

"A charity thing that Roz told you about?! Fuck sakes, I was invited to that! I changed my mind at the last minute! Fucking hell!" he hisses at me. Standing there stupidly, I watch dumbstruck as he storms away to climb back up into the chair above the pool. Wrong-footed, I feel the urge to cry, so half-run to the changing area and away from whatever it is that just happened.

I haven't heard from him all day and have felt stressed and unhappy. Opening Facebook, I decide to draft a light and friendly message. A sort of veiled enquiry into why he acted like he did. "Hi! Are you ok?"- it's pretty basic but I'm unsure what else to put.

The message doesn't get delivered. It just sits there in the online ether, laughing at me. There's a rush of blood to my feet and my heart falls off rhythm. What the actual fuck?! He's blocked me. Just like that? He's blocked ME?

Of course, he hasn't blocked me. It's a glitch. Maybe I've lost internet signal. The weather's bad tonight. With trembling fingers, I type his name and search for his Facebook page. It's gone. I can't find it.

Grunting a sob of frustration, I realise that absolutely he's blocked me. Me? His favourite person, ever. Or so he said.

Its oddly like being dropped off a cliff. The surprise and shock floods through me. Confusion and loss follow next. Am I being punished for taking control? I don't understand what's happened. I'm ashamed that losing contact with him makes me feel so lost.

I lie quietly crying on the sofa, like a child in a blanket tent, until creeping into bed with Niall at sunrise to pretend nothing has happened.

It's Easter break and we are at Mum and Dad's house on Mull with the children. The weather is unseasonably warm and the children are racing around in excitement, squeals and shrieks so high-pitched and frantic that they could be mistaken almost for fear instead of thrill.

Dad has shouted up the stairs that porpoises are playing in the bay in front of the house. I'm standing at the port-hole-style window upstairs and searching the sea for a glimpse of them. I've been sitting up here pretending to read. In a mild depression, I feel extraordinarily lonely and ashamed. Moody and pale, I cry late at night and fake smiles when I need to.

Watching the water turn and spit as the porpoise roll and dance with each other, I lean my head against the cool glass of the window and momentarily close my eyes. When I open them, the porpoise have moved further down the sound. Smaller now, I can just see foam and movement and not the lovely detail of their almost mythical forms.

They are heading to deeper sea, perhaps to Coll or Iona. I step back and wipe away a small greasy mark on the window pane with my jumper sleeve. Cold constantly at the moment, I've borrowed one of Dad's big Arran jumpers he uses for his work as a wildlife expert. It smells faintly of grass and cow manure. Sitting down on the chair outside my parents' bedroom door, childlike with my head between my knees, I close my eyes. Memories of picking field mushrooms, waiting for long-awaited otters to surface and falling over unexpected molehills racing down to the shore of white sandy beaches give me a lump in my throat.

It's been 5 days since I last heard from Jonathan. The sudden change in temperature in my life is stark. I feel as though things have lost their colour. It's almost like my skin, my clothes, even things around me have faded and become washed out.

I leave the chair to sit on the top step to watch the children occasionally dart below me. The staircase is a wrought iron design based on marsh reeds intertwining. I push my palm onto one of the cold metal leaves and feel the soothing nip of pain. At least now I am feeling something other than almost overwhelming twists of shame and confusion.

I stand up suddenly- this is pathetic. Ok- he might have been great company. But, but, fucking but! He has acted like a dick this time and a crappy 5 months of chasing me round a swimming pool and making me feel like I mattered is not the stuff of grownups. I'm a mother and a wife and I need to sort myself out. Slamming my fists onto my thighs, suddenly I stand up.

"Right- let's ask Grandad to get the telescope out and see if we can see these porpoise properly!" It's an almost convincing spurt of positivity. "Boys! Where's Grandad?!"

We've driven to a nearby beach with a bold plan to dig in the mountain stream that slithers into the sea for the small, sweet, freshwater oysters free to collect every year. The sand is

23

dark grey and the children look almost like war casualties washed up on the beach.

Rufus's nose is pink from the late spring sun and he is angry the sand is stuck to him. He hates mess of any kind and gets extra bad-tempered when things don't do as he expects.

He thinks the sand will just brush off- it won't, it's wet and sticky and I try to console him. His chubby hands frantically swipe left, then right, up, then down on his shorts, and I keep batting them away to help him.

"Wait- let mummy do it Roo-Roo." Leading him closer to the shore, I pick a small rock pool and gently rinse his little legs. He smiles when he sees his clean, white, freckled legs reappear. "Tankoo Mummy," he says, smiling up at me.

This is what life is all about- not about fucking cheesy, seductive charmers or hotel swimming pools or cheap bikinis and blushes in the effing showers. It's about my sons. A life- a good, normal life.

Suddenly I feel better now, looking into his big round turquoise eyes, determined I'm going to put this embarrassing, stressful mistake down to experience. I really was stupid to let my head get turned. Really fucking stupid.

The pictures I choose to post online later are classic Easter Holiday. Niall and I looking tired and hungover, arms around each other's waists, smiling at the camera. The kids, spiky-haired, sat on a pier with legs across each other, looking out at a tin foil sea.

My parents watching TV on separate sofas, refusing to look at the camera. Mum with a large red wine in her hand, her glasses perched on the end of her nose, Dad intensely watching the football munching cheese & olives like he hasn't just had an entire roast dinner.

Sitting next to the fire, I read through all the nice comments on our photographs and I think about what was very nearly cheating on my husband. So, so close and look what nearly happened! I've been naïve, blind, greedy and selfish. I know this. My dinner settles hard in my gut and want to be sick.

Reaching for yesterday's newspaper now, I've been logged out of Facebook for only a minute or so before I feel my pocket buzz.

"I need you. I want you. I can't lose you." Out of nowhere, he's back.

I catch my breath and look over at Niall. He's watching the football and occasionally sipping from a bottle of beer I opened for him a few minutes ago.

"I'm going to bath the boys," I say, faking a stretch and standing up. My hands are shaking as I put my own glass on the coffee table. "Hmmm. Ok. Cool," Niall says without looking at me. "Mind and don't use conditioner on Rufus's hair. It makes it greasy and flat," he says, still not looking at me.

"What do you want?" I type as soon as I get upstairs "You fucking blocked me last week. You made me feel a complete dick!"

"I got scared. I was falling for you." comes his lightning bolt reply. I have to sit down. "Well, that's no way to treat someone you've got close to. No way to treat someone you like!"

Waiting for the apology, I can't help but feel anxious. "Ok, friends again?" he types, all laughing emojis and green hearts.

I don't like being tugged backwards like this, but his reappearance in my world makes me feel so good. With the rush of relief, I tingle like I'm coming back to life. Not wanting to push for an explanation, and unsure what to say to avoid him being angry again, I try to sound casual about this recent blip between us.

"Ok, but don't do that to me again. Whatever this is should at the very least have a semblance of kindness and what you did was unkind," I type back. "I can't bear huffs or the silent treatment, Jonny!"

"No problem. Scouts' honour!" he replies. I smile and mutter to myself, "You better not" and sign off.

Listen to: Katy Perry: "Hot and Cold"

Red Flags:

- *Shock Tactics.* One minute *"how are you today"* and the next *"I want to fuck you right now"*. It is these surprise pieces of flattery and aggressive attempts at seduction that keep Narc *targets interested and on tenterhooks waiting for the next time it happens. Because let's face it, in the main part, it feels good.*

- *Editing the Past. is rather narcissistic. Posting online to suit the stories they tell off-line. They will often delete entire relationships, weeks, months or years in one fell swoop once they choose a new victim. Beware the person who easily just deletes/blocks other human beings who once were special to them. Online life and offline life should be honest and reflect each other. If it doesn't, this person is duplicitous at the very least and someone you should be wary of.*

- *Isolation. You are often adrift and alone in these complex early days of the relationship because the Narc has either chosen you because you HAVE to be discreet, or made it clear they prefer it that way, PLUS it's embarrassing isn't it, your beloved being so....hot and cold. Why would you tell anyone who respects you that you feel like a puppet?!*

- *Hoovering. This is the term for those sudden passionate messages, half-apologies and compliments that the Narc will randomly cast your way after giving you either your marching orders or a period of silence. They won't necessarily apologise for what they have done to hurt or upset you...but they will shower you with their feelings for you and hopes for the future.*

May 2014

"I can get you in for free so now you have no excuse not to come with me," Jonathan says as he guides me gently, but rather fast, down the corridor away from the pool towards the hotel gym. "Go on then," I say with a smile. He puts his arm around my shoulder and we walk together.

Only yesterday I'd said for the hundredth time "I don't want to join the gym. It's just a meat market for pervs to chase women in Lycra!"

"That won't happen- you're with me now," he said, his dark eyes on mine. Day by day I'm discovering that he is everything I could ever want in a man. Strong, safe, passionate and romantic. He's perfect.

"I'm leaving hospital. I need your help. On my own and really ill" the text reads.

What the hell has him so ill he's been in hospital? Maybe a gym accident or something worse? In a panic, I'm already trying to think up an excuse to go to his rescue.

"Give me half an hour. I'll come across town and bring you some food and get you settled." I send. Where are his friends and family? Poor guy. Immensely sorry for him, I'm also absurdly flattered he has contacted me asking for my help.

Already wearing fresh gym gear, I've told Niall I'm going for a park run. Worry smothers the pang of guilt that shoots through me as I read the address off the text that Jonathan has just sent me. The taxi-driver looks confused and I'm not surprised.

In the centre of town, near to where he lives, I buy a chicken and some pasta along with some garlic cream cheese, good olive oil, parsley and lemons. I'll make him something comforting and wholesome like a friend should. It's a deliberately quick meal to prepare. I don't have long and must get home.

The door opens and yes, he does look ill. He's even hobbling a bit. I cook and chat as he sits at the small, white table he has up against the window in his decent-sized kitchen. I've never been in his flat before so feel a bit awkward and even a little shy. Chattering away and trying to ignore big butterflies, I'm probably talking too much. He's relaxed having declared he is "absolutely starving".

"I can't stay long." Avoiding eye contact, I pour sauce onto the pasta and stir. I catch his reaction out of the corner of my eye. His face falls then noticing me see this, he juts his bottom lip out in a sad wee boy face. "Stay as long as you can, please? I'm really rough, Lucy".

"Give over you! I'll make you some food then I have to go. You're a big boy. Man up!" Hot, garlicky steam rises up as I tip a portion into a bowl in front of him. Leaning back away from it, I giggle. "You are smokin'!" Jonathan says in his best Jim Carey voice. Retorting with "Shut up and stay sick!" I walk away to start the washing up.

For the next 15 minutes, I watch him play with the food, turning it round and round. Eating small mouthfuls, slowly. "I feel so ill, Lucy. I can only eat a bit." Sliding the bowl away from in front of him, I start to stand up. He catches me round the hips and tugs me forward quickly. Standing over him now, I stop breathing as he looks up at me.

"You do know I will have you, don't you?" Firmly and confidently, he doesn't blink saying this. I'm shocked. He's so direct! Blushing, I look away. There's that intense look again.

"No chance! Never gonna happen. You're having my pasta, not me, mate." Laughing a tad uneasily, I pull away.

Stepping backwards towards the neutral safety of the oven hob, I frantically brush down my denims, trying to remove any trace he's touched me. "Come on then, let's have a coffee," he says, and before I can respond he's beside me and reaching over my shoulder for the kettle. "Jonny- I really need to go. Honestly...."

He's already got two cups out and starts to deftly spoon coffee granules in. "A quick coffee then I'll let you go. I'm rubbish on my own," he says, looking at me & smiling. He has colour in his cheeks now and moves effortlessly around the kitchen finishing the hot drinks I really don't want to stay for.

20 minutes later we are still sat on his extremely uncomfortable and rather small, red leather sofa. We've spoken about my swimming, the gym, the kids. He's complained that the baby is due in only a few months but he still hasn't seen the mother nor had anything to do with any appointments.

"That's fucking terrible Jonny, you need to get that sorted because when the baby arrives, she will be tired and bad-tempered and won't let you see it anyway. Get a hold of her now while you can. While she is excited for the birth," I advise. He looks at me and shrugs "Nah- it's pointless. She's a psycho. I just have to get on with my life," he mutters and throws back the last of his coffee.

"I'm honestly really sorry for you." He looks out of the window as I say this and I wonder if he's on the verge of tears. His face in profile looks handsome and sad. I really need to leave and go home to my husband. I'm afraid of the growing care I have for Jonathan.

In a heartbeat, the sofa squeaks as he slides towards me, all comedy coy. Now he's different. Not sad. Now he's more....

cheeky. Teasing. Suddenly, like a naughty child, he sticks his tongue out at me. He has actually, just stuck his tongue out at me!

"Jonny-, I mean it. Give over. I'm friend-zoning you!" Trying but failing to be firm, I can't help but laugh. Leaning back awkwardly, I'm trying to get some space between us. Squashed against the arm of the sofa and him, I have nowhere to go. Instinctively, I know he's absolutely going to make a physical move on me if I don't leave. Maybe it's the medication, but he looks different. Much better.... excited...a little predatory in fact.

"Jonny. I have to get the kids." Half-sliding off the sofa, I must look ridiculous! A quick push of my hands and blessedly I'm standing now, a foot away from him.

My phone's buzzing in my pocket so I get the 'sad little boy who lost his toy' look again. He withdraws his hand from the arm of the sofa nearest me. "Go on then. I'll let you go," he says, stretching his arms across the back of the sofa, uncaring if I stay or leave now, he looks completely at ease. When he walks me to the door, he walks in no obvious discomfort. The prostate infection he said had him in hospital today, seems to have solved itself.

In his long, slightly gloomy hall, we awkwardly stand too close together as I wait for him to open the door. He leans in to kiss me so I step back and bark a laugh. I wag my finger at him and he shrugs. As I step into his stairwell, I turn to say goodbye but the door is shut in my face. Maybe a gust of wind from the open kitchen window pushed it a bit harder than he meant.

Walking fast down the road towards the city centre, I feel intense relief I didn't do anything silly. I just want to get home. A shiver runs down my spine so I put my gym top on, pull the hood up over my head and start to Run.

Listen to: Tom Jones: "Mamma Told Me Not to Come"

Red Flags:

- *Masks Slipping. Quick changes in manner when a Narc doesn't get what they want. They can simply make you disappear by slamming a phone down, shutting a door, walking away or (as already mentioned) blocking you on social media.*

- *Not caring that being cut off or blocked upsets you. This is because they simply don't care that their choice to stop contact (for whatever reason) hurts. They have no empathy and are most likely focusing their interest on another target while you cry and beg to communicate or get answers. Doing it again and again even after promising not to, is a form of emotional abuse.*

- *Hero Making. Casanova Psychopaths will make you their hero. Their saviour. Put you in the position of caregiver even though they have friends, family, parents or colleagues who would be more appropriate. They know it will make you feel useful and special and is also another test to establish how much you care about them.... It can also be a way to get you alone with them.*

- *Making a joke out of any inappropriate or harmful behaviour. They will say any embarrassment they cause you is "just messing around". They will minimise what in essence could be borderline sexual harassment, especially if it is during a time you should not expect it or when they have you there for some other (innocent) reason. You might wonder if you imagined any "passes" because it's so quick and out of place. may even consider if it was your fault or if you are being silly or over sensitive. This is why they get away with it for so long.*

- *Incredible tenacity and persistence in pursuing you and any other goal. They will be absolutely dogged in how they chase you. You will not see that to them, this is the best bit. The chase along with the slow erosion of your ability to say no.*

June 2014

My deliberate absence from the hotel leisure spa means I haven't seen him much but it's been a useful break from the swelling, expectant intimacy between us. His misplaced pressure in the flat put me off him a little and I'm rather relieved.

It's hot. Really hot. I've taken on the habit of gathering all 3 kids in an evening for a walk in the warm. Tonight, I've posted up some pictures on Facebook of us all looking tanned, happy and relaxed. One of me standing by Rufus's pram in a strapless baby blue sundress, hair up in a bun, smiling widely. One of Niall and I, seated together on the sofa, kissing in a bright sunbeam. He grabbed my face as I went to take the selfie and stole the kiss.

He suspects I have the lifeguard on my friends list but I can't help but feel suffocated and confused.

Riddled with guilt about the emotional betrayal I've committed by liking someone else behind Niall's back isn't really reduced by the fact that we haven't even touched intimately. Whatever this is, it is not acceptable for a married woman, no matter how unhappy I am and how wonderful Jonathan is.

My eating disorder is in full relapse as a result. Smothering my guilt and confusion with food then purging the feelings soon after sometimes helps, but sleep is not easy on any level. To help the sleep issue, I've started drinking a little more often and Niall's started to make catty comments about it.

I've been asked to help out at a school trip. They want me to accompany Charlie's class to a local park for a morning. I'm to chaperone and make sure the kids don't steal trees, fall in the river or eat squirrels. It could be a difficult job.10 minutes after I post this little volunteer task on Facebook, Jonathan texts me.

"Come and meet me, sit in my park in the sun". Unsure & still deciding what to say, I don't send a reply fast enough for him and he tries again. "The wee park is right near to my flat in case you want a coffee!" he adds, along with heart faces and little coffee cup emojis. Excited to spend time with him, I'm remaining determined not to go up to the flat again. The park, in public, is not a bad idea. This is what friends do. But we aren't friends. Shit, I don't know what we are.

June 7th 2014

Walking up Sauchiehall Street, I stop at a shop and buy 2 large bottled beers and a newspaper. I'm going to keep this casual and friendly. He beams when he sees me walk around the corner. In fact, he practically ran towards me!

Without asking him where we should sit, I walk ahead of him and choose a sunny spot right in the middle of the park. Desperately trying to resist any chance that a physical boundary might get crossed, this seems a smart idea. Yet I'm still here, with him! Completely torn in two by this whole thing, my head and heart are at war.

As he throws himself down beside me, all 12 stone of tanned muscle, he wafts aftershave and I smell retro Lynx. Closing my eyes for a second, memories flood in. The smell reminds me of when I was a teenager desperately chasing better-looking people than me. "Why are you smiling?" he asks.

"I can't imagine anyone not wanting to kiss you, Lucy," he says when I've finished explaining. That intense look again. "Oh, trust me- I was a no-go area. I had an English accent, mousy, spaghetti hair and I was never out of Laura Ashley clothes for fuck sakes. No one was interested in me until I grew boobs and finally at 17, had my first boyfriend then yeah, I was... popular;" I make quote signs with my fingers. "but I genuinely was never actually a bike or anything like that until I had my heart broken at nearly 18. Yes, then.... I went a bit wild. I was just looking for love; someone to fix my broken heart." Babbling away, it's like I can't stop. He has an incredible knack for making me nervous and awkward!

"I'm sorry babe" he whispers, then before I can move, strokes my face and cups my chin. At his touch, I soften. He hasn't called me a term of endearment before.

"You look stunning now anyway. Especially today." I have on white lace shorts and a white vest top. It's summery but it's sparse. I'm tanned and slim from sunshine and anxiety.

Now he's looking at my legs, then my breasts. As we lock eyes, he winks at me. I purse my lips in annoyance. But the only person I'm annoyed at right now is myself. I shouldn't be here. This is all my fault. I'm the one in a relationship. To break the tension, I start to root about in my bag. He laughs, of course. I think he enjoys making me squirm a bit. I've never, ever met anyone so confident in their own ability to charm others! I can't help but feel thrilled at how much this guy fancies me! I'm just a wee mum of three me!

Offering him a beer, I easily open the other one with my teeth. "Oh- alcohol doesn't like me," he says, waving it away. "You have one though. It's not a problem for me."

Must be because he's so heavily into health and fitness, I think to Myself and take a long pull on the icy beer. Closing my eyes to enjoy the sensation of the bubbles, he takes the opportunity to flirt again. "Very nice knickers," he says. In surprise, I look at him. He's specifically looking at the small gap between my shorts and my leg. Changing position, I cross my legs but feel more flattered than embarrassed.

I wag my finger at him in mock annoyance, but he grabs it and kisses the tip. We lock eyes and again that "Stare" sucks me in. The tension is palpable. I see an old man on a bench a few feet away watching us and he smiles. I smile back. Jonathan's watching me again.

"Come up to the flat with me- get a coffee," he wheedles. "I know exactly what you want and it's not coffee. NO way am I coming up to your flat again!" Throwing my head back with a cackle, my reply is firm. "I'm not daft, mate!" Now He is standing over me, blocking out the sun & not saying anything. I've embarrassed him. Why do I keep upsetting him? He shrugs. "No probs. See you in 5," then he walks away.

My heart's racing and I'm glad I've said no. It's now almost exactly 6 months since I met him and so far, I've managed to keep him at a distance. Definitely the longest I've made anyone wait!

Sitting in the park, waiting for him to come back, I try and read the paper but can't concentrate. My head is buzzing & I feel a bit sick. I've lost nearly a stone this last few months and it's not just the swimming.

Jonathan is a really great, respectful guy to stick around chasing me, especially as he is single. Only the other day he said he was lonely and looking for love. I'm starting to see that maybe he is worth the risk of a fling because he has not treated me like one. I've never met anyone quite like him. The beer is making me giddy and reckless with these stupid thoughts, so I quickly pour it away into the longer grass in front of me.

At some point, he's back and lying close next to me now. I feel awkward sitting over him, pretending to read the paper, so I put it away and lie down next to him. As soon as we are side by side, he leans over & kisses me. I don't kiss him back but I don't push him away either.

This isn't my husband; this is another man. It is just a kiss on the lips but it lasts several heartbeats and is gentle.

Moving away, I sit up and wipe my mouth. "You're bad, Jonny". He laughs. "I couldn't help myself. You are so stunning and tempting. I'm sorry. Not sorry."

To fill the slightly awkward space between us now I check my phone and see it's gone half two.

"Shit. I have to go!" Standing up to straighten the hem of my shorts and reach for my bag, I watch as he reaches over and picks grass off the front of my vest top, just by my left breast. He looks me in the eye, smiling that Cheshire cat smile again. Turning around, I walk away a little unsteadily. I can feel him watching me. It's like the sun on my back. As I around the corner at the bottom of the road and stop to decide which way to walk down to the station, I feel my phone buzz. "You are fucking amazing," the message reads with love heart eye emoticons and a green heart. I don't reply. I'm trying to regain control here- he wants me but I'm not letting him know I feel the same. Not yet. I need time and space to think carefully about this because when it starts, I don't think we will be able to stop. Walking the 3 miles out of town, up the road towards home I can't stop the "what ifs" going around and round my head. Another line's been crossed. The risk, the badness of it, the feeling as though I am all he wants is intoxicating.

The confidence I feel by resisting him makes me feel powerful. Little do I know; he is the one in control.

Why did Jonathan target me? Pick me out of the dozens of other females walking around the pool and gym? What did I do right (or wrong!) that meant he spotted me and thought "That's her- that's the next one"?

There is no coincidence in how we come to fall into the clutches of Narcs. Because they are always hunting. Always seeking out new fresh meat to feed their appetite for sex, attention, support and adoration. It's not about you- it's about them and their hunger; the hole in their soul that they fill by taking everything you have and everything you are.

If it hadn't been me, it would have been someone else. The reason he targeted me was because I was there and I was his "type". When I was first with him, I assumed his type was pretty, petite, blonde and chatty with sporty hobbies and a love of fun.

When I discovered he was a narcissist, I had to force myself to understand that his type is actually so much more than that. It's Darker! Casanova Psychopaths want women who want to be loved. This is why the Love bombing Stage is often classic "grooming" for what will most likely become adult sexual abuse if your Narc is a Casanova type!

These seducers & charmers are sirens to vulnerable, weak, easily distracted people. Vulnerable people who are hurting or who have been hurt in the past, are perfect targets.

These toxic sirens sing a song we've always wanted to hear. Hypnotised, we fall from relative safety into their clutches and what's so sad is, we go willingly, and even sadder still.... we think it was our choice.

This last week Jonathan has been particularly intense. Not pushing him away in the park and continuing to have contact since he kissed me has fuelled him. He can tell I'm falling for him and now, after all this time I don't think I care.

Constantly following me around the pool, swimming with me when his shift finishes and loudly telling other staff he thinks I am amazing, stunning, incredible, the seduction is flowing at an extreme rate. We are the only 2 people in the world. The rest is just blurred shapes and white noise.

I feel it. No, I know it. That he is in love with me too. Enveloping us is the musky smell of hope, opportunity and lust. God how I've missed true love!

Actively being encouraged by colleagues and friends to "go for it"; "life is too short", I can't help but sometimes imagine what it would be like to be his and for him to be *mine.*

Losing keys, blindly crossing the road at the red man and smiling at strangers like an idiot, I can't sleep and eating is a chore and when I do, I'm sick later.

Jonathan is persistent with his sexting although I am yet to sext him back to the same level. Rather than feeling like harassment or sleazy nagging, I believe he is just so adoring of me he can't help himself.

In other news, Niall is nagging me that the dinners I cook are not as "fancy" as usual and I don't have the candles lit or the hoovering done before he comes home each evening. Waving him away he can no longer get to me and it's getting on his nerves. Often, I just sit in the bathroom to breathe deeply, desperately trying to stay calm and not give away what is going on inside me. I want to scream and ask someone, anyone, for help to make sense of all this. To stop me but there isn't anyone I trust with these bad, immoral, out of control thoughts.

My husband knows I'm off-centre. I think he senses something bad waiting, hunched and quivering in the shadowy corners of our future.

Niall knows me well enough to recognise that I am easily led when I'm complimented and given attention. It's how he seduced me himself after all his own hollow promises, adoration and lies swept me up and carried me to this place. A place of infidelity, shallowness and greed.

His sexist, naggy criticism is pushing me further away. Jagged, sharp-edged words again and again. A stony face. Flat-eyed looks.

In our world, I am trying so hard to be what he wants, but tragically failing to be completely focused on our business, his delicate well-being and the ideal of the perfect housewife & mother.

It has been almost 2 months since we last slept together. He tried to grab me from behind and force a kiss last night and I tensed like stone, feeling like he was the interloper on what I have with Jonathan.

14th June 2014

Today the energy between us was tangible. Shimmering and electric.

Jonathan has his intense look on again and I've barely been left alone the whole time I've swum. He must have approached me to chat a dozen times and it's got to the point where even customers are laughing at the besotted lifeguard and blushing young woman he's so clearly in love with.

Like a dog on heat, he wanders around after me or leaves his station to crouch over me as I float the water below him to catch my breath after each dozen laps. It's like he is in heat. I bask in it- I admit it. Being adored this way is simply intoxicating.

Here in this place, with him, I feel like I belong. The connection between us is so obvious we can't help but enjoy the "are they, or aren't they?" gossip. He loves being the centre of attention; our situation has him right up there with me completing the picture.

Rushed and swearing to myself, I'm in cubicle 37 as usual. Checking my phone, I realise it's after 2 and the kids are out at 3. Frantically I rub my hair to dry it a little, swipe cream across my face and spin back and forth, round and round looking for the 2nd of my two sliders. "Fuckety fuck, fuck!"- where the hell is my hair bobble? Right there, ok- where's my purse? There, good, ok.

There's a light knock on the door but I'm topless and wearing only bikini bottoms. This is not good timing- I really have to go. Fucking Jonathan and his obsession with me! I smile at myself. When a man wants something, he wants it and losing a bobble or a flip flop won't stop it.

"Bugger off you!" Giggling, I open the door a crack. He's stood there smiling without a care in the world. "Jonny- honestly love. I need to..."

Before I can finish, he pushes the door open and leans in. Roughly kissing and taking advantage of my surprise, he pushes me fully inside, locking the door adeptly behind him. Slipping his tongue inside my mouth confidently, I give in. Weak with shock and lust, he easily lifts me up, wrapping my legs around his waist. He pushes me hard against the cubicle wall and uses the pressure to keep me there. We kiss passionately and he deftly slides down his shorts and enters me.

We have sex there and then as quietly as we can. He finishes quickly and breathes hard into my neck. He sets my feet back on the wet floor, pulls my bikini bottoms aside and goes down on me. I press my hands against the wall of the cubicle, spread my legs and close my eyes. Trying not to make a noise, I can still hear the normal sounds of normal people outside- this is dangerous and wrong and right and good.

His radio crackles and we pull apart quickly. He stands up and kisses me again. A promise that this is not just.... this. I put a finger to his lips to remind him not to talk. Shhhhhh, our eyes say to each other.

"I need to go- they're looking for me," he whispers. "I know- go!" I whisper back, bending down to start picking up damp clothing which has found itself on the floor. I gently slap his chest "Go!" He kisses me gently again, smiles and quietly backs out of the cubicle and closes it comically like a jester. A sweep of the hand and a small bow and he is gone. "Idiot," I say under my breath. Sitting down on the bench, I'm still topless and realise I'm shaking. I liked it but I didn't. I don't know how to feel. Is it fear or exhilaration?

Later he tells me he explained away his wet and dishevelled uniform by telling colleagues he picked a crying child up to comfort them while he looked for their neglectful parents. This cover story sits a little uncomfortably with me, like a small jagged stone in my gut.

Walking up the road 20 minutes after the encounter, I'm still a little bit jangly and stunned about what just happened. It's a lovely, sunny, warm day but I can't help but feel dazed and anxious. I keep seeing images of us together like a film reel and strangely I want to turn them off. Half-way home and walking over the bridge on the motorway, I stop dead when I hear the determined toot, toot, toot of a car horn behind me.

Ready to stick 2 fingers up to whatever white van man is abusing his horn for me, I swing round fast and see that it is

Jonathan in his car. He pulls over, opens the door and tells me to get in. So of course, I do.

Listen to: Billy Ocean: "Get outta my dreams, get into my car"

Red Flags:

- _Outstandingly perfect starts._ Casanova Narc victims will speak of the beginnings of relationships like this as incredible, different, more extreme and more intense than anything they had before. Extreme highs and sadly, soon the extreme lows.
- _Lies that make them look good._ When Narcs lie, they tell the best lie they can think up. A believable lie that almost always casts them as a hero or as a wonderful person. This is a symptom of the incredible grandiosity and need to feel like a good person to attract as much "human fuel" as possible.
- _The "super couple"._ Watch out for a person repeatedly making new partners "the one". You will have little instinctive moments where you feel you are being shown off and maybe even helping to make the Narc look good. The 2nd time Jonathan and I met to have sex, we randomly ended up going a drive after it and he took me on a tour of his home town and I met his family! At the time I was flattered but now...I realise its odd and creepy. A fast-track process to be "his" in front of people he wanted to impress.
- _Early on in the relationship, you will start rationalising abuses of trust or inappropriate acts_. The initial love bombing stage has us in such adoration of our future abuser that we see only the "good" in the Narc and no bad. Narcs always have excuses for slip-ups and you adore them so much you let it go. This is the "mind fog" fog seeping in also.
- _Excuse Planning._ In my case, Jonathan started the process of setting excuses aside for any times where he would/could hurt me. E.g. Narcs will make sure we know they have responsibilities or ongoing physical and mental health issues. This allows them to have ready-made reasons for acting oddly, ghosting or discarding you

PART 2.
The Devaluation

July 2014

There is no excuse for infidelity. I know, I hear you. However, when you are dealing with a Casanova Psychopath, you can be the most faithful, loyal person and yet have those qualities eroded away. Narcs will choose victims who give off an air of sadness or loneliness. We might never have cheated with any other "average Joe", but Narcs wear us down and build us up at the same time. This complex mix of pestering, manipulation and perfectly placed charm is to the right candidate, impossible to resist.

Niall and I met in May 2009 and he was so lovely, calm and charming in the early days of our relationship. For the first 4 or 5 months, he was quite simply wonderful. Like Jonathan, he was apparently perfect.

When he was caught out lying about his age, it was strange, a little shocking and actually very funny. I thought it was kind of cute he thought I was only in my mid-twenties so chopped 8 years off his own age and hid it for 7 months. Yes, it was embarrassing when my friend and travel agent called me to suggest I have a chat with him about the difference in age he gave when I was there versus what was actually in his passport. I let it go, just a silly story to tell the grand-kids.

It wasn't quite so funny when, only a few weeks before our wedding, my bridesmaids got together to gleefully announce that the flat he was "renting" to them actually belonged to our local housing association. The three witches laughed and joked about what a "farce" our wedding was going to be since the flat he told me he owned was actually a council flat. The flat I'd visited hundreds of times during our courting. The flat I encouraged him to let out to my friend when she found herself homeless after a family dispute. The flat he had proudly announced he would sell to help us get a larger family home one day. Nah, that wasn't a laughing matter.

I lost 3 friends/bridesmaids in my shock and subsequent anger. In denial, I refused to accept the bombshell, called them liars and eventually had to accept that their spiteful claims were indeed true. That whopper almost completely destroyed my trust in him. For 3 years he had lied about owning property and the plans we had made regarding joining both mortgages up for a large family home with a garden, disappeared in an instant.

The final nail in the coffin came quickly after our wedding. The sudden screeching (in my face) announcement that he was carrying some income tax debt was a shock. My demand for details on how much came with promises that it was £8,000, then, half an hour later, actually £12,000. Ten more minutes later, the final sum declared was £20,000. Unbeknownst to me, I had been carrying him, not because he earned too little, but because he owed too much.

So, the chilled-out, independent, confident and solvent man who had wooed me and allowed me to plan a financially secure life, a wedding and carry a child for was actually a habitual liar. Chuck in some confidence bashing, and 5 years after we met, I was ripe for picking.

In researching personality disorders and Narcissism, I have read many articles giving names to various types of Narc. I think Niall sits quite high on the scale with the huge ego, lies, cruel language & reputational damage.... but I'm unsure if he is a truly dangerous type of Narcissist. Jonathan...? I'm 100% he is!

My counsellor reassuringly said that we all have some Narc traits and we all fall into some sort of Personality Framework. This framework spreads itself between Emotion and Logic. At its most simplistic, we all have varying degrees of that mode of behaviour. We lean to various ends of it- the healthiest sit in the middle. Lucky sods.

By the time we came to the last year of our relationship in 2014, I could list Niall's favourite insults: "No one loves you"; "you are not as good as you think you are"; "it's your fault we have no money"; "you are demanding"; "you are stupid"- over and over. I could never forget these insults no matter how I tried.

When I met Jonathan and he said the exact opposite, I let myself get swept away and will forever regret it.

In the days after that first sexual encounter with Jonathan, I went over and over how it could have got so far.

Barely sleeping and struggling to eat, I was riddled with guilt yet had no desire to stop. Niall appeared not to notice anything was wrong, but if he had, I would, of course, have lied. I wanted to continue whatever it was we were doing. I needed it. Jonathan made sure of that. In those first few weeks of the affair, I started to turn into someone sneaky, distracted and greedy for time to either message or meet with my lover.

After the encounter, Jonathan was quieter with me, not quite as intense. I told myself firmly that he had chased me for 6 months and now we could relax into something more equal, more normal. How wrong I was!

Narcissists read people within seconds of setting eyes on them. Jonathan will have spotted me immediately that first day in the pool and seen the tasty attributes that Casanova Psychopaths like him desire.

"Why is she here alone?", "Why today, out of nowhere-what's happened to trigger this lone visit?"; "Is she new to the area or just to swimming?"; "Nice bikini and not a full costume... but she looks nervous. Hmmmm, confident or faking it?"

Jonathan would have noticed me if I'd been in before, so these pre-attack queries will have flooded in as he readied himself to approach me.

He'll have decided that I was his next target and most importantly planned to present himself to me as everything I could ever hope for because that is what Narcs do. They are masters at gifting themselves to others. The perfect friend. The perfect lover. The perfect colleague.

It's important to note here that this is how Narcs make up their pool of fuel... the swarming group of various sources of ego and support around them.

I refer to these later in the book, however I need to mention "Flying Monkeys" at this point, as they tend to act up and show their worth to the Narc once the devaluation stage has kicked off. Flying Monkeys, as a term, refers to the air-born, vicious minions of the bad Witch in "The Wizard of Oz". As in the film (and book of course!), they surround the witch and do her bidding, attacking her victims, ganging up and relentlessly "pecking" at and pulling apart targets. I don't need to go further into the explanation, I think you get the drift!

So- watch out for the friends, family members, colleagues and social media buddies who seem to.... peck away at you and later, work with the Narc to destroy you. Healthy, normal people don't do this and they certainly don't surround themselves with minions of mass destruction!

Around mid-July 2014, Niall seemed to react in an effort to adapt to the new stilted, cooling dynamic between us. Randomly coming home with flowers and trying to kiss or embrace me at any opportunity, he worked hard to defrost me. Sadly, it was too much, too late. As he pushed and pushed for me to thaw out, I knew I deserved to feel the flood of shame and guilt that swept in every time I looked at him or heard him talking to his son.

I wasn't sure if I was going to end my marriage to him but I did know that I wasn't prepared to end the affair with Jonathan. It was just too rewarding when he was into me and too tragic and painful when he wasn't. The 6 months of love-bombing me had done its job, spectacularly. I was hooked.

Rufus and his Nana P are away on a week's holiday to Blackpool, leaving Niall and me in relative peace to decorate the flat a little. I wonder if she timed the break deliberately, picking up on the miserable wall of silence growing bigger day by day between her son and I.

Even today in the quiet of the flat, sweeping rich deep teals and greens across our bedroom walls, the tension between us is bubbling away like lava, so I'm waiting for the explosion of rage that allows me to grab a gym kit and leave. Niall doesn't disappoint and starts to complain about the cost of the "fucking stupid fancy paint", I paid for a few days before.

An hour later, breathless and giddy with passion, I slip up, muttering into Jonathan's warm chest that Niall and I are updating our bedroom.

My lovers' whole body has suddenly frozen and his face shows the same level of fury I remember from the time by the pool, when I'd told him about the night out where we all nearly met.

"You hurt me when you talk like that. About him. About your life," he says. "I thought you loved me," with a childish wobble of his bottom lip. I watch, silent, as he turns away to get out of bed. In his anger and haste, he pulls the bedclothes off me.

"It's just decorating! It's my fucking house and not Niall's anyway!" I exclaim, and reach for him. Jonathan's eyes light up and he changes posture slightly. "Well, I'm too hurt now. You've ruined it. You need to leave." He's going to get dressed and with his back to me!? What the fuck?!

"Oh, come on Jonny!" I reach out again to tuck a finger playfully in the waistband of his boxers. He shrugs me off and stands up to pull up his denims.

"I said, you need to leave Lucy. Just go." The last word is shouted from the hall. He stomped out of the room and left me there, used and naked. Our sweat going cold on my skin, I wait there to see if he'll come back and say sorry. Trying not to cry, I decide to get dressed and leave. A few minutes later I'm shouting goodbye into what feels like an empty house.

As I cross the road to walk towards home, I look up to see a shadow move from the kitchen window then wonder if I saw it at all.

Later he blocks me on social media, ignores my messages apologising for upsetting him and only resurfaces with a YouTube love song link the following evening. "It's the pressure of the baby and feeling like you're not serious about me! It's driving me crazy," his excuse reads.

The next time he does another one of these "post-fuck discards" is startlingly only a few days later.

Spooning together, Jonathan is stroking my hip and butterfly-kissing my neck, wittering on about how to deal with the woman due his child.

I can feel him getting wound up, going over and over the same complaints as usual so I try to help calm him down with practical advice. "Look, I'm sure she's reasonable and is just waiting for you to crawl. Women can be.... manipulative. She's got what she wanted from you, but she can't legally stop you from seeing the child if you want to, sweetheart..."

"I don't want to talk about it anymore, Lucy." Jonathan's voice is suddenly Steely but I keep talking like a fool. "Well, it can't go on. I can help you draft a letter or find a solicitor. In fact, I called one yesterday, I meant to tell you about..." Suddenly, I'm not where I was. He's pushed me off and is sitting facing the window. "Jonny, you need to calm..."

He spins round and looking into his dark angry eyes, I shut up. "Stop trying to control me! She's a nutter and you're one too!" The words slap me hard in the face. My heart stops at the sudden change in manner. He storms out and stomps down the hall to the bathroom. Pulling my dress down, I put my knickers on quickly. Ashamed and embarrassed, I don't know whether to follow him or sit and wait on the sofa we just had sex on. "Here we go again," I whisper, re-tying my ponytail and slipping on my shoes.

I can hear him in the bathroom- even his pissing sounds angry. Have I finally had enough of this strange and torturous affair? This is supposed to be easy, fun, sexy. For 6 months he has been, easy, fun and sexy and now.... now this is prickly, difficult and tentative. I keep making mistakes and feeling like shit! Go, go- Go! A voice in my head says. A sudden surge of adrenalin has me shouting at an empty doorway.

"You're a dick. Moody as fuck!" My chest thuds as I hear him stomping down the hall back towards the living-room.

He stops dead to gawp as I start to dramatically shove things in my hand-bag. My red silk nightie, a hairbrush and hair-dryer. "Sorry, Jonny-but this isn't for me." He trots after me as I stomp round his flat, grabbing stupid pointless things- 76p off the top of the fridge, my orange glitter nail varnish off his bedside table and my tatty purple toothbrush from the bathroom.

Putting on my navy work blazer, I argue with my earrings & bracelet, arms and hair all over the place, trying not to cry with anger and frustration. "Baby I.... it's her...." he starts to stutter as he realises I'm almost ready to leave.

"I can't handle you. You make me ill with stress and I'm only ever loving to you! I don't get it! You're *impossible!*" Shouting the last word in his face, I falter as he stares at me, agog. Rattling the door handle and trying to turn the keys in the lock to get out, I start to cry. It's over.

"Baby, don't be like this," he says, as he half-reaches for me. "You're a moody bastard and she's a fucking problem not just for you, but for me now!" He turns the key for me & the blessed door swings open. Before I can change my mind; I walk straight out and jog down his stairs without looking back. My throat's tight & I feel like I want to scream.

Running across the street with my gym bag on my back, I don't look back but know he's watching me leave. Gritting my teeth, I run faster.

Within 2 hours, Niall and I are in the car and on our way to Blackpool. Behind big sunglasses, I cry quietly all the way there. I just couldn't bear to share the same city as Jonathan right now. The break will do Niall and I good.

My husband watches the road and sneaks sideways looks at me sipping at the bottle of water I brought for us both. He doesn't ask what's wrong. I'm glad. For every mile travelled, I feel worse and worse, slowly starting to regret my decision to end it with Jonathan, the most wonderful man I've ever met. Going over and over all the amazing things he's done and said this last 7 months and how good we are together when he's calm, I start to lose hold of the shock and anger I felt only a few hours ago. Regret at my too hasty decision starts to take root and fear that this was all my fault casts over me like the shadow of a lunar eclipse.

Sick with sadness, the first few days we were in Blackpool I spent far too long crying in toilets and enduring tense, puffy-eyed dinners with my husband, my youngest child and my mother-in-law. I ate only enough to prove I was fine- absolutely fine. I drank too much to prove I was fine- absolutely fine. Staring into space while Niall and his mother talked about things I used to be interested in, I was distracted and kept forgetting things.

Twice I locked us out of the room, and most days I had to run back to the bar to get Rufus's sun hat. Walking behind Niall and his mother, deliberately slowly, I disconnect from their conversation and struggle to make eye contact.

"What's her problem?" their eyes say to each other. Thank goodness neither puts an arm around me or asks me what's wrong. Constantly on the tip of my tongue is the marriage-shattering scream that I'm broken hearted, and not by my husband this time. The words sit in my throat like broken teeth.

Blackpool's sweaty and sticky - salt and vinegar hot. Neon that hurts my puffy eyes almost everywhere I look. Loud, jostling families arguing about who spent too much at the slots or who dropped their ice cream.

I stop to watch a couple holding hands. He's broad and dark like Jonathan. She is petite and blonde like me. They could be us. Staring, I watch them kiss deeply and giggling together, almost fall into a cafe. They don't notice anyone else but each other. It hurts so I put my sunglasses on again and walk fast to catch up to my family.

I've checked my phone every half hour since we got here. It's been three days now. I lick ice cream off my wrist where my little boy has spilled it being too hasty in grabbing it from me 2 minutes ago. I need to get a fucking grip. Time to put on the big girl pants, fucking sort my shit out and go back to my marriage.

On day 4, we return to our room, pink and tired from yet another scorching day. Feeling lighter and more positive, I wait for a bath to run while Niall potters about next door. Sitting on the toilet seat, I post an update on Facebook; "At the beach- Blackpool over Barbuda any day"- adding a picture of myself making a leap 3-foot high along the shore. I am in a bikini that I often wore to the swimming pool. I'm making a point, suspecting that Jonathan will hear I am away on holiday with my family.

Posting several more pictures, I choose one of Niall 's mother and I, arm-in-arm in a beer garden, smiling and dressed for dinner. Then one of Niall and I in shorts and matching white T-shirts. Just an average married couple in the sunshine. My smile is stiff but Niall is beaming widely, apparently proud of his wife. Enjoying the sun.

Lying in the bath, I realise I haven't cried today. I feel bitter and ashamed rather than hollow and sad. It's over. It's done. Maybe Niall and I can go to counselling or go away somewhere, just the two of us.

Rising up out of the water to reach for a towel, I glance at my phone. It's lit up with a message saying I missed a call while I was under the water.

"She dumped me. I'm gutted!" comes Jonathan's distinct gravelly voice. Pressing the phone close to my ear, I'm unashamedly clenching my knees together & holding my breath, desperate to hear what he says next. There's rustling and more muffled talking. It's a bum call but he does sound sad. He's been talking about me and seeking solace from a friend.

Breathless and shaking, I'm perched on the side of the bath like a needy fool. I replay the voicemail message again and again until I hear Niall banging about in the room next door. He's woken from his nap. "Can I get in, Lucy? I need a shower before dinner". Frantically shoving the phone inside my pile of clothes, I open the door for him. My smile too wide & legs like jelly.

We're in the hotel beer garden and the heat has got to us all. In fact, Niall and his mother are loud and a little drunk. Slipping away outside onto the outside seating area, I realise I can't talk to Jonathan here, it's too busy. Crossing the road quickly, I jog down the steps to the beach and step under the canopy of an old stone bandstand. Its cooler now and blessedly peaceful.

Jonathan picks up within 3 rings. Unusually quick, I wonder if he's had his phone nearby.

"I never called you. No. Not me." My heart clenches. "You did - I can see it here about 3 hours ago. It's a 4-minute message! You were talking to someone about me. You were upset that I dumped you. Dumped - that's the word you used. I promise."

"No Lucy, I never called you. I swear it. My phone's playing up. I'm fine." I don't get it; this is fucking weird. "Ok. No problem. Never mind." Unsure now and ready to cry, I'm waiting but he doesn't talk. "Well. I have to go. I snuck away because I thought you were upset... Sorry." Three more seconds of silence. I take a breath in to say goodbye, again.

"Well. You look like you're having a good time..." He's talking. This is a good sign. He's interested in how I feel- an even better sign. My heart lifts again. I feel a bit dizzy. I've missed him so much and he's missed me too!

"It's ok, really fucking hot!" I try to sound happy and not at all upset by this weird conversation with my ex-lover. "Yeah. Hot here too.... but it's shit without you. I've no one to sit on the big steps in town with. I'm fucking bored shitless. Plus....I need my balls emptied." He laughs. He sounds totally different to the voicemail.

My groin clenches at the sexual reference. It's out of place and sudden. Then I feel relief again. This confession means he misses me and wants me. The sex has been off the scale between us and I squirm at the bigger, louder twitch in my gut.

I imagine him wandering around the town centre alone, top off, trying to strut and look proud, but actually missing his lover dreadfully. I imagine him going home early to sit in his shady flat looking at pictures of me on holiday without him. I feel sorry for him & want to be with him to comfort him.

"Well, I'm home in a few days. Maybe we could talk about things?" I say this tentatively. "Yes. I would like that baby," he says smoothly. Sliding down the wall to sit down on the cold stone step, I close my eyes in relief. I've missed him and know for sure I never, ever want to break up again. "Ok- well I'll message you when I'm back in Glasgow."

"No problem. I'll message you later...... I miss you," he says. Not trusting myself to speak, I end the call and sit in the shade of the bandstand for another few minutes trying to breathe properly.

Niall and I hardly speak on the drive home. Rufus is travelling back by train with his Nana in a few days' time and I'm insanely pleased he isn't here to pick up on the storm brewing. I've made my decision and fear Niall's reaction with every cell in my body.

As we cross the border, the rain starts. It comes fast and hard, and it's almost tropical. Opening my window, I lean my face out into it. Feeling Niall watching me, I don't turn around.

As we walk in the flat, tired and sunburned, I blurt out my plan to have geographical space between us. He stands there getting redder and redder with rage, but still I power on.

"Niall, I'm really unhappy and I think you are too. Some of the things you say and do have harmed me. I'm struggling with it all. The lies were bad but the criticism and emotional neglect has just made it all worse. We never go anywhere as a couple and let's be honest you're not the most romantic or... passionate of people...."

"Oh, not that again. For Fuck sakes!" he shouts, as he grabs his holdall off the top of the wardrobe. "I told you to leave it. Why can't you leave it?!" He's grabbing shirts off hangers and shoving them in his bag.

"I can't leave it, Niall. The issues with us as a couple are a problem, but the lies you told were huge! They were life-changing fucking lies that made me fall in love with you and plan a future with you. The wedding was nearly ruined and I lost three good friends! It's like all of our marriage has been a lie because you're not who you said you were when we met!" I sit on the bed behind him and watch as he gets angrier and angrier.

"It's done now. You know the truth now, so what's the point? What do you fucking want from me? Yes, I was skint when I met you. Yes, it wasn't my flat. Yes, I didn't pay some fucking taxes but it's in the past now!" He stands up to shout in my face. I go stiff with fear. This is when it gets bad. He never just loses it then calms down. He loses it then gets angrier and angrier as though fuelling himself.

"I know what you've been doing anyway! You've been fucking about behind my back! I checked your phone when you were bathing Rufus 2 days ago! It's why I tried to have sex with you last night. To humiliate you!" My heart stops & slowly I wipe his spittle off my cheek.

"Ok. well, now you know. I need space from you. I need to get my head together Niall. This is a separation whether you like it or not. You've destroyed my confidence and I'm sorry......I think... I'm in love with him"

In an instant he rears back, reaches out to grab my right arm and drags me off the bed, pulling me out into the hall, he manhandles me into the living room where he eventually drops me strangely between the coffee table and sofa. Standing over me, he screams and shouts solidly for 2 minutes about what a cunt, whore, slut, selfish bitch I am. How I'm ugly, old and stupid and he's going to kill Jonathan and I. I weep and beg him to stop but of course, he only does this in his own time. Sitting on the floor, my shoulder starts to throb and I tell him so.

"I don't fucking care! You've hurt me! You and that ugly bastard have ruined my life!" he shouts in my face, kneeling down to look me right in the eye. I'm terrified. He stands up then slumps onto the sofa suddenly. I can see he's tired now and the shock of what's happening is starting to seep in.

"Look, Niall, let's just have some space. A few days apart. It will be good for you too." I bum shuffle backwards away from him and back towards the door.

"Fucking whatever. Fucking selfish bitch. I have to work. You've fucking made this decision without me. Where am I fucking to go?! I gave up my flat to live with you!"

"Stay at your mum's. No? You work there anyway. She still has a spare bed. She will love having you there!" I carefully open the door out into the hall. If he flips fully, I can lock myself in the toilet.

"This better be a separation. I'm not having you embarrass me in front of my family and my friends who spent a fucking fortune on your stupid fucking joke of a wedding!" He pushes past me & I flinch. What he's saying hurts. That was our special day. A day we planned together for a year. It's cruel insults like this that have us here- broken and in pain- and he still doesn't get it.

"I'm going to my Mum's. You better fucking let me see my son!" He is standing in the hall with the front door open. "Of course, I will. Jesus, Niall - you love him! You're an amazing Dad! I would never stop you!" This is the truth.

My husband storms out, slamming the door behind him. A picture of a kingfisher I painted in school falls off the wall. It doesn't break and gratefully I gently hang it back up. I take this as a good omen.

Listen to: Little Mix: "Hair"

Red Flags:

- _Gaslighting._ *Narcissists will lie about little things like this bum call to offset your mood, make you question your eyes and ears and disrupt your natural decision-making. It's a little test of your nerve and trust in them. It's a good way to see how adamantly you stick to facts. You give in to their insistence that you absolutely are wrong seeing or hearing something because you just want things to be calm and them to be happy. You also adore them so much you WANT to believe them; the alternative is just too painful. Gaslighting is a HUGE red flag and gets more and more common the longer you are in a relationship because it truly does send you crazy making it easier for the Narc to abuse you.*

- *Traps to make you reach out to them. The "mistake" phone-call was simply bait for me to jump at Jonathan's contact and allow him an opportunity to sound me out for hoovering. It also gives the Narc the ego-boost of you making the first move in what became making up. He knew I would call him. Narcs do this a lot.*

- *Possessiveness. Jonathan had been watching my Facebook. Seeing me appearing happy and settled Again, aggravated his ego & encouraged him to make contact to hoover me back in. He couldn't allow it, so Absolutely had to disrupt my recovery. Initially, you'll find these particular acts flattering and think it's jealousy because they love you; later you will see it as possessive and controlling and mean. It's also exhausting. Narcs never want to fully let you go, this is why you must go and MEAN IT.*

- *Sudden Sexual References in the context of missing you. Casanova Psychopaths in particular use sex as a weapon. They use it to tame you, make you theirs, to tease and manipulate you and later to hurt you. It's difficult to admit as a victim, but you will likely find that dating a Narc will result in some of the best sex of your life and you will find it exciting and intoxicating so will miss "it" almost as much as your lover/partner during discards.*

August 2014

My marriage pretty much over, my lover now gone, I couldn't eat or sleep at all. My G.P. also confirmed Niall had damaged my rotator cuff in my shoulder. "It's similar to what happens to your shoulder sockets in a car crash," she had told me, as I winced at her soft touch as she bandaged it up.

"This is too much pressure for me. I need to let you go," Jonathan texted, when I told him about the separation.

"It was my decision. He was too intense and I was going to tell him about us simply to get his fucking hands off me, Jonny!" He reads it but doesn't reply. I've made a mistake. I've referred to Niall touching me. Shit, shit, shit. Now he really will dig his heels in and we will be over again! My hands start to shake as I wait for his reply.

"Have you had sex with him since you met me?" reads the text with no kisses.... "He tried it with me a few days ago, when you and I were broken up, but we didn't actually have full sex. I had no idea what was going on and he is ...was.... my husband!" I have no idea what else to say- this is such a mess! A confusing, traumatic mess!

His angry reply comes in fast. "I've not been near anyone since I met you. Yeah, I shagged her, the Sinead one, once! Like, last November! But it's always been you! Only you! I'm away. It's over. You cheated on me."

Suddenly, Jonathan's picture disappears. He's blocked me, so absolutely devastated, I cry non-stop for the rest of the day and stop only to stumble to the off-licence before getting so drunk I manage to get some sleep.

Nearly 2 days later, Jonathan is back. "I miss you. You make me want to be a better man. I lost it out of jealousy. I adore you. You're so amazing! I never thought you would choose me over him. I was just scared baby," all green hearts and kisses. This message is followed up by a love song to seal the deal. He knows how to get me on side. I cry with relief and type my reply.

"Please don't do it again. This ending us & going in a huff thing is horrid. Please stop doing it."

"I will baby. I promise, no more. We'll be fine." I believe him. Of course I do. So, it all began again. Hoovering then discarding, over and over.

Living in a constant state of anxiety that was either blanketed by an intensely wonderful sense of being either his partner or the dreadfully horrific sense of being his ex, became the norm for me very quickly. The adoration periods were always far longer than the discard phases, so I trained myself to think he loved me more than he hated me.

This is where Narcs are very, very clever. They know the opposite of love is not actually hate, the opposite of love is actually apathy. It is feeling invisible & of no importance to the person who is supposed to love us. It's being ignored while we cry and beg for not just forgiveness but answers to why this abuse is even happening in the first place.

Most Narcs use ghosting, social media blocking, ignoring techniques because they are passive aggressive. They can't be blamed for actually DOING anything obviously horrible to you and while you are pushed to the side and left in the dark, they are creating a whole new opera of what your relationship is or was like.

Their audience of "flying monkeys" suck it up because they don't and can't hear your side. They think, how can "ignoring" someone be cruel or evil? Surely you (the victim) should just grow up and go away instead of (as the Narc says) hanging around waiting for some explanations or attention?

Listen To: Stereophonics: "White Lies"

Red Flag:

- *"The Victim Cloak". This is where Narcs start to set out their stall on who and what you are to allow them to seek support and attention from their followers and any possible other sexual supplies. Narcs have their Victim Cloaks tailored to be perfect! While they are a victim of your "obsessiveness" and "controlling behaviour", they can misbehave and ghost you and it sets the scene for the inevitable reputational damage at the end of your relationship.*

- *The Narcissistic Rage is classically displayed by Niall when I told him I wanted to break up. The verbal insults, physical violence and unreasonable reactions are classic Narc behaviours when faced with the truth that you (as victim) can no longer supply them with your loyalty/love/time/trust.*

- _Discards._ When the Narc has what they apparently wanted. Watch out for them ending the relationship when you "finally" commit to them or choose them over that family member/ partner/job/child. Narcs enjoy getting what they want but even more, they enjoy throwing it back in your face and testing your resolve to maintain the relationship now it is pretty much all you have. They have manipulated you into giving up virtually everything for them, so removing themselves at this point is a rejection of responsibility, and it is a true thrill and ego boost to know you adore them that much.

October 2014

"Let me take you out for dinner, baby. I won't see you for a whole week so let me treat you," Jonathan says, as he starts the shower up. Cleaning my teeth at the sink, we are companionably getting ready to go to the gym together.

Thrilled at his proactivity, I rinse my mouth out, I drop my own towel and slide into the shower with him. "I'm going to miss you so much! I'm going to go crazy," he mumbles into my neck as I lean forward into the tiles and feel him press up against me from behind. I go on holiday with my friend Annie to a 4* hotel in Gran Canaria tomorrow, yet sickeningly, I don't want to leave him. I had booked the hotel with Niall several months before it, long before Jonathan became of interest to me. Niall was refusing to come even though we had separate rooms. I partially understood. I had after all apparently broken his heart.

Later:

I'm wearing a new burgundy wiggle dress and matching burgundy suede heels. For a change, Jonathan's made a bit of an effort with a black T-shirt that appears not to have been hung up on the floor.

As we eat, he blethers away quite happily and looks longingly at me, going on and on about how much he's going to miss me.

"How do you know about this place then?" I ask and take a sip of my beer. Leaving dark red lipstick on the rim, I wipe it off with a napkin. Jonathan's quiet suddenly, so I look up at him. He looks a little pale and I wonder if he's eaten too much.

"Oh yeah, I erm... came here for a work thing a while ago- thought you'd like it," he says, taking my hand and smiling widely now. "I do like it. Never heard of it- good choice!" I reply and kiss his hand.

Nearly two years later, I discover that he did not go to the restaurant with work colleagues...

In the taxi to the airport, my Facebook pings with a notification. Jonathan's posted up a selfie of us taken a few hours before. "Going to miss my baby so much!" he's written along with the picture. We look like we are holding on to each other for dear life. Immediately, I don't like the picture. My hair's thinned quite badly and it's a good 3 or 4 inches shorter than this time last year. The stress of the last 3 months has started to get to me physically.

I resolved to try my best to stay as connected to him as possible while away. Jonathan had successfully made me extremely anxious about leaving him "all alone and with no one".

My plan was to send him as many pics and videos as possible. A supremely sexual couple, we were having sex at least 4 or 5 times a day- anywhere he wanted it and often that included his work. Strangely we only had sex outdoors once and never in the car. I now wonder if the thrill of sex in his place of work was a... thing for him, considering the context.

Jonathan & I had never been apart longer than the 5-day "split" that spanned Blackpool. Jonathan had also instilled in me the knowledge that he masturbated almost constantly when I wasn't with him, so I dreaded him mourning me and perhaps even cheating on me if I wasn't there to personally satisfy him.

"When you're not with me, I get anxious and depressed, baby," he'd say, although this made little sense considering he was the one who would choose when I was allowed in his life and when I was cut out of it.

By this point, Jonathan had successfully led me to understand that sex calmed him, made him feel happy and wanted. I knew the worst thing in the world would be him getting depressed or frustrated and discarding me while I was thousands of miles away and unable to fix it.

By now I was his pleaser and my own approaches to sex and intimacy were being twisted and manipulated, mainly to appease him and reduce my own fears of abandonment.

Let me give you some (cringey!) examples of how I kept Jonathan "calm" and "happy" when we were together- I saw it as making him feel loved and respected. "Too many people have let me down, baby. Used me. I need you to teach me how to love and be loved. You are the one," he would say when he made up with me after a discard. "You make me want to be a better man and you can teach me."

Every Sunday, or at least once a week, I would give Jonathan a full-body salt scrub and olive oil massage. My suggestion was to do this to help with the skin issues he had. When his skin was bad, he'd complain he couldn't sleep and when he struggled to sleep, he was bad-tempered and moody with me. I just wanted him to be nice to me so started this little ritual. I would also buy zero PH creams and shower washes for him and make sure my own toiletries were hidden away, because once he used one of them and was angry it made his skin worse.

Another thing I would do to keep him happy would be to clean his house. Now as you know, I had my own, quite large, 2-bedroom flat across the city, but every time I stayed at his house, I would give it a full hoover, dust, tidy and clean either for him coming home from work or the next day. So, when he came home and I wasn't there, he could relax himself in a nice, clean and tidy flat.

If was in the city centre shopping, meeting a friend or at the gym, I would use the keys he gave me and clean his flat and leave him a meal in the fridge for when he came home. "You are amazing, baby!" he would text, so I'd glow knowing that I had survived at least another day in his favour and tonight I could try and sleep, believing he wasn't stressed or angry with me. Most importantly, feeling safe that a discard wasn't on the horizon.

Listen to: Annie Lennox: "Walking on Broken Glass"

Red Flags:

- *Sexual Manipulation. This is tied in with the interesting, passionate and regular sexual appetite your Narc will have and pass on to/demand from you. In time, you come to realise sex is a way to their "heart" and a way to feel safe that they won't cheat on you or discard you. You will do things you haven't done before and the amount of sexual contact you have will be extreme even when you are apart. You learn tips and tricks to soothe your Narc with sex, even when you're not really the one getting pleasure or in the mood.*

- *Self-Induced Slavery or excessive "pleasing activity". Like all domestic abuse victims (in particular), we will start plotting to protect ourselves from harm of all types. It is very common for victims to tiptoe round the Narc, doing tasks and helping them profusely because we will be rewarded with longer periods between discards and harm and we will feel "needed" and "special", so trust it's less likely we will be replaced by someone better than we.*

- *You are more giving/loving/caring/generous/with this particular partner than anyone you dated before. At times you wonder why other partners didn't get this level of "love" from you. However, you will rationalise it by believing this is because a) the Narc is more vulnerable and needs you more than past partners, and b) because they are indeed "the one" and they "deserve" this much care and attention because they shower you with amazing Love bomb and Hoover phases!*

November 2014

We've heard that Sinead has now had Jonathan's baby. To date, he hasn't seen the child and has made no efforts to see her.

The baby, registered without his presence (so he said), was born also without his presence and my heart pulls for him when he complains about it.

"Why don't you write Sinead a letter? Maybe appeal to whatever good side she does have? If she lets you get involved, she gets a babysitter and the child maintenance!?" I place my hand on his cheek and turn his face to look straight at him, hoping he will do as I suggest. We've just had sex over the kitchen table. He'd grabbed me as soon as I arrived. Afterwards, while I sat on his knee and he kissed my neck, he'd started talking about Sinead and the atmosphere darkened, again.

He brushes my hand away and stands up abruptly I virtually fall on the floor. "No point. She's a psycho. She's wanted another kid for ages! It was all she ever talked about and it drove me mad! She's a crackpot with real issues and I'm done!" he storms in my face.

My gut clenches and my heart starts to flutter out of control. I shouldn't have said anything. "I'm just trying to help, Jonny. Don't shout, please?... I'll agree with whatever avenue you want to take. You know that. I just don't like these times when you freak out because it causes issues for us. It ruins nights out. Evenings in. Days away. You might need to put your foot down with her or this will roll on. If it's your baby, you should see it."

I blurt all this advice out, knowing full well I should just shut up. I can't help it. I want to help, and rather selfishly, I want an easy, peaceful relationship and right now any presence she has, be it via social media or a text to him, causes a drama far bigger than is required.

"No. Just leave it. In fact- I don't feel well. I think you should go home. I'm driven mad by it all. I want to be on my own, Lucy. If this keeps going as it is, I'm going to have some sort of breakdown and maybe kill myself."

He's stood by the door now, staring at the wall behind me, clenching and unclenching his teeth. My top is on the floor at his feet and I'm watching him angrily buckle his belt 8 feet away. What just happened?!

My eyes sting with the promise of tears. "Jonny, please- don't do this. Please. You're making it all so much worse. We can just forget all about it and her and go to dinner. I booked it already, you know that!"

I hate the sound of my panicked voice. I want to be sick. Dinner is not what I want- I just want the nice, calm, quiet evening he promised me only half an hour ago. Why hasn't he just blocked her on social media? Blocked her on his phone? If he doesn't want to force the baby issue and avoid it, he needs to damn well AVOID it and not keep picking at the scab and complaining when it bleeds.

I don't say these words. I know better. If I criticise how he's handling this, he'll discard me and maybe this time, for good!

"Leave, Lucy. I mean it. I don't want another relationship. I'll lose my mind! She made me crazy with her nonsense and obsession. I can't go through it again."

Openly crying now, I put my top on and reach for my bag. For a few seconds, I can't see through my tears. Disorientated, I'm unsure where my coat is. Then, I spot it on the floor by the door where it was passionately thrown only 30 minutes ago. Panicked by the reference to suicide and him wanting to be alone, I've no shame and want to get to my knees and beg. I've been back from holiday a couple of weeks and it's been amazing.

I truly believed the time apart had taught him that when we are not together, we grow almost sick with grief. The last few days have been heavenly. In the airport, at arrivals, we'd run towards each other and he had swept me up, swinging me around, kissing me fervently, not caring we had an audience of more than 200 people, most of whom were laughing, smiling and clapping.

I no longer feel pity for this female.... I feel the first flickering, spitting flames of hatred towards the interloper, the unwanted passenger in our relationship. Sinead - the baby-wielding psycho.

Two days later we are back on again and I make no mention of what happened and neither does he. I'm learning what things I am, and am not, allowed to talk about...

A Week or So Later

Flicking the telly to mute, I answer the call from Jonathan's mum, as fast as I can. She gets bad-tempered if I don't answer quickly.

I put it down to boredom and loneliness and make a real effort to be patient with her as much as possible. Chattering away about our respective days around each evening has become fairly common for Jonathan's mum and I. She struck me as a little lonely, and like myself, welcoming of a new friend.

"Where's Jonny tonight then?" she asks me, after we've discussed what I'm making for dinner, how the kids are and how my job search is going. "Not sure. He said he had some sort of meeting or something. It's probably a work thing. He didn't say love"

I'm trying to hold the phone and file my nails at the same time. I can smell the boeuf bourguignon on the hob and gesture madly to Sonny to go and stir it. It smells a little smoky. That usually means it's reduced too much and needs shifted at the bottom.

Leaning forward off the sofa, I can see out of the living room into the kitchen & watch Sonny stir the casserole carefully. The look of concentration on his face makes me smile and I lose the train of conversation for a few seconds. Jo's nattering away in the background and I catch the word "anonymous". My heart flutters before my brain catches up. "Sorry love. Say that last bit again. I wasn't with you then." Before she says the full sentence, my mouth goes dry. "I said," and I hear her sigh of impatience "it's probably an AA meeting. Not work. It's Alcoholics Anonymous"

I can't freak out. Not now. "Oh! Ok! Yeah, of course. I'm daft. The kids are shouting something; I need to go. Sorry. Call you same time tomorrow? Ok. Love you. Bye!"

I can't speak to her right now. I don't know how to compute this. An alcoholic? Going to meetings? Who? Jonny? My Jonny?

My heart's racing. I stare blankly at my hands and taste stomach acid. This doesn't make sense! Why hasn't he told me? Why has no one told me? I've known him a year? A fucking year?! My partner's an alcoholic? What does this mean?

No- it will work. It's fine. It's fine. I try to breathe evenly. The real issue here is not that he's an alcoholic, more that he's managed to keep it from me a whole year. He's avoided bars and clubs with me. Never drank anything. I truly thought it was just his thing.

A gym thing. He let me believe that!? No- I never asked. It's my fault. I should have asked. It's not his fault. He never really lied. He just hid it.

That little voice again. The distant chiming of warning bells.

Eager to reassure him that I was perfectly fine with his AA membership and ongoing sobriety, I messaged Jonathan as soon as I could stop my hands shaking enough to type.

I wrote and rewrote the text, desperate to say the right thing and not trigger a discard. "I don't know why you didn't tell me you were in AA! You silly! I love you! It's no big deal. I'm impressed and proud of you!"

The message fell on deaf ears as of course he read it, blocked me and discarded me- yet again. His mother then waded in, texting me, calling me a "psycho" and a "nosey bitch". This was new as to date; she'd always been fine with me.

Devastated, I tried to appease both of them to be met with continued abuse. Whirling from the shock of the revelation in the first instance and desperate to try and calm my vulnerable partner and his apparently completely paranoid mother, I spent the next 18 hours crying.

Late the next day, he unblocked me and sent a link to a song. Something about a guy needing a woman to teach him how to love. The text reads as standard waffle about "wanting to be a better man" and being "ashamed" etc but I didn't care. He was back. Thank God.

"I'm sorry, baby. I just needed time to get around the fact you know now. I think I thought you already knew because you never asked. It's all good! I'm nearly 8 years by the way- I'll show you my coins. You get one for set times you're sober," comes the message late morning the next day. Weak with relief, I try not to hear the little voice asking me how he hid this huge secret so well....

My technique for verbally (and not just sexually) appeasing Jonathan had improved a bit now we were several months in. My messages to him after a discard would be exactly what he had expected at this stage of the process.

I started referring to myself using words he and his mother used, such as "nosey", "selfish", "stupid", "clumsy" and "thoughtless". As long as I described myself this way, he would eventually come around and re-enter the relationship. No discard was ever a break-up- it was a punishment and a test.

Like an evil dog trainer, he'd withdraw treats and leave me out in the cold until my whining and keening reached the level he accepted. I was devaluing myself to make him happy.

"Let's do the leg press, Luce," Jonathan says, hauling me up off the gym floor. "You are fucking great at the leg press!" he declares proudly, hugging me tightly and kissing me full on the lips then my forehead.

Big hands on my backside then up my neck, he kisses me again. I catch him looking over my shoulder to see who is watching. He likes us being watched.

He's squeezing me so tight I can hardly breathe. Being out of puff from the 50 stomach crunches he made me do makes it even harder to laugh as I push him away.

I hate stomach crunches and it delights him to push me past the number he told me we'd do. "Just 20, baby. Just 20," he had said as I sigh and get down on the floor to start. At 20 he said, "we are going to 50, baby." It was painful.

He'd laughed, standing over me with his feet on mine, keeping me weighted to the floor. I huffed and puffed through 30 and then 40. He used his phone to video my agony in the last 10. I'm a bit embarrassed about it and he knows it. I watched him and cringed as he showed the video to colleagues while I waited for him to set the leg press up.

He steals another kiss then pushes me away a little roughly. He's hyper today. Maybe even manic. It's been a good week- quiet and drama-free. It looks like something's come up job-wise. I haven't told Jonathan I'm really struggling with money.

He winks and reaches for the leg press, making a grand theatre with a "your turn Madam" sweep of the hand. He takes a silly half a bow as I step on. My Prince Charming. I smile, stroke his face and feel a pull of love.

He's always more buoyant when there are no "circus dramas" as he calls them. "Not my circus, not my monkeys," is one of his favourite sayings.

Five minutes later, I step off the leg press and bend down to re-tie my trainer and feel a tell-tale prickle on my neck that signals someone watching me. Standing up abruptly, I turn to face the entrance to the gym.

A woman with a head full of red frizzy hair is stood there. Stock still. She's staring straight at me. At us. She's not in gym gear and she stands out because of this.

Frowning, I tilt my head in a silent question to her. I expect her to wave or smile but she doesn't. I look at Jonny to see if he's noticed her, but he's too busy kicking out and grunting hard on the machine next to me.

Turning away, I bend to fix my other trainer lace. "Weird, starey dude," I mutter to myself. "Did you see that woman? Just stood staring like a weirdo, Jonny?" He isn't listening. Red-faced and straining, he's focused on the press.

Maybe just someone getting a show-around ready for joining another time, I think to myself. His voice makes me jump "Stop messing about, baby! Go get an 8-kilo medicine ball. Side crunches next!" he pants. When I turn to do as he asks, I look back at the entrance- the woman is gone.

Later That Evening

"Sinead says I can see the baby!" The sentence hits me with a thud. "That's great news." I know it should be, but for some reason, I feel unsure.... "When and where?" I try to sound casual. "Her house. Tomorrow evening!" and again that thud, now with a louder bell. "Why can't you have the baby on your own? Take it a nice walk in the park or at your house or maybe to visit your mum?" I'm trying hard to sound casual.

Only an hour ago, I'd posted on Facebook that we had plans for dinner tomorrow. I don't remind Jonathan of this. I don't want to prick his bubble.

"She says she doesn't want the baby away from her and I need to get to know it while she is there."

"Ok- well you should take a present. I'll be at yours for 2 or 3 I think; do you want me to come and help you choose something?" I need to make an effort. "Yes, baby. I'm going to get a little silver bracelet for her."

"Love you baby!" he hangs up, too excited to say goodbye. I've never been in this situation before. Never dated a guy with kids. Maybe it's normal to sit with your ex on child contact visits? I don't know. Just go with it- if he sees the child, he might settle down and finally we can enjoy the relationship we promised each other. This could be a good thing. A really good thing! I pray it goes well and that this is the start of him being able to be a father to the child.

"She's a fucking psycho crazy cunt bitch!" he's shouting. "What, what, what? I don't understand! Calm the fuck down, Jonny. Tell me what's happened!" My heart's racing and I hold the phone so close to my ear it hurts. Yesterday it was all fine. Today he's seen the baby. I don't understand why he's shouting.

"She fucking wouldn't let me in! I haven't seen it!" I hear him hit his hands against the dashboard. He's furious.

"She won't let you see her? Why?" I try to speak calmly, even though now I want to scream and shout myself. Here we go again!!! Fucking Sinead and her games with that kid. Another date ruined. Likely another 3-day discard, as this will all be my fault. I have to calm him down. Stop the bus. We have dinner booked and I bought a new dress. I fucking wish he'd see the fucking solicitor I keep arranging!

"She knows about you. She's gone mental. That's it, I'll never see my daughter now!" Before I get a chance to reply, he slams the phone down. Blocked and alone again, I sit and cry in my new dress until past midnight when I realise he's not going to change his mind.

"It's none of her fucking business," he'd said, shutting me down when I first (and last) advised him to be upfront with her about being with me. "She might not be a proper ex, Jonny, but she has got pregnant and when the baby comes, things could get difficult."

"She's got her kid and that's it. I'm not telling her. None of her business who I see Lucy," he replied.

On making up after that particular discard, Jonathan talked a lot more about Sinead being the main issue affecting our relationship.

"She drives me potty, baby. I'm sorry. It's her- she's a psycho and I was upset. I just want to see my kid and she's fucking it up."

"It's ok, I understand," I message back. "Can you call me and tell me what happened and we can try and fix it together? I promise I will do whatever I can to help."

Later, he sets out the new rules of the relationship. "I'll give you her number to block her on your phone and WhatsApp. Right, her full name is Sinead Lorrimer, so now you know her second name you can block her on social media. She has a few fake accounts and I'll give you the names of those too. It's best we just get on with things and maybe be a bit more careful about what we post about. She will watch us. It's what she does. She's a really unwell person. Ok, baby?" I listen to this wordlessly. That warning bell again.

This all seems overkill... but then again, of course, it's good he's being careful and protecting me.

After the Bracelet Debacle, things actually were quite calm and chilled. As I recall it, we had several weeks of "peace". Putting this down to the only difference in our life- Sinead was gone. Angry at him being with me, we didn't hear from her and I was absurdly pleased.

I started to plan Christmas at my place as a family and Jonathan invited himself along, much to my delight. Adoring him absolutely, I again started to hope that this was it- this was all going to be ok. He was again the man I met. Indulgent, passionate and intense. We got even closer and things felt solid and safe finally, after all.

Is there an emotion more dangerous than hope? I have come to realise that there really isn't.

Listen to: The Police: "Every Step You Take"

Red Flags:

> *Using people as supply. Narcissists need people to fulfil varying needs and to supply them with sex, escape plans, witnesses, confidence, acceptance, popularity and so on. People are there in their lives for a function only.*

So, it's not just romantic partnerships/sex that Narcs and Casanova Psychopaths need people for. They need other people for 2 other reasons:

For cover and camouflage. To help them play out the theatre they want prospective victims and flying monkeys to see. These people support the Narc and give them alibis and lie for them while they act out behind your back.

For an escape route and "rebuild" plan. For when they discard you. This is the buffer against your (totally true) accusations of cheating, lies and abuse. This is their support network while they destroy you. This helps them stay exactly the same and start the process all over again with the next victim.

Threats of harm. Narcs will not just threaten to end the relationship if they want to manipulate or punish you for some reason, they will threaten to harm themselves. Suicide, relapse or even cheating are ideal threats to scare you half to death and make sure you don't just toe the line, but that while you are discarded, you sit in fear and chase them incessantly to make sure they are ok.

Hidden Addictions. There are theories that Narcissists and people with other personality disorders are more likely to develop addictions. I'm inclined to agree. Narcs are naturally arrogant and selfish. They enjoy indulging their impulses. They also will suffer stress in their attempts to live the two or more lives they enjoy, so drugs or alcohol will help them stay as calm as they prefer in order to do this.

Enablers (e.g. family members) being vicious. When you unsettle the Narc with truth-seeking or accidentally uncovering lies/secrets. Narcs don't just have the "flying monkeys" who support them from afar and watch the pain you are in- they also have closer supplies who will lash out cruelly and blame you for any perceived disruption. They feed off the drama almost as much as the Narc does. You will struggle to engage with these people but try, try, try again because the Narc claims to need you to get on with them. Enablers are usually best friends or close family members and are often Narcs or Sociopaths themselves.

Refusing Advice that clearly will make things better. Narcs have no interest in reducing drama or crises in their lives, nor in dealing with anyone causing you or both of you pain. They enjoy the stress that it places on you, because it shows them how much you care for them. You will gradually get angrier and angrier at whoever the Narc says is causing this stress, and in my case, it was a very common Narc supply- The Malignant Co-Dependant warm supply ex.

Being Self Critical. Appeasing your Narc with negative comments and unnecessary apologies to "calm situations down" or get them to talk to you or see you. Apologising when it's not your fault and using phrases that they like to use on you- You're not helping, you're "controlling". You're not supportive, you're "nosey". You're not passionate, you're "demanding in bed" and so on...

January 2015

Roz, the woman I swim with, came across as a bit of a busybody, but I liked her. She had been using the centre that Jonathan worked at for several years, and was often in swimming the same times as me. Accidental meetings in the leisure club had led us to plan more organised meets, such as this lunch.

She wasted no time in giving me a detailed description of what she thought of Jonathan- describing him in glowing terms. "Funny, kind and helpful and oh so charming"!

Then I heard the word "engagement". White as a sheet, I listened to her prattle on about how it was such a coincidence her daughter was on the same degree course as Jonathan's ex-fiancée, Sinead. Then the room tilted a little.

Again, that awful rock in my gut and now a new thing, a strange blurring of my vision. Roz is still babbling on as I try to breathe correctly. I blink repeatedly and hold on to my chair for dear life. Thankful she's stabbing away at her salad with vigour and not looking at me, now the room starts to spin and I break out in a sweat.

"Oh yes. The red roses on the mantelpiece and that lovely card! Such a nice picture to share on Facebook. So sweet!" she's exclaiming.

I want to be sick right here, right now. I want to shove her fucking plate off the table and watch it smash on the floor. I shift in my chair and try to calm the fuck down.

Crunching away and still talking, she goes on and on, but I can't hear her. There's a radio turned up high in my head. His voice. Other peoples. My own instincts. "She's bonkers!" "She was just casual." "I never wanted her." "She's obsessed." "She needs to get over it"; over and over. It's like a ghost train ride that just won't stop.

The screaming hurtling cart suddenly comes to a stand-still. I remember when we first connected online. Fuck! Of course! His page said, "engaged". That time he said she hacked it. Fuck!!!!

"She shagged plenty of people between the times of me shagging her. I never really liked her, so I wasn't bothered. I hoped she would leave me be when she caught some other poor guy that way," he said only last week when I asked why they never got together properly.

Roz has a glint in her eye now. She's mid-chew. I realise she's rather enjoying this. She has picked up on my shock and the change in atmosphere. She has some dressing at the side of her mouth and I don't tell her to wipe it off.

"I don't feel well, Roz. I haven't felt well all day, to be honest. Let me pay." An apology. I'm sorry." I rush the words and don't look at her. My chair squeals in pain as I push it back. I grab at it to stop it clattering to the dark slate floor.

At home, before turning a single light on or even shutting my front door, I make a drink. My hands spasm as I pour it into the glass. I drink it in one and stagger to the bathroom. The floor is moving like I'm on a boat. Washing my face doesn't help. It's blotchy and puffy. I look ugly. I look bitter, scared and damaged. I don't know if I can ask him about this. I know I shouldn't.

With it being Wednesday and the boys at their dads', Jonathan would usually come here to mine and I'd make dinner for us even if he was backshift. Today I'm dreading seeing him. I know he will take one look at me and know.

Three gins in and I'm still sitting in the dark. He messages me, "That's me on the way up the road, baby. Can't wait to see you!"

I'm in a panic but sufficiently tipsy to think I can skilfully pretend I am fine. Gathering plates and cutlery, I nearly drop them and my heart speeds up again. With shaking hands, I light candles and plump cushions like an idiot.

Going through these little habits helps a little. I sit on the sofa and pretend to watch television. I have another drink but drink it too quickly. Hearing the familiar slam of his car door, I rush to clean my teeth. Bending over the sink, my shoulders prickle as though he is already in the flat watching me.... judging me.

As I walk out into the hall to meet him, he swoops me up in a bear hug. Clenching my eyes shut, I inhale. His familiar smell makes me want to scream.

He lets me go and steps back to look at me. His face folds in confusion and quickly changes to anger.

This is why people with personality disorders like Narcissism are often confused with empaths- they can read people like books and sense emotions, almost like smelling something dirty.

Stepping back, his eyes darken and his jaw sets. I've drunk too much to be careful.

"You were engaged to Sinead. You lied to me!" My voice cracks. I know confronting him is dangerous, but I can't help myself. I have to know what is going on. I have hope he will sit down and tell me the truth and we can get past this.

"Away and take a fuck to yourself. What the fuck are you talking about? You're fucking daft! I am away UP THE ROAD!!" he screams in my face, as he backs towards the door. He shoots me a look of complete hatred and grabs his backpack. "Please, Jonny. Please! I didn't mean to upset you! I don't understand! I'm just trying to understand!" I beg to an empty hall and the echo of a slammed door. Sliding down the wall, I sit on the floor to sob.

In the following days, I lost 2 more pounds in weight and had zero sleep clutching my phone, waiting for him to come around and be mine again.

By the Friday, he'd told me Sinead had bought herself an engagement ring, bought herself a card and posted the pictures on social media to "force" him into looking like they were engaged, even though they never even dated. She apparently did it once she knew she was successfully pregnant. Comparing his story to her strange behaviour and the tales his friends told me, I took this story in and believed it completely. You would have too....

Listen to: Sabrina Carpenter: "Lie for Love"

Red Flags:

Running Away & being angry. When lies are uncovered Narcs live with so many lies and juggle so many masks to hide them, that when they start to get found out they will be vile. They will refuse to discuss it, blame you for being "nosey" and even gaslight you, saying what you have seen or understood to be true is simply "nonsense". It will be such a shocking change in demeanour and so confusing, you will almost immediately regret finding the truth out and make yourself responsible for it.

A refusal to "talk over" issues or problems. Narcs don't like "talking it out" or explaining themselves. They see honesty as a weakness and as too high risk. Talking calmly and like an adult is virtually impossible, unless they are doing it in a Hoover phase to get you back on side after already refusing to talk or explain away a lie or problem such as the "engagement" I discovered. Their tantrums are also a good way of training you to hide any feelings you have at being lied to, and you will eventually stop confronting them. You will keep their secrets inside yourself or simply start to live in denial. It is toxic and unnatural and will destroy you in time.

April 2015

Niall is still furious about our marriage ending, but I never ignore his calls. On this particular day, I'm walking through the park having done some shopping for dinner for Jonathan and I. Answering Niall 's call, I brace myself for the usual barrage of abuse.

He's shouting like a maniac and it takes a few seconds to even capture the essence of what he's talking about. "Some fucking nutter messaged me on LinkedIn. About you and that ugly bastard. Get it stopped. I want to fucking get on with my life! The life you fucking ruined, you cunt!" I'm pretty used to his vile rants, but usually, he just calls me names; this is of a different theme. A flicker of fear twitches in my chest, and having not eaten today, I put the shopping down at the first signs of a sugar low.

"What? I don't know what you're on about! Calm down! What's the name on the account?" Abruptly, I sit down on a grassy bank but realise the grass is wet. Frowning in annoyance, I'm not yet aware of what is coming. A train hurtling towards me.

"I'll fucking check. God sakes, hang on. Wait there." I hear him tapping at his laptop and muttering obscenities about me. Then, suddenly I know who it's going to be. Who it always is.

"The name on the account is Sinead Lorrimer. Her fucking messages, all 3 of them, say you ruined her life. That you and he ruined her life! Just like me. Life-ruining bastards! Look what you've done you stupid cunt!" he shouts. My stomach lurches. I knew the peace wouldn't last. She's full-blown stalking me. No, us.

"Block her. Send me the screenshots of her messages. I'll get Jonny to stop her. I promise. I'm sorry. She's been stalking us too. She's not well. She's in AA. He was single when he met me. They never even went out!

She's just obsessed with him. I'm really sorry" Babbling and fully crying now, the shock has me shaking like a leaf. This is bad. Really bad. Really, really bad

Then it gets worse. "I didn't tell you, but I had 2 calls just before Christmas too. November and December! Some woman, drunk and shouting, calling you a home-wrecker and a slut!" She's called him too?! Oh my God. I feel faint.

"Just fucking deal with it. Oh, and because of this, I can't afford the usual maintenance for Rufus. She's upset me. I'm ill. I'm cutting the money. Fuck you!" he says, and slams the phone down. Another month where I will default on my mortgage, but I can deal with that later.

For the *first time* in what has now been almost a year of Sinead punctuating my relationship with Jonathan, I make contact with her. I don't even make it upstairs to my flat, but stand outside in the street. Leaning against the wall on the street outside my house, I tap her name into Facebook. I feel a flutter of surprise as I see I'm not blocked any more.

"That's odd timing.... no, it's clever timing." White-hot rage spreads through me. Suddenly I don't care about Jonathan's excuses, or that kid, or what she has to say to me. This has to stop and it's time I stepped in.

"What is wrong with this woman?! What sort of person behaves this way? A professional woman in her 40s. A mother!" Ranting to no one in particular, I'm losing control.

I don't want to flip out, but I'm struggling. I haven't had any contact with this woman, yet she's stomping about my already really difficult life. "Why is she doing this?!" I shout at my phone.

An old man walking past me jumps in surprise. "Sorry! Sorry!" I say in a rush. "Women are mental, aren't they?" My voice catches as I try to laugh. He smiles but looks frightened. I'm not surprised. I look nuts.

On the screen is a selfie of her and oddly, it's her sat in his living room. Oh my God, she is the double of the woman I saw stood in the gym last year... oh fuck. Fuck, fuck. Fuckety fuck!!! It was HER! This is the first time I have seen her face. I was never interested before. She's the woman from the gym. She stood and watched us; that's why soon after it, all this stuff started happening. She found out about me because she was stalking Jonathan. I feel faint and slide down the wall to sit on the pavement, not caring how strange I look.

Before I can stop, I'm typing a message to her on FB messenger. I don't know what else to do, so this seems an opportunity to draw a line in the sand.

I try to be polite but get a little patronising and passive aggressive at points. Being this upset, I have to try hard to keep my temper. I don't swear and make no threats, but I probably am being a little bit rude in suggesting she leave us alone to be happy and go find someone else who "does want" her.

Without taking my eyes off my phone, I fumble for my keys and let myself into my stairwell. Breathless and disorientated I almost trip going up the stairs but actually, yeah...I feel exhilarated. This will all be resolved today. We can maybe argue it out or at least discuss what each of us wants surely?

"You're bonkers"- ping. That's all she has to say? All her stalking, trouble, dramas and accusations and that's it?!

I sit on my top step and try and make sense of this. "I'm the bonkers one? What the fuck?"

I start to type a reply. I want to know what she means and ask why she is doing this to us, to me. Her picture disappears and my gut drops.

She's blocked me! A year of weirdness and meddling, and her reply is to call me bonkers and block me?!

My phone rings as I struggle out of my coat, drop it on the hall floor and stagger into the kitchen. "What the fuck are you doing!" my beloved's shouting. "She's going mental! She says you swore at her and threatened her! I'll never see my fucking kid now!" he screams.

Don't lose it, Lucy. Don't flip out. "Jonny- she has been stalking us. She has contacted Niall at least 3 times. He's going mental! I have a child to him! It's not my fault! It's yours *and* hers! I can show you the message. I made no threats and I didn't even swear. I can prove it!"

"I don't want to see the fucking message. You've fucking ruined everything! You can deal with it now. I'm fed up of all of this!" he shouts, and I hear him cut me off.

Dazed and battered, I lean against the oven and stare into the sink. There are 2 coffee mugs from Jonathan and I this morning. Closing my eyes, I count to 10 and try to stop the impending panic attack that seems so common now.

I wish I could go back in time to this morning. I wish I was stronger and I could somehow get Jonny to defend our relationship. Be more defiant with Sinead. I wish he wasn't so afraid of not seeing a child that he's only seen 2 or 3 times. I wish he'd just tell her to fuck off and go to see the solicitor I've arranged for him 3 times now! I look up at the ceiling in silent

prayer and my eyes fill with hot angry tears. I need a miracle &
I need help.

*It is around now, I believe, I started to develop the narcissistic
infection. I think I'd been bullied, tormented and confused for so
long and not just by Jonathan.... that my brain simply started to
fuse and react to it. In a sort of survival state, I began to try and
manage what was going on by developing anger issues towards
who I felt was responsible, I got very nasty and mean about
anyone or anything hurting Jonathan or our relationship and my
manipulation skills improved so I knew what and how to talk to
him or about him to keep the peaceful times lasting as long as
possible. I started to mirror my abusers to try to second-guess
them and at times, passively aggressively take control of what I
thought was going on. The infection only got worse because, like
all Narc-Victim relationships, he and his flying monkeys got worse
and worse. I became addicted to keeping Jonathan sweet, to
protect myself. I lost sight of my parenting responsibilities and
began to try to "scare" Sinead off with posts on Facebook
whenever I knew she had unblocked me to watch us.*

By mid-April 2015, Jonathan and I'd known each other for 18
months and we decided to book a week's holiday to Tunisia.
Having had a wee job since December, I had the cash handy and
paid for it myself.

"We can have some time together, no dramas and away from
all the jealous bastards trying to control us," he says, when I show
him a screenshot of the booking confirmation. Absurdly pleased
he was "into it", I didn't bother asking him for a contribution
towards it. As far as I was concerned, this was a way to bring us
closer and have time away from Sinead and our other haters.

I'd enjoyed a long charity sector career prior to meeting
Jonathan, but hadn't had a job or income since Niall effectively
sacked me from our business for ending my marriage to him. So, I
was delighted to be headhunted in the November before, and to
have had a regular income across late winter and into spring 2015.

Jonathan started his usual pre-discard nonsense the night
before I started the job (late November 2014) and almost
completely ruined it. This time he didn't blame anyone else, but

claimed I deserved better and should get on with my life without him. He timed this declaration of false modesty and desire to "set me free to find someone better" late in the evening as I prepared for my first day at work.

With less than an hour's sleep, a white face, puffy eyes and shaky hands, I delivered my 3 children to school and staggered to my new office the following day. Broken and shattered that the love of my life again didn't seem to want me, I don't think I made the best impression.

Across the time I worked there, he discarded me many, many times, to the point where I lost the job in the end.

Colleagues grew fed up of my regular visits to the toilet to cry, beg-text him to end a discard, or to be sick. Understandably, they grew fed up of our intense make-up phases, where he barely stopped messaging me and I was distracted from work. They also couldn't understand why I was so madly in love with such an obvious cunt-bag idiot. They lost respect and patience rather quickly. Even though my contract was extended from 3 months to 6 months for meeting my targets, I was let go just before we went on holiday. In all honesty, I was relieved. This meant I could focus entirely on Jonathan and keeping him... & us...right.

It had been a pain in the backside getting Jonathan his time off, as he said the staff kept losing his holiday forms. When I said I would mention it to his line manager, he reacted swiftly and said he would make it happen himself. The holidays were approved 9 days before we travelled, to my utter relief. I now realise he was stalling on the holiday as best her could although the answer as to "why" came much later.

I still don't like reflecting on Tunisia. I struggle to think about how much I enjoyed it and I can't even look at the photographs we took. I threw out the turquoise wrap he bought me as well as the little matching bag. My face tightens and my heart twitches when I see pictures of it or hear about the gun attack on the (now iconic) beach only a week after we left. Anything about the place now makes the bile rise in my throat.

On the first day of the holiday, we (well, he) got chatting to two women from Scotland in the restaurant at breakfast.

Jonathan heard their accent as we walked past them and of course, stopped dead, spun on his heels and strutted over to chat. Abruptly left alone in the middle of the dining room, I went to make up our plates for breakfast. I knew he'd be a while.

We saw these 2 women, Jemma and Marie, a few times by the pool, but they never swam and were often covered up with big blouses or towels- we didn't chat again, which I thought was a shame seeing as Jonathan was so excited to meet people from home.

The resort was cobbled-streets-bobbing-sailboat-pretty craft market-gorgeous with a long, white, sandy beach a mile down the road. That week we had boat trips, took stupid selfies with a camel and had a ridiculous press-up competition with a group of Tunisian school kids. This produced hilarious photos of Jonathan and I displaying our abs and guns proudly. I wore a lot of red that holiday as it's Jonathan's favourite colour, and in one picture you can clearly see how slim I was.

Tunisia was a bubble of happiness for us both- away from "dramas" and Sinead, he seemed very relaxed. It was the happiest time of my relationship with him and it seemed to be one of his with me. We spoke of coming back for our honeymoon as we lay in the sun, frying in tan accelerator together. He thought it hilarious to choose the one called "Addiction". Handing over my £20 at the airport cosmetics counter, I laughed along with him.

Towards the end of the holiday, I made one of my mistakes.

Jonny was almost as brown as I was but still agitated that his skin was peeling while mine was glowing. "It's because you try too hard! You need to let the tan develop, not burn and hope for the best," I say and rub cream on my stomach. "But I want to be darker than you!" he complains, lying back on the lounger and putting his sunglasses on. "I want to win the tan competition." His petulant tone makes me laugh. Seeing him happy, I relax, just a little.

Over the top of my sunglasses, I take a quick look at him. He's watching me apply cream to my legs now and not looking at my face.

I can't hold it in any more. I've felt sick all day- ever since I overheard him telling one of the bar staff he went to Turkey recently. "When was it you went to Turkey, babe?!" There, it's out. I've asked. Fuck!

The silence between us is painful and I want to take the question back. Pack it away and never mention it again. The cream has long been absorbed, but extremely anxious, I can't help but keep pretending to rub it into my skin. Realising my hands are shaking slightly, I reach for my towel and grip so tight it hurts.

Behind the Ray-Bans I bought; I can see Jonathan's face set into that familiar look. His cheek now has a small pulse going in and out and I know I have said something wrong. I should have listened to my instincts. My nerves were a warning to stay quiet.

A few more heartbeats of silence. Now some teeth-grinding. That familiar fucking sound of him being angry with me.

"I went on holiday with Sinead and her 2 kids." He says this clearly, staring out at sea now. The pulse in his cheek gets even faster.

A plummeting feeling takes over and my mouth goes dry. I lick my lips and taste the banana flavour of the tan cream. A bead of sweat prickles my chest and dribbles down between my breasts.

My heart feels like it is going to stop. Who goes on holiday with a "casual" sexual partner for a week AND with her two kids!?

"I don't understand," I say blandly. "You said she was just someone you had the odd one-night stand with?" The words get stuck in my throat and I almost choke. "...one-night stand with?" I repeat more clearly.

He turns slowly to look at me. It reminds me of Arnie in Terminator when he spots a target. "For fuck sakes, just leave it! Why are you so fucking nosey?" He swings his big legs off the sunbed and I hear a creak as he stands up.

He angrily shoves on the sandals I bought him and storms down to the water's edge to kick at the shallows like a petulant child. Dumbstruck, I'm rooted to the spot. It's not waves I can hear, it's voices. His voice. His mother's. People telling me Sinead was a nobody that Jonathan barely knew. My breakfast rises up in my throat and I cover my mouth as the sun lounger seems to sway beneath me. It's another panic attack. Anxious he doesn't see me; I stagger to the toilet in the beach bar behind us and sit there for nearly an hour. When I go back to the beach, he's lying snoring with my sun-hat over his face.

Later in the room, I get more of the story. "Sinead booked the holiday to Turkey" without his permission and "forced him to go". He went on to say she was in "relapse at the time and drinking a lot" so he was worried about her children travelling with her alone. He said it was a "crap" holiday and that she regularly disappeared and he believed she was off drinking, taking drugs and probably "sleeping around" with people while they were there.

Nearly a year passed before she came looking for him again and they slept together once, and that was the time she got pregnant. "That's why I call it a one-night stand. Because it was, baby" he whined, as I simply lay there, naked, next to him, looking at the ceiling. Desperate to believe him and go along with this entirely believable story, I accepted it. Immeasurably glad he wasn't shouting at me, calling me nosey or saying he wanted to go home.

It sounded just like him to go on the holiday to avoid a drama and keep her 2 children safe. When Jonathan fell asleep, I quietly left the room. I need peace, quiet and a drink.

My heart sank when I spotted a mother and daughter I'd got friendly with sitting in a booth by the bar. I'd hoped to sit alone and get some space to try and make sense of why Jonathan kept lying to me about the past.

The mum seemed to signal to her daughter, called Shona, and as I sat down at my table, she stood up and walked over.

Shona looks nervous. Without asking, she slides into the seat opposite. Suddenly, looking at her pretty face, I'm glad she is here and the words just fall out of my mouth. She sits quietly listening to me prattle on about Jonathan and how we got together and his mad ex and the kids he wants to see. At one point, she gets a napkin from the bar for me to wipe my face on. "I've got to get my shit together- he hates it when I cry. I'm going to ruin this holiday with my nonsense."

"You deserve better than him," she says suddenly. "He's not good enough for you."

Staring at her in surprise, I start to defend him. "He loves me to bits! I just think he fibs about her because he doesn't want to upset me. She really is crackers. You don't know the half of what he has told me about her. It's a bit of a shame, really. She's not well. She makes his life a misery."

Then Shona says something really odd. "Do you think he is a bit of a...erm... Sleaze...?" She's whispering and leaning towards me, her pale blue eyes searching mine.

I recoil and laugh at the same time. I do it so fast that I almost spill my drink. "No! Don't be daft! He is a terrible flirt, but then so am I. He's just the same with old grannies as he is with anyone else. He's just really friendly."

I crunch an ice cube viciously. Reacting to her insult of the man I adore has pushed my defence buttons. I want to see him. Kiss him. Laugh about all of this. It's so ridiculous. This is a beautiful place and I am here with him and he is here with me. I want to go up to our room and get dressed for dinner. Forget about all of this muddy, shitty, historical crap.

"Honestly Shona, he's not like that! He adores me. You can see that! He's just over-confident and a bit of a show-off, love."

Shona looks a bit embarrassed and sits back. I watch as she carefully sips her drink.

She blinks and with a slight shake of the head, stands up. A decision made. "Ok, no probs, Luce. Do you want another drink? I've got to go get mum one anyway." Walking towards the bar, she stops suddenly and stoops to hug me. "Stay here with me and mum, honey," she whispers in my ear.

"No, love. I have to go get ready. Plus, if he naps longer than an hour, he is grumpy!" I laugh humourlessly. I feel strange.

Listen to: Robert Palmer: "Addicted to Love"

Red Flags:

- *Puppeteering.* Narcs enjoy setting up cat fights and watching the fur and claws fly. They will play people off against each other and be supremely entertained by the fallout. Narcs would choose drama over peace any day of the week and it's why any relationship with them just feels like a constant rollercoaster of dramas and yet the Narc never really steps in to take control, stop it or help you!

- *The Narc creating a FALSE circle of safety and trust between you.* They drip feed the idea that it's you and them against the world. In excess, it can lead to Stockholm Syndrome and encourages you to become totally bonded with your abuser. You will lap up your abuser talking like that because it makes you feel special and safe, and most importantly, like we were uniquely tied together know this feeds your (already fragile) ego and encourages you to agree that yes- it's just the pair of you against everyone who is "trying to ruin" what you have. A by-product of this means you will doubt any negative stories about your abuser. He/she has ensured you doubt these "haters" before they even report anything to you!

- *Sabotage.* Disordered people will try and sabotage pretty much anything positive happening to you or anyone else they are challenged by. They do this because a) they are jealous of you doing "normal" things and b) their ego is fed by your response to their created drama. If you cancel your "thing" to pander to them or rush to their side, OR get upset and beg when they cancel something mutually-planned "for" or "with them", they are fed. They are feeding off your reaction.

- *Lying about your worries and feelings to "protect" your partner or keep them calm.* Pretending to be fine or not asking questions that you think will result in some sort of argument or worse, a discard is mental torture that is very common in abusive relationships. Narcs, in particular, see pain/hurt/fear as weaknesses and they are a reflection of the bad behaviours your Narc has exposed you to. If you cry, your Narc has to see it and quite frankly it fucks them off. They think you're

83

"punishing them for not being perfect" by crying when you discover a lie or other betrayal and soon you will learn to hide your tears. They prefer it that way.

- <u>*Backing out or ruining plans for extended intimate time together.*</u> Do you find your Narc initially thinks a holiday or party or family dinner is a great idea then as it looms closer, they have more excuses than you can shake a stick at? Do you feel like you are put in a position where you must make it work for them to attend? These events represent intimacy. They are also a time when they are away from whatever secret life they also want to maintain. It's stressful for a Narc to be away for hours or days from the seclusion of the places where they sit quietly and plot and hunt and hide from the truth. Watch for this *"panic mode"* when you have some extended time together coming up.

- <u>*Losing a passport, forgetting insurance, not booking the hotel or not putting holiday forms in are classic pre-holiday sabotage acts*</u>. Narcs really know how to keep us on our toes and frighten us when we are looking forward to something. They enjoy teaching us who's boss and reminding us they are in control.

May 2015

Early on in the holiday, we'd already made quite a few new friends, including Shona and her mum. Shona had grown close across the week. Her mum had developed a bit of a romance with one of the members of staff, which left Shona on her own quite a lot.

As Jonathan seemed quite relaxed and at ease, I accepted an offer of a game of water polo with Shona and some staff. In my absence, Jonathan made small talk with an English couple holidaying with their teenage daughter who was called Elizabeth.

Later he tells me (nearly choking with laughter) that the daughter is "daft" and completely "thick". Apparently, she said something about Anglesey being in Spain or something similar, and he thinks it's hilarious that she is so "stupid".

I thought he was being a little cruel and told him off. Frowning at me, he walked onto the veranda to play on his phone. Again.

The English couple's daughter is a very attractive girl- big, bouncy boobs and a pretty face, but having spent some time around her I would say yes, she is certainly vulnerable.

Shona says she parties at night with Elizabeth and some other younger ones, so I get the gossip every morning after breakfast. Erica apparently has a different member of staff every night and apparently isn't backwards in coming forwards about having an STI and recently having had an abortion! It's pretty grimy and rather sad stuff and I felt really sorry for her. When I tell Jonathan, he refers to her as a "slut".

Shocked at his judgement of her, I scold him again. "Hey! Don't speak like that, Jonny. It's not nice. If she's acting like that, maybe there are other issues there behind the scenes. Men are taking advantage of her!"- I playfully slap him on the backside and shove him off. We've been in bed for a quickie before dinner.

Later in the shower, I mull over his odd language about the girl and remember it's actually not the first time. There's a young girl who hangs about the reception at his work, who's recently had a baby- he also calls her names every now and again and yet, to her face, is all fatherly and respectful. I've never really noticed it before...

On the last day of the Tunisia holiday, I was packing us both up, and on an impulse, I set aside a few pairs of pretty shorts and tops for Shannon. I felt sorry for her staying for another week without us while her mum played tonsil tennis with Sporty Pants.

I leave the clothes neatly folded up outside their room. Thirty minutes later Shona knocks on our door and walks in. She's in just a towel. Although she's 17, she looks a lot younger. Very pale, some freckles and certainly pretty, she could be 14 or 15.

She hugs me and, reflected in the bedroom mirror, I can see Jonathan smoking a cigarette on the balcony. He has his back to us but I can tell he's tense.

Shona releases me, but stays holding both my hands. She really is a lovely wee thing. I'm definitely going to ask her to be our childminder when we get home.

"You are a star- I hardly brought any shorts! I didn't expect it to be so hot!" She laughs. "It's no problem. Jonny bought me some things out here in his bag, so I don't have much space to get stuff home anyway. Glad you like them!" As I finish talking, I watch her walk out onto the veranda. She takes a cigarette from Jonathan and he hip bumps her. It's nice they get on so well.

A few days into the holiday, he'd fallen off the wagon with his smokey dokey (one of those fake cigarette e-cig things) and bought some cigarettes from a shop down by the beach. I wasn't bothered- "it's just some fags, Jonny!" I had said, laughing and hugging him. "You're 8 years sober for God sakes; a few fags won't make a difference to that amazing achievement!" Him wittering on about little things like "taking up a fag", "being sore from the gym", or "having no money" always set my anxiety off- his little mini-panics often led to a discard. I've learned to jump in and stroke his ego quickly, and it sometimes staves off any emotional upsets, but often it doesn't.

Spikes of their laughter punctuate the next half hour and I get on with packing us up to travel home.

"He's fucking lazy, Lucy," she declares loudly and hugs me from behind. Turning round, I glance at Jonny—he won't like her criticising him. "I don't mind doing it. He gets pissed off packing and I'm good at it."

A shout from outside. "She's my good girl!" As he walks back in, I see he's topless, the favourite red t-shirt now draped over the veranda.

Pulling me into a bear hug, he kisses the top of my head and inhales. I look up and see he's eyeing up his own reflection in the mirror and flexing his muscles as he squeezes me tight.

"Dunno what I'd do without her, my Luce," he says, and fully lifts me up off the ground, making Shona crow about what a cute couple we are.

Earlier that day at breakfast, a group of us had made plans to go to the Irish pub down the street, near the beach. A sort of last hoorah. This would be the first time we had been out of the hotel resort at night and I was actually really looking forward to it. I had sensed Jonathan's mood darkening across the latter part of the afternoon and my anxiety started to creep in.

I'm running a bath while Jonathan sits on the bed playing on his phone. Leaning out of the bathroom to have a quick check of him, my heart plummets when I see he's hunched and taught again. His bag lies packed at his feet and mine is still unfinished on my side of the bed. Frowning and quiet, his manner a stark contrast to the jokey happy charming man at the pool bar less than an hour ago.

It's a cooler evening, misty and electric as though a tropical storm is brewing. The hairs on my arms suddenly stand on end, so I wrap my towel around me and sit on the toilet waiting for the bath to run, not wanting to annoy Jonathan by what he calls "hassling" him or "pressuring him to cheer up". The bath is taking an age to run and as a chill settles over me, I can't help but crave the heat of the water and a quick departure out of here. His mood will improve once we are out and about and around other people. It always does.

Turning the taps off and sinking into the hot foam a few minutes later, I hear shouting from the bedroom. Rising out of the water fast and badly splashing the floor, I catch only the end of what he's said. Something to do with him not "feeling right" and being "anxious about going to a pub". My heart thuds with an almost painful surge of fear. This was the first time he had ever mentioned he was struggling with his sobriety. Having been to dozens of AA meets with him, I knew that a relapse of any sort was going to devastate his life and mine. This is almost certainly the first stage of a discard. Fuck!

I should have seen this coming! Of course he's freaking out. All the prattling on about "taking up a fag" and giving up on his e-cig, then the "guilt shame and remorse" crap he often talks about in AA...I need to stop the bus on this fast or not only will the holiday be ruined, but his 8 years' sobriety!

"I'll stay in then!" I'm already getting out of the bath having literally got in only a minute ago. "We can play pool and cuddle in the saloon bar!" I won't drink. "We can have an early night, if you know what I mean!" I try to laugh, but I'm panicking so badly I make a shit job of it. Wrapping my towel round my head, I pad out to the bedroom to find him smoking on the veranda again.

He turns around and flicks the cigarette butt deftly over his shoulder into the hotel gardens below. "Nah, baby. You go. I'm fine. I just need space"- at the last word my stomach tenses. Oh my God, please don't do this! Walking towards me, I realise he looks calmer than I expected. In fact, he's eyeing me appreciatively. I'm naked bar the towel on my head. Relief surges through me. "Honestly, baby. Just go. Have fun," he says, smiling as he pulls me onto his lap.

I let him kiss me and he runs his hands down my wet back and over my naked buttocks. He squeezes them a little and I catch him watching himself in the mirror behind me again.

Playfully slapping his chest, I pull back away from him to see his face properly. It's true, he actually does look ok. "Give over! If you're not well, you're doing great to hide it! I have to get dressed anyway. I'm meeting them lot downstairs in less than15 minutes!"

He lies back on the bed, cross-legged, playing with his phone and sucking on his e-cig. Happy now I'm leaving him to have the room to himself, there's no atmosphere at all. I try and ignore how this makes me feel. He slides behind me and zips up my green, sequinned, mini dress and kisses my neck, whispering "have a good time, I'm fine" into my hair.

Three hours later, we are still in the pub and I'm sober as a judge. There's something wrong, but I can't place my finger on it. He hasn't messaged me to see if we are having a good time, nor to let me know he's ok. I've messaged him but he's blue-ticked and not replied. Desperate to show him I'm capable of socialising without him and able to give him the "peace" he so regularly demands, I pretend I'm fine and resolve to stay until closing time.

At some point around 10 pm, Shona picks up her phone and says he's Facebook messaged her. Frowning in confusion but extremely relieved he's ok, I read the message she shows me. "Hi, babe- not in best frame of mind for the pub. Enjoy"- not a word about me. A shard of anger slices through me but disappears as I remember this is one of his techniques to passively communicate with me. He likes to use third parties to pass messages on when he's in a funny mood with me. I'm just so fucking glad he's talking to the person he knows I'm right now sitting with. As long as he's talking, there is no discard, or at the very least, it's over! "Let me know when you're coming back" is another message he sends a few minutes later.

Knowing he's ok means I can relax a bit, and I manage to enjoy the last two hours with my friends. As we tipsily fall out of the lift and loudly shout "byeee" to each other, Shona and I go our separate ways and mutually stagger into our rooms at the same time, making us laugh uproariously. Taking my shoes off, I tiptoe in, but Jonny is still in the same position I left him in. Wide awake, in bed and faffing about on his phone. He seems absolutely fine and the relief I feel is intense. I relax and fall into bed beside him.

Waking up in the morning and still a bit groggy, I automatically rub my face and feel a pain in my cheek. Looking in the mirror later, I can see that I've been bitten by something nasty. It's a raised bump, almost like a wart! The prominent bump has 2 puncture wounds.

The little bump stayed on my cheek for more than a month. I still have a slight scar now and in a sinister way it represents that holiday- a little spidery vampire bite to symbolise the long, slow process of him sucking me dry.

Waiting for the buses to travel back to the airport, our friends appear one by one to hug us and wave goodbye. Everyone bar Shannon's mum and the older couple come and say goodbye. I find it a bit odd, then put their absences down to hangovers from the night before.

The trip home was pretty uneventful and we chatted away with an attractive dark-haired girl sat at the window end of our 3 seats on the plane. It turned out her boyfriend was also a hardcore gym-goer, so she and I talk most of the journey home- sometimes mocking our menfolk for being moany bastards when their bodies are sore from too much time in the gym.

Just before we land, I visit the loo and thank the lord the flight had no turbulence- I'm not a great flyer these days.

As I seat myself back down between Jonathan and the girl, I notice she's gone quiet. She's staring out of the window and hasn't even turned to acknowledge I've sat back down. Looking inquiringly at Jonny, he seems not to have noticed. I watch as he throws nuts into his mouth and bobs his head along to whatever music he's now decided to listen to. I let out a sigh of relief that he seems really upbeat. I expected the home journey to trigger a bit of depression in him as this means a return to the dramas we have suffered with his children's mothers, but he seems fine. Thank God.

We walk off the plane, hand in hand, and I remember to turn around to say goodbye to the girl who sat with us. "Oh! She was fast, Jonny! I wanted to say thank you to her for helping keep me occupied on the flight,"- he's not looking at me. Too busy turning his phone on and patting his pockets for his e-cig. Finding both in the same pocket, he looks at me, smiles and grabs my waist. "Come on, baby. Let's hurry up. I want home to get a take-away and have sex. In.... that.... order". A firm, passionate whisper in my ear.

Listen to: Gin Wigmore: "Written in The Water"

Red Flags:

- *Sudden cooling of people around you. Watch out for strangers, people you meet, acting oddly when you return from leaving them and your Narc alone. He/she will quite possibly have said or done something that is in distinct opposition to how they have behaved when you were there. In Casanova Psychopaths, it's likely your Narc has attempted a come-on or been observed doing so.*
- *Watch out for their quick excuses when you suggest dinner or drinks or exchanging numbers. Listen to your "that was weird. I thought we got on. Why have they gone chilly?!" internal voice. Your Narc will blissfully carry on as though nothing odd happened. He will claim to notice no change and maybe even accuse you of being oversensitive or paranoid.*
- *Mini Panics over Mini mistakes/flaws. Narcs won't ever be honest with you about bad behaviours, but to release their own tensions and taunt you at the same time, they will prattle on and on about something relatively minor citing terrible*

guilt, shame or remorse! The example I gave here was Jonathan blethering on about "taking up a fag" when actually, behind my back, he was sexting all bar 1 of the women in our group of friends on the holiday and necking street Valium like a bacon addict pops Rennies.

- *Toxic Triangulation. This is very common in Narc-victim relationships. It is the act of bringing in another person or group into the dynamic of your relationship. It belittles the victim and can make them feel insecure, left out and even encourage them to vie for the Narc's attention. It's gutless and immature, but worst of all, it also places you at the centre of a childish game where your innermost feelings are observed by their chosen witness/es. Toxic Triangulation (rather dangerously) makes the 3rd person, the mediator, feel important.*
- *It is very clever manipulation and helps the Narc gather supporters for their cause as a victim of your "craziness" and "controlling behaviour". Because Narcs also enjoy having multiple sources of ego-fuel, this almost "group chat" about their worries/your behaviours/decisions about the relationship is delicious for them, but poisonous for you!*
- *Huge Confidence. You may catch a Casanova Psychopath looking at their reflection often or regularly talking about what they do to make themselves look good. Keep an eye out for how they are around other people- do they give off an air of feeling and looking gorgeous, especially to the opposite sex? Do they easily approach people and flirt? Do they get affronted when turned down instead of easily accepting a 'no thanks'? They will strut and stride about like they own a room and initially it will absolutely be charming.*
- *Hypocrisy/Mini slips of the mask. Your Narc will appear empathic, kind, loving, sweet then out of nowhere, make a homophobic or sexist or nasty comment and you wonder where it came from. Narcs' masks slip when they feel vulnerable themselves. When they have a target in mind also. When they tire of you and when they want to test your loyalty.... There is no consistency. If they hate or dislike*

someone, then there is something else going on behind the scenes that you are not yet privy too. In my experience, Jonathan was cheating on me with the vulnerable young girls he referred to as "sluts".

- *The Mind Fog. When you are with a Narc, you will not notice the little oddities that would usually disturb you or make you suspicious with any other person. In essence, I know your reading this and guessing EXACTLY what was going on behind my back and sometimes right in front of my face! When you're engaging with a Narc, the Fog sets in during the Love Bombing Phase. It becomes most useful to the Narc in the Devaluation Phase, however. Under a spell, you miss the signs you are being lied to, used and cheated on. This is why it's so devastating when you finally are forced to see the truth after the relationship ends. The shock of realisation hitting you full force is excruciating and you truly hate yourself for being so "stupid". For a long time, you may also punish yourself more than you punish them but that passes.*

June 2015

I've been discarded again. It's his 40th Birthday in 48 hours. The £450 lovingly spent on food, helium balloons in his football colours, venue hire and countless hours of marketing the party to his vast Facebook network means nothing to him. Right now, it means nothing to me. Grieving, sleepless and publicly embarrassed, having been automatically removed from the event page on social media, I can't help but sit in wait for his message permitting me back into his life. It takes 2 days but, as usual, in the early hours of his birthday, I am allowed back in.

"It was the pressure of the party, baby. All those people! Turning 40. My kids not being allowed to come...it just got too much. Please try to understand." Flooded with relief, I message Lauren and tell her I will be in work today after all. I let her down yesterday and simply lay in bed all day, crying and clutching my phone like a lunatic.

The party I'd planned and looked forward to for half a year, was at best...unpleasant. All false smiles and pained "Hello, how are yous?!" I played waitress, cook and hostess for long enough for people to start to notice and ask me if I was ok.

Grubby apron over the strapless white lace dress bought specially for the occasion, I watched from the shadows of the kitchen area as Jonathan danced wildly to our song with his best friend Jaydee.

Virtually ignored all night, things got too much around 10 pm, so I dared to indulge in a cigarette and a quick cry on the fire escape when he seemed distracted enough for me to hide for a bit. Bashing through the rusty metal doors like a deranged cowboy 5 minutes later, he'd noticed my absence quickly. Knowing me well, he knew I would be outside and not heading home like any sensible person would. The spurt of rage when he caught me being comforted by a work colleague slid from his face fast when he realised, I wasn't sitting alone.

His family left without saying goodbye, so we tidied up just the 2 of us, as best we could. Later, while he slept, I sat in the living room alone and wondering how such an eagerly-awaited event could have felt so wrong for me.... for us.

About 2 pm, Jonathan gets up with some grunts and stumbling around. I quietly make a coffee and 2 bacon rolls for him. "Do you want me to run you a bath? I can give you a salt rub too if you like?" I say, as he leans away after kissing me. He gets tomato sauce on my jeans but I cover the spot with my hand so he isn't annoyed by it. "Yes babe," he mumbles through a mouth full of food. "Good idea- I feel shattered." Summoning a smile, I take the empty cup he's just handed me and go to make him another one.

After his bath, we are sitting together on the sofa choosing a film to watch. He takes my hand, places it on his crotch and gives me the look. He's been grumpy and distant since the party last night. It's not the first or the last time he will ask me to please him sexually to take the edge off whatever has him in a bad mood.

Afterwards, Jonathan goes for another sleep. I've bought several pretty throws for his sofa to make it more homely and comfortable but nothing seems to work. I wrap myself in the larger throw and try to watch television. There are re-runs of Come Dine With Me on, so I turn the volume down low and pour a glass of old red wine.

Settling down and emptying the glass, I try to forget the events of the last week as best I can. Looking out of the window at the drizzle, my mind just won't settle down. Things feel out of control now- I'm unhappy but love him so much. I can't concentrate on anything. My periods stopped 6 months ago and at times like this, in the shadows of a discard, I really struggle to find the sense of joy I had when we first met.

Listen to: Camilla Cabello: "Never Be The Same"

Red Flags:

- *Hyper-Vigilance. It won't take long for your Narc to train you to become tuned to their moods so that you are pretty much constantly on high alert for any sign that you are about to be discarded or ghosted. They enjoy picking and choosing when to expose you to whatever sign/s they use. In my case, if he was openly tired (or claimed to be), bad-tempered, quiet or even just gave off a "dark mood" type of energy. I also knew if he was quiet on WhatsApp or other social media and took longer to message or reply, a discard was imminent.*
- *You are sometimes invisible. At a party, wedding, other special occasion, the Narc will simply forget you exist (unless it suits them to show you off). You will busy yourself with other activities so as to quell unease at being suddenly of no matter. You will feel uncomfortable and they will know but not care. If you make it clear you are unhappy with their behaviour, you will see spurts of anger but others around you may not.*
- *Physical ailments. Physical ailments flaring up, your concentration and focus starting to suffer. The fight or flight response causes spikes of adrenaline and cortisol when we feel panic, fear or danger during a discard, then a hoover, then a discard again is extremely harmful to our bodies. Human*

94

bodies are designed to cope with these spikes on occasion, but not for them to happen so regularly and so suddenly.

Over time, we can actually form problems with our body naturally regulating these hormone blasts and it's possible to develop illnesses associated with hormone deficiency or hormone hyperactivity. I know I have a problem myself and have developed not only C-PTSD symptoms, but I also display problems associated with hormone irregularities attributed to emotional and psychological abuse.

- <u>*Coercive Control.*</u> *is defined in law as a pattern of behaviour a person is exposed to by a person "connected to them". The behaviour makes the person feel isolated, scared, vulnerable and controlled. The person making you feel this way has to know they are likely to be harming you in these ways for it to be illegal. For example, to have been told by you that it upsets you. In this example (although there were many in my relationship), Jonathan makes it clear that sexual favours or sexual acts between us would improve his mood and make me feel more secure a discard wasn't on the horizon. By this point, I had been discarded or ghosted by him so many times, that any negative atmosphere or mood around him, meant I knew one was coming.*

Coercive Control is a term developed by activist and academic Evan Stark and is now illegal. It is a form of domestic abuse.

July 2015

He's started putting his hands round my throat when we have sex or flipping me into different positions fast without asking my permission. I close my eyes and get on with it. He'll settle down soon. I'm sure of it.

True, his appetite for me always was high, but there are times when instead of just 3 or 4 times a day, he's pulling me into whatever relatively quiet or private place he can. Many of these are in his place of work.

7th July - My 35th Birthday

Taking selfies for Facebook, we are sitting in a pub near his flat and discussing where to go this evening. I feel almost relaxed today, having not been discarded since his birthday. Jonathan seems happy and, dare I say, hyped up?

His phone buzzes and immediately the atmosphere clouds over. I know whatever's punctured our afternoon together isn't good. My stomach hardens to rock and I feel my armpits go clammy. I want to scream and slam my fists on the table- here we go again.

"It's fucking Jaydee. Some big long message about how I need to focus on Sinead 's kid. Look, it's fucking like 3 messages long!" Jonathan is livid. He's gone a funny colour. My mouth goes dry.

"What does he mean? I don't understand!" Not this time, please not today! I make fists under the table until my hands hurt. Closing my eyes for a heartbeat, I dare to open them with the falsest smile possible. "Ignore him. Please, Jonny. Please don't let him ruin today!"

That voice, whispering in my ear again "They're watching your Facebook. They're all watching you. Its only minutes since you posted those pics. A deliberate bomb thrown in on your special day."

Jonathan is reading and re-reading the messages and his knuckles are white, wrapped hard around the phone.

I want to run away. Feeling sick now, I push my plate of food away and slide his empty one beside it.

"Your right. Fuck them. Fuck them all" he says suddenly, and I jump. He grabs me and his eyes are just a little too bright. "Fuck it. Let's stay out. Go play pool together. I'll buy us dinner later!" he kisses me. I feel weak with relief. Thank God.

The hatred I feel for his so-called friend and the female at the centre of this all goes up a notch.

There's a group of guys all playing over near where we decide to sit in the pool hall and I catch Jonathan noticing a couple of them eyeing me up. He starts to sweat and his neck is oddly tense.

I have on a red ethnic-patterned halter-neck dress and red stilettos. My fine hair is up in a loose French twist. I can sense him getting pissed off. His jaw is twitching. Fuck sakes, he's looking at them more than me. Picking up my wrap and bag, I reach to take his hand and walk us to a table in a quieter corner. He relaxes and I breathe a small sigh of relief.

As I walk back to the table from a quick loo visit, I pull my chair out and stop. My phone screen's lit up. Like most modern mobile phones, it does this when it has been touched or accessed in some way. Jonathan is sat at the table on his own phone and not looking at me.

I enter my password and it displays the login page for Facebook. Apparently, the "wrong password" has been entered.

Jonathan slowly looks up at me, smiles and says "do you want a game of pool?"

Listen to: Labrinth: "Jealous"

Red Flags:

- *Jealousy and Paranoia with no grounds at all. This is your Narc not trusting you because they are lying to you. They want to check out how you behave when they are not there because they are misbehaving when you are not there. They will gaslight you and deny acting this way, of course.*

  Narcs will also not shy away from accessing your accounts and not just taking information away to use at a later date, but by pretending to be you and perhaps upsetting or harassing people to frame you. Change your password daily if possible.

- *Flying-Monkey Sabotage. You will feel like you are being watched and wonder how exes and cohorts (Flying Monkeys and Supplies) could know about and want to permeate romantic dinners or private time. The Narc will claim to know nothing about it, maybe even saying it's just not possible and it's all in your imagination-even though it's almost certainly happened in PREVIOUS relationships!*

  You are not paranoid and you ARE being observed and stalked. Narcs love this and actively encourage it and certainly won't moderate their own behaviours to help reduce it, and almost certainly will ask you to moderate yours. Narc exes are often so damaged by the relationship (and often "bread-crumbed" to stay around) that they will have the need to watch the Narc and his/her new partner- they show signs of the Narc Virus in this behaviour as well as severe Co-Dependency....

- *Hyper Vigilance/Sixth Sense around your Narc. You will develop an incredible awareness of your Narc's moods and behaviours mainly around how they affect you. This is very dangerous because your instincts for your own wellbeing get suffocated and replaced by instincts for his/hers. It is also a great concern, because while you are waiting in fear for that text, call or visit from someone who you KNOW almost always precedes your Narc hurting you, you are not seeing the OTHER signs that will protect you from the other, less obvious behaviours.*

    You become fine-tuned to your Narc's moods, but most of the time they are not real! The Narc can easily fake anxiety/ depression/anger/sadness/desire for peace to simply discard you and do as they like without you being there.

August 2015

In mid-August, my little eatery (now 2 months old) suddenly became a target for internet trolls. Out of nowhere, two people posted nasty reviews back to back. Same day. Same time and same sort of language.

What made these reviews stand out wasn't just that they were the first negative ones I had received, but that the two women posting on the page were not based in Paisley (where I worked) or even Glasgow. One was middle England and one was Northern Ireland!

"Yeah. The waitress was really ugly. Huge chin," one post reads. Nothing about the food or bar itself. A strange thing to mention as well as I don't actually have a big chin, in fact, it's so small that in certain lights, I look like a Simpsons' character!

However, in one photograph in Tunisia that Jonathan had posted on his page, we had a sort of half-hearted bicker on his feed about me disliking a picture he chose to post, because I looked like I had a huge chin. Had these customers gone and looked at my personal page?

"Yeah- she was rude to me too. Really abrupt. The fish and chips were terrible!" the other female has typed. I don't even have fish and chips on the menu- it's not the sort of thing I make. I am also out of my way chatty and nice to everyone who comes in and can't place one person who I would think thought of me as rude.

The comments go on to link up as both women seemed to be almost talking to each other about me, slagging me off openly on my works page. A page with thousands of followers- both from the pub and my new little business.

"When did you visit and what did you order?" I know I shouldn't bite but this is a pile of crap. It's not fair to just have some random trolls do this! I work hard and my food is good! My looks are nothing to do with where I work too! "If you visited here and had such an awful time, why didn't you say anything when you were here? I don't recognise either of you and I'm the only staff here. I'm the chef manager, not a waitress but I serve customers. All of them! Oh, and ladies, I don't serve junk food like fish and chips! Go troll someone else!"

They go quiet and I wait to see if they dare reply. Shamed and shown up for being malicious idiots, they disappear and we block them from both the Pub and eatery's Facebook and Twitter pages.

Constantly simmering with paranoia and rage these days, I start to search through their pages for clues as to why on earth they set about me like this. Lauren, the bar owner has locked herself in the bar office to permanently delete the posts. I can hear those little bells of doom again...

5 minutes later, scrolling and making notes, a migraine starting- a familiar name pops up on both their friends lists - Sinead Lorrimer.

I want to fucking kill this bitch! What the fuck is her problem?!!! Breathless with rage, I call Jonathan. He doesn't answer but I leave a tearful, ranting message, demanding that he sort this female out. Unsolicited, she has now messed with my ex-husband as well as my work. "I mean it, Jonny. You need to sort her! Enough is enough. It's been over a year now. Please. Please fix this for me." I sob at the last part and slide down to sit on the kitchen floor where customers can't see or hear me.

I need him to protect me from myself now. I can feel I'm close to flipping out and I know it won't go well. How far does he expect me to be pushed?!

"Just fucking ignore her - she's a psycho. Passive aggressive. Delete it and block her," he messages only a few minutes later.

I almost throw the phone at the kitchen wall. I grunt in frustration and slap my own head repeatedly with my hands.

"Why can't you deal with her? Please! Just tell her to stop and we can get legal advice and take control about the baby. Please help now. Make things better!" I message back. I'm praying my man will end this.

"It's nothing to do with me. I can't make her be normal. She's a psycho." None of this makes sense?! I take a sip of the brandy Lauren poured to calm me down, then throw the rest back. A decision made.

For the first time, I go public and out her on my private Facebook page. I've blocked her and the fake account she has, so I'm confident at least one of her friends or family members, watching me, will step in and advise her to leave us alone.

It takes just over 30 minutes for the world to explode yet again. Sitting in the train station, tearful, tired and stressed, he calls me. "Well done! You're a fucking idiot. She's cancelled my visit to see the baby again! It's all your fault! You should have just left it alone!"

Yep- you guessed it. I got discarded again. This time for 3 days. Almost used to the torture now, I stocked up on gin, sent my boys to their fathers and didn't leave my bed for the duration of the silence. I cried and ranted and shouted at my lonely four walls and begged someone, anyone, to please help me understand what the hell is going on and why, most importantly why?!

Jonathan had started to be more openly cruel now that I was growing weaker under his manipulation and harm. He knew I was completely addicted to him by this point. My begging for his help with the toxic people around us, alongside my snivelling, pitiful pleading for his love, gave him the ultimate ego boost and confidence that no matter what he did to me, I was his. Completely.

He had successfully made me entirely co-dependent on him. Like all Casanova Psychopaths, this is their ultimate goal. To enslave you, use you, harm you until they feel ready to move on to the next target or go back to an old one...

Narcs escalate - they need constant fuel so you will see in your relationships with them a growth in the volume of negative behaviours (e.g. discards) and you will experience a wider, often darker variety of abuse. They will start off fairly discreet and slowly become more obvious. August into September was my time for things to "ramp up"- Later, you will understand that a sudden increase in harm often signifies a sudden increase in hidden bad behaviours and pressure on your Narc...

It's late August and I'm in the kitchen making high protein food for Jonathan to take to the gym. Singing along to the radio and occasionally throwing a shape, I've got my back to the room. I love music and if it's loud enough I can't hear my own thoughts. I've had one gin, just to take the edge off the biting sand flies of worry and anger that seem to crawl all over me most days now.

He's having his usual post-work nap, so I'm pottering about getting the flat ready for an evening in. The windows are open and it's a lovely sunny evening. For a second, I close my eyes and breathe in. I wish it was like this all the time. I wish it more than anything.

I've opted to wear a cute little summer dress with the shoulders exposed. Deciding the butternut squash and ginger soup could use some cream, I hike my dress up to more easily bend down to the fridge.

In a heartbeat, I feel someone behind me and before I turn fully, I feel a sharp stinging pain on my neck. I yelp like a cat and jump up and away from the fridge to sit on the floor. It's him. Jonathan is smiling down at me. His eyes are dark and glittering and the grin is cruel. It's like everything is in slow motion. My eyes fill with tears, but before I speak his faces changes. It's normal again. In his hand is the large metal spoon I was using to stir the boiling soup with.

The night-time frights he sometimes did as a "joke" escalated that summer too. Jonathan knew I was extremely afraid of the dark and have been since I was a child. He had already done little nasty things, like turn the light off on me when I was in the loo. I'd scream and scream for him to put it back on, not knowing if he was in the bathroom with me or far away down the hall.

He also started jumping out at me from other rooms as I scuttled back from the loo, desperate to escape my imagined ghouls in the hall.

He also developed this thing about rushing in when I was on the toilet or in the bath as well. While exposed, he'd take a photograph of me gaping at him, the words "Don't, Jonny!" not yet out of my mouth. He found this invasion of my privacy hilarious.

He even took a photograph of me when I was having sex with him "reverse cowgirl". He'd placed himself and the phone at the right angle where you could see my backside and his penis meeting. I heard the click and immediately spun round and demanded he delete it. He laughed and showed me the phone while he deleted the image with that nasty, dark smile on his face. He actually hadn't deleted it- I found it 4 months later.

Listen to: The Rolling Stones: "Paint It Black"

Red Flags:

* *Malignant Co-Dependants Using Flying Monkeys to Harm you/your life. Narcs have such toxic relationships they create toxic people and can create toxic exes. Malignant Co-Deps will stop at nothing to affect your life, your work, family, even your children will be targets. It is a sign of the Narcissistic Virus and the longer it goes on, the worse the infection*

becomes. This is why you must stop contact completely when you end your relationship with a Narc, because you almost certainly will become so desperate to have them back you may even recruit friends to upset the partner of the Narc you are obsessed with. You may even gather your own flying monkeys, just like the Narc has done.

- *Invasions of privacy. Often sexual, are relatively common in Casanova Psychopath relationships. As already shown, they don't respect you or your boundaries. Even when you ask them to delete that video or pic or stop taking them, they won't. They get a thrill out of this type of power and control. They can revisit them later with friends or alone and enjoy the rush over and over again. The taking and posting of pics you have already said you don't like or feel ashamed by is disgusting and if they are sexual, this is against the law and called "revenge porn". You must report it!*

- *Escalation from covert abuse. Escalation to more overt abuse Narcs will push and push and grow in their need for fuel from you. It is around now that things may become physical- like the spoon example. Little sharp reminders they are in control and that they know you well enough to do these things 100% confident you will accept it. This is also them testing you for more extreme physical abuse later.*

September 2015

By September 2015, the jumping out at me with the lights off at night wasn't giving Jonathan enough of a thrill, so he took it up a level. He started to lie on the floor in the dark in either the kitchen (by the loo) or the living room (by the bedroom door) so that when I was running back to the bedroom from the toilet, he would suddenly reach out and grab one of my ankles.

On more than one occasion, I fell and hurt myself while he bellowed with devilish laughter. On easier occasions, I would just scream in shock and terror in the dark and almost cry with panic thinking tonight was the night. In the dark, I could just hear him move away from behind the door and walk casually to the loo or back to the bedroom himself.

He'd carefully plan these little night-time attacks so that days or weeks would pass and when I least expected it, he would do it again and I'd get the ultimate fright, having dreading it happening the whole time it hadn't. I would beg him not to do it and he still did. He puppeteered my fears and loved every minute of it. "chill out baby. It's just a joke" was his response when I crawled into bed half crying.

Walking out of the gym into weak Autumn sun, I'm chattering away to my beloved. Hyper-anxious, I talk and talk even though he isn't talking back. Picking up on something darkening the air between us, I prattle on anyway.

"Can we go via a shop? I need to get some bits in for tonight. That was a good swim. I did 85 laps. If you like, I can get us a takeaway maybe? Download a film or maybe we could get a game if pool?" I can't stop talking.

I reach for his hand as we walk through the hotel car-park, but he snatches it away. He's in the car and starting the engine by the time I've shrugged my backpack off. I have a strange thought he might just lock the door and leave me here. The rush of relief when the door opens for me when I try it, is sickening.

"What's the matter, Jonny? What have I done?" I start to cry as usual. I already know what I've done.

He keeps starting the car then turning the engine off and this toxic teasing is escalating my pleading. "Please, baby, don't do this. I'm sorry. I didn't know. We were just chatting. I didn't ask anything. I just mentioned you were upset. I was honestly only letting off a bit of steam." Quickly I wipe my nose on my sleeve. Shit, I'm hyperventilating. This is new. I've had panic attacks this last few months but I've never really struggled to actually breathe this badly.

"You're fucking nosey. You can't help yourself. It's making me ill. I'm going to relapse and drink with your pressure.... So, I'm sorry, I have to let you go. It's over. For good this time." Bending forward to rest my head on my knees, I can't stop the sobs escaping as he continues to rev the engine.

104

Earlier, in the Pool

"So, how's the big man then?" A colleague of Jonathan's called Phil is asking after him. Checking to make sure my partner isn't around; I partially lift myself up out of the water to rest my arms on the side and kick my legs back out into the water for balance.

"To be honest, he's struggling. That's all 3 kids he's got issues seeing. Mad bitches, the lot of them. It's causing all sorts of problems for us. It would be good if you could maybe make a bit of time to cheer him up. I'm not getting anywhere with him and think another guy's advice would be good." Oddly, I want to cry but don't. Not here. "The Cherry Anne one who has his middle boy? She winds him up now and then too! Calling him up every few months, like 8 am, demanding Jonny take the wee boy to school! That's after not talking to him for ages and him not getting to see the kid!" Treading water now, I rub my hands over my face in tiredness & frustration.

"Shame she won't let him see that kid. I mean, they were on and off for like 3 or 4 years. She always was a cow, man," Phil says, before trotting off to scold a child for running on the wet tiles.

Holding onto the side of the pool for dear life, I don't dare turn around to face the pool.

What the fuck is Phil talking about? 4 years?! I thought it was a few days at most?! I was told she got pregnant deliberately on a wild drink-fuelled weekend almost a decade ago. I was told she had secretly carried Dan without Jonathan knowing, desperate for benefits and an excuse not to work. Jonathan told me all this. No one said any different. All of this information came from Jonathan. Letting go of the side of the pool, I sink to the bottom and swim back up fast, trying to calm those fucking doubts in my head again. As I open my eyes, I see Jonathan standing rigid, watching me- he glances at Phil then back at me. Before I can smile at him or wave, he walks away.

The atmosphere's horrendous. Jonathan is staring out of the car window. I can hear his teeth squeaking as he grinds his jaw. The smell of car fuel is intense and my head hurts.

His face shows pure disgust. He's raging with me for meddling and being nosey. I'm horrible and selfish. I feel so ashamed. "You've ruined it all again!" he shouts, driving too fast out of the car park. "You've embarrassed me. Phil will talk about me now. You looked a fucking mess when he walked away- he will know I lied to you! Why can't you just fucking leave things be!"

His flat is south out of the hotel spa car park and mine is north. As the car swerves left towards my house, my heart plummets like a stone. I was right, here he goes again. I beg and beg for him to please not take me home and leave me there, but of course, he does.

Last Friday in September 2015

Steam rises from the school uniforms in front of me, so I stand back out of the heat. I fucking hate ironing but someone has to do it! As I iron one of Jonny's T-shirts, his familiar scent rises up and I close my eyes. It's been quiet this last week or so and he seems very upbeat and positive. I'm doing everything possible to keep the consistency. The only blip recently was a parking ticket from outside my house the other day. His face darkened as he reminded me Sinead had recently requested regular maintenance payments. I paid the ticket for him before he'd even parked back up at his own house that same day.

My boys stare, transfixed by the tv. Three lovely little elfin profiles. Sonny's hair appears to have grown suddenly and he has floppy blonde curls falling over his brow. Wondering if he can see properly, I gently reach over to flip them away and they flop right back in the same place. Stroking Rufus's head as I walk back to the iron with another pair of school trousers, he doesn't react. This reminds me to chase the speech therapy appointment that precedes the autism assessment the school has recommended.

"How much longer will you be baby? I'm up for ordering this food. The kids are starving!" I message my beloved at 6pm. He blue ticks the message but doesn't reply. My gut drops.

Oh God, not again. I walk fast to the kitchen with a plan to make a drink to settle the nerves that have just flooded in.

Ding, ding - he's messaged me back! Racing back into the living room, I scrabble for my phone and all three angel faces turn to look at me, as worried as usual. Flooded with relief I slide to sit on the pile of washing piled up on the chair. It's him- he's ok. We're ok. It's fine. I read the message and stop breathing for what feels like an age. "With my Harry - been accident. Harry been stabbed at meeting. Going hospital." Harry is Jonathan's sponsor from AA. "Mummy, are you ok?" comes a little voice beside me. It's Sonny. "Yes sweetheart, it's ok. Give me 2 mins. Everything's fine." I rub his back and he turns back to the tv, not reassured at all.

Still sitting on the washing like a demented house-wife, I try to compose myself. Oh my God! Poor Harry! What the actual fuck?

I quickly message back "Omg- what happened. What can I do? Call me as soon as you can?! Do you want me to come to the hospital?" My gut rumbles and tell-tale cramps signal the urgent need to go to the toilet.

That night I had my first bout of I.B.S. I have never ever had a fully "dicky tummy" when I am anxious up until this point. I used to get cramps and acid reflux with Jonathan, but never had I actually had to rush to the loo with fright.

Never. Not after being made redundant a 4th time. Not telling Niall I wanted a divorce. Not waking up after being raped by two strangers a month after turning 17. Not even when I left home for the first time at 18 years old, nor after an attempted suicide after a bad bullying experience with my new flatmates. I've never ever felt the need to go to the toilet out of sheer fear. Never.... until I started dealing with Jonathan.

For the next hour, I pace the flat. My poor partner and lovely Harry. Harry's wife must be frantic! His daughters too. Running through possible scenarios, from stitches to amputation to full-blown death, I've decided to wait & just sip and sip at a pint of water- I think I have a urine infection again.

The atmosphere has shifted to a darker place and the boys will know why. "He is just with his friend. He'll be home soon," I say as I pace about and stare stupidly at my phone.

The phone rings at 6.45 pm and I grab at it. It falls on the floor and all 3 of my boys turn around to look at me. They look frightened and I feel a jolt of shame. Pressing it close to my ear, I pray for good news.

Before I can even speak, I hear an unfamiliar voice in my ear. A nasal, slurred voice. "Aye man- pass me the fags." A man. Then there is scuffling.

Oh my God! Shit! Someone's stabbed them and stolen their phones! Then I hear the love of my life laughing.

Everything goes blurry. There's a ringing in my ears as though a bomb's gone off. Blankly, I look up at my 3 children, innocently sitting on the sofa with the tv turned down. I take in our ironing all piled up in its organised sections, mine, Jonathan's, Sonny's, Charlie's and wee Roux's. This is my life. This is the life we have. What's about to happen to it?

Fifteen minutes later, I'm in a taxi heading to an address that Jonathan's new BFF easily gave once I promised to bring more vodka and some fags. My neighbour, David, is watching the boys and my main focus now is saving my man and saving what we have. Strangely numb, I make a plan and stick to it. It's easy. I can do this.

"We're about to go to a house I've never been to before and my partner is in the house at the beginning of what I think could end up a serious alcohol binge. It's his first in 8 years. I need to get to him as soon as possible so I can bring him home."

The taxi driver next to me looks uncertain. I don't blame him. My neon pink jumper, denim shorts and navy Wallis deck shoes are clearly not a convincing alky rescue ensemble.

He can see from my pleading face that I am worried, but he can also recognise the set of my jaw and the strength of my words: "Please help me," I say without so much as a blink.

"Will he hurt you?" the driver asks. Smiling sadly, a fat tear escapes and plops onto my hands clasped tightly over the seatbelt. "No - not like that. He would never do that, he loves me."

Soon, we pull up outside a corner house in a council estate near Rutherglen. Leaning across the driver a little, I can see the curtains to the living room are open.

A sob escapes when the unmistakable outline of my lovely Jonathan's face tips up and back as he lifts a bottle to his lips.

Rigid with shock, I see him take a draw of a cigarette next. Fear grips my bowels and time stops.

Standing on the weedy cement steps with my back to the house, I give the driver a wave, the signal he can leave me here. He drives away into the dark, and for a moment, I feel more lost than I think I have ever felt in my life. My breath is coming in short gasps & frantic little puffs float like smoke around my face. I want to go home. Desperately.

This is worse than I thought. He's happy and he's partying. He is loving life. His sobriety and I mean nothing right now. Nothing. NO help is coming. It's just me.

I compose myself- this is what alcoholics do, Lucy. This is the illness. This is what you sign up to when you commit to them.

I walk up the steps and open the door. Why just walk in?! Fucking hell, I don't know. For some reason, I want to catch him unawares. Maybe a girl there as well? What? No. Fuck sakes, Silly! He would never cheat on me. Never. I enter the hall and turn slowly left into the living room.

I'm across the room and sitting on his knee kissing him before he can say a word. Mind you he's plastered so saying any word right now might take longer than usual.

To him, I'm thrilled to be here at this super cool house party with the heroin addict in a football top, my extremely drunk partner and the old lady in the corner. She's smoking roll-ups, drinking whisky and is hooked up to some sort of breathing apparatus at a small table next to her by the kitchen door.

Yep- this is not freaking me out at all. I'm not screaming inside at all. I'm not feeling like I could be sick & shit myself at the same time.

Jonathan looks up at me but is struggling to focus. I'm treated to a blurry smile and fervent kisses. It's working. He's happy to see me, in fact.... I might actually fix this.

His breath is disgusting and I wonder if he has cleaned his teeth today. In a year and a half, I have never noticed bad breath on him. He doesn't even smell like my man. "Hi- I'm Lucy. I'm Jonny's partner. What the fuck is all this?" I declare sweeping my arm around the room. I even manage a short bark of laughter. By god I'm good.

Looking pointedly at the old lady, I smile charmingly. "Can I have a roll up, love?"

She relaxes immediately. Maybe I am one of them. Maybe I will fit in. As I sit down next to her, I joke "when I make roll-ups, they look like fucking old shoes some cunt left by a swimming pool after a Majorcan stag-do!" She guffaws, then coughs madly and beckons to the freaky-looking NHS machine keeping her with us. I pull it closer to her and she nods and wipes her face with a hanky.

She smiles as she finishes making my cigarette and hands it to me. I see her papery hands are shaking. She's extremely unwell.

Jonathan laughs behind me, "that's my girl. Her patter's fuckin great" and the atmosphere warms up a notch. Behind me I sense someone walk in.

Turning around fully and lighting my cig, I see a bald, mean-looking guy, about 40 years old with cruel eyes. I sense immediately we have a problem here. He is 5ft 2 if he's an inch, and he's as hairless and sweaty as a freshly boiled egg. He is going to be vile. I just know it.

"Who the fuck is this?" he says and points at me. He sways a little. Not just drunk- he's high. Very high. I've decided to call him Rat Guy (in my head, of course).

Smiling sweetly, I draw on the smoke. "I'm here for my Jonny. He's not well. He's been sober for nearly 9 years now. I'm gonna take him home. Ok?"

"Are yeh fuck," he says. "Jonny boy, you're having a fucking great time, aren't yeh?" He walks across the room taking a small detour to the window seat to balance himself when he nearly trips. Rat Guy shakes Jonathan's hand as though they are at a fucking board meeting. I want to rip his veiny arms off and shove them up his Kylie Minogue sized backside.

Jonathan laughs. "Yep!" he says and takes another drink. He doesn't look at me. He knows this is wrong.

The battle lines have been drawn. Jonathan has to pick between his partner, supporter and lover AND this nasty, druggy bastard who has no care whatsoever that he's ruining someone's life. No, several lives.

Jonathan has his favourite black jumper on. It's ribbed and some sort of cotton/Lycra mix. I bought it for him last Christmas. I can see it's grubby & has several marks on it. He stayed at home last night saying he wanted "a rest before spending the full weekend" with the kids and I.

Eying up the marks carefully I see they are pale grey, or maybe white? I think he's been taking coke. The shock of this feels like a punch to the head. I've never seen him take drugs- fuck, he hates himself when he even smokes a cigarette!

Glancing at the bottle Jonathan has in his hands, I see it is indeed the old school alcopop, Hooch. My laughter is like knives at a target, as I point at the bottle: "Fuck sakes, if your gonna relapse, you might as well drink something decent. That's fucking shite!" My eyes are glittering and cold, but I'm persuasively funny enough to have Jonathan guffaw again with pleasure.

I love my man more than I've ever loved any man. I want to go home, back to the life we've built. This person is not my Jonny... I don't know who he is.

Jonathan hoists himself off the sofa and reaches out to take something from Rat Guy's girly little hand. He goes upstairs- I feel nothing. Not even shock. So far into this horror film, I'm completely on autopilot. Grandma and I chat quietly in the corner and I shoot occasional looks at the doorway, waiting for my partner to return. It's now been more than 10 minutes since he staggered out of the room and stomped up the stairs.

Rat Guy is not impressed. He seethes quietly in the corner, drinking a dark, orangey beverage. It looks like a very strong vodka and coke. I've worked out he's not a relation to Grandma and Jonny, being new to the dynamic, has money and time, just what any dealer needs.

Grandma offers me a drink. I don't want to say no, but I do. "I can't drink right now. I've my boys up the road, waiting for Jonny and I to get back- we've ordered a Chinese. Feeling the urge to cry, I swivel round to lean towards her more closely... "So, we really need to go."

She looks at me and I think there's a spark of understanding. Perhaps her life, too, has had its heartbreaks and bad men. A lump forms in my throat as I hear her ignorant words. "Let them have their fun," she says and takes a slurp of her drink. She spills a little on the table so I wipe it away with my sleeve. This is not going to be my life. Not a fucking chance.

Slowly, carefully... I lean in even closer. Whispering in her ear, she smiles at the intimacy, then her face freezes "If you don't fucking let me take my man home now, I will fucking scream and shout so loudly your neighbours will call the police before any cunt in here gets a chance to stop me. So, to be clear, to be FUCKING clear... I'm taking him home NOW and you are the one to help me do it."

The chair creaks as I lean back, re-cross my pretty legs and slowly take a drag on the fresh roll up she has (expertly) prepared and lit for me. Smiling a crocodile smile, my eyes glitter in sheer determination. "Ok?" I mouth. She is paler than she was 2 minutes ago- I didn't even know that could be possible.

In two heartbeats, she says "Come on boys. I'm knackered and this wee lassie has weans up the road waiting on her and her man." She's shaking all over now. Scared and unsettled. She underestimated me & I don't care.

Jonathan comes down the stairs just as the taxi I ordered arrives. There's coke on his right nostril and some caught in his stubble. He's sweaty, red-faced and weaving on his feet. His eyes are bloodshot. He looks horrid.

He takes my hand when it's offered and tries to kiss me. Pushing him away, I manhandle him out to the taxi I'm about to pay my last £10 for.

The driver asks if he will be sick. "No, love- he's not the type," I say as I buckle Jonathan in. I get in the front seat. Getting in the back with him isn't an option- he's not my partner right now. He can sit alone.

Facing front with him behind me, I let big, fat, salty tears slide down my face all the way home. The driver speaks only once.

"Are you going to be ok with him?" He looks in his mirror at Jonathan, slumped and dribbling in the back seat. I nod. "Can you help me get him up the stairs?"

At one point, Jonathan urinates in the back of the cab. I feel a heartbeat of complete hate. I must survive this. I must focus. I don't tell the driver and I feel so guilty that I tip him a fiver in change. It's all I have left.

The driver pulls up and helps me manhandle Jonathan up the 3 flights of stairs to my flat. On the journey up, Jonathan is demanding alcohol. Asking who the driver is. Ranting about C.I.D., asking why he is being arrested, "my bird lives here- she'll go nuts, man. Let's go," he says as we reach my landing. Three plant pots, a battered snow sledge and some footballs make it mine and he knows it.

Now somewhere safe and familiar, I feel dizzy and sick. Jonathan is ranting "my daughter is dead. She died of cancer today. Don't arrest me!" he's panicking & talking absolute crap. Fumbling with keys, I ask the driver to hold Jonathan up for a minute while I rush the boys into their bedroom. I don't want them to see him like this. He is not our "Jonny". I can't let them be exposed to this. My boys shouldn't feel anything but love and respect for the man they nicknamed "bad Tony". Not on my watch.

The boys know something is afoot, so hustle to bed no bother. "Go to bed babies- Jonny's not well. I'm going to sort it out," I whisper. In 2 minutes, we are in my living room alone. "Baby, what happened? Why did you do this? Tell me why, please?"

Crying but trying to stay in control, I feed my man 1 mouthful of cold Chinese at a time and stroke his face. He can barely sit up.

It will all be fine tomorrow. It will be ok. Harry will come. Jonathan will get sober. They can go to a meeting and start the 12 steps again. He has me. He has a life and a job and he is strong. He has done many years already and that is incredible and he will do another year, then another. I haven't lost him. Tomorrow is a new day and he will be back to normal.

Having put Jonathan to bed covered in partly-eaten Chinese, I'm now sitting quietly in the dark in the living room. There's a strange ringing in my ears and the smell of the takeaway he marked my carpet with is making me want to vomit.

His phone is on the coffee table where he left it after taking it out of his pocket to lurch onto the sofa. He looks after his phone like it's a small child and it's rare for me to see him more than a metre away from it. I realise I don't have his sponsors number.

Typing in his year of birth to open the phone, I almost miss the first line of a message on the screen. My blood runs cold.

"Yeah- always up for a shag, you know that," 3 kissing emoticons and 1 laughing one. Bending over the phone in a prayer position, I lean forward, my forehead on the coffee table- hoping that this is just a bad dream. Abruptly sitting up and now cold to the bone, I have to accept the messages are still there. This isn't a nightmare, this is real.

The discussion is fresh. Only a few days old. It's a woman I know from AA. She knows we're a couple, that he isn't available and hasn't been for well over a year now. The sexual banter back and forth, agreeing to meet for sex when they are both available, blurs my vision.

He is in relapse and they all say that when people relapse, they go completely mental- they do things they don't mean. I believe what these people say. They are in AA and AA is honest. It's safe. He's safe there. Everyone is. Come on…. It's just one daft, manky female.

With shaking fingers, I close this message stream and dare to scroll down the list of people he has called and messaged recently…… I see the first few words of another message to someone called Lynda AA. "I want to lick your arsehole." Sent by my beloved, last night around the time I was freaking out that Harry might die from being stabbed.

Bile rises in my throat and I can't breathe again. Is this what a heart attack feels like? The pain is intense- an actual physical pain right in my heart as though it is shrinking and pulling away from my insides. I want to fold inside myself. Crumple like paper and disappear with the wind.

Please God, no.

In the next few minutes I read a total of 8 message streams to different females- some with names like "Health suite", "Jemma Hotel", "Amy Jackson" and "Michelle AA", and others are just mobile numbers and not stored with a name. Almost every message is sexual. There are hundreds.

There are videos of him masturbating and these females doing the same. Many of his videos I recognise as ones he's sent me.... There are disgusting pictures of these females' vaginas, breasts and backsides and even more of his penis. My heart breaks just a little bit more when, in amongst the hardcore filth, I read a stream that is far more vanilla. A dozen or so messages to a "Jen Cruise Conference".

He is speaking quite nicely to her, offering to be an advisor and "help her" through whatever it is she is struggling with. Initially, it's friendly, but soon he goes in for the kill with "I fancy you," and she responds with "I fancy you too". I feel sorry for her- she sounds...nice.

The ones from Amy Jackson are as recent as 2 days ago and there is a picture of her big, veiny tits in a bra in one. He has replied with "Wow. Send me one with the bra off."

I see in one he has sent her a picture of his penis right after this. He thinks it's bait. He's in his work shorts...well, poking out of them.

The penny drops; I know who this person is. This is the scrawny, vulnerable girl who sits in the cafe in the hotel reception! She sits and watches us. I thought she was lonely- she wasn't. She was waiting for the gap I leave when I'm not there. When I go home to my children or go to get changed to swim or gym.

She's a girl he says he's known since she was 5 years old. I'm horrified. I've known her for over a year. I've even held her new baby, bought her a hot chocolate!

The picture messages to Jemma Hotel are extreme. Far more hardcore than he's ever sent me and certainly more extreme than I have ever sent him... After seeing the picture message of Jemma Hotel's neon pink fingernails grasping at her own (not designer) vagina, I run to the toilet and throw up bile and snot. I know I'm in shock. I can't stop my teeth chattering.

His call log is almost boring- he hasn't called these females much. Classy guy just texting with what seems to be little or no "real" interaction. But my chest throbs when I see 2 outward calls to a number without a contact name last night when he was at home.

It's just a mobile number, but because it was dialled twice and the person didn't pick up AND it was in the last few days, instinct tells me it means something... something important. I note it down on a piece of paper and resolve to try and call this person over and over until I find out who they are.

In my bed, he sleeps. I stagger out of the toilet into our bedroom and sit on the carpet, with my back against my wardrobe. I look up at him snoring away on my bed. There's a snake stirring in my belly, up to behind my eyes. It feels like hate... how can I hate my partner? The love of My life?

Uncoiling, I leap onto the bed and hiss loudly in his face, "what the fuck have you been doing? You've been fucking cheating on me!". I grab his law and shake it. His tongue flaps about uselessly then suddenly his eyes flick open.

He wakes up like a vampire. Lips curled in a snarl of pure hate, he looks me straight in the eye, lifts his legs back and kangaroo-kicks me straight in the stomach.

He does this so quickly and so hard I'm flung off the bed backwards into the television in front of the bedroom window. He's panting and snarling on his knees on the bed like something possessed.

Half-crouching in the space between my television and the window, I start to beg. "Jonny. No. Please No. No. No. I'm scared. You're scaring me!"

In a second, he flips himself up off the bed and is in front of me, lifting me off the floor by my throat and spitting in my face "you fucking cunt. You're a fucking psycho. What the fuck are you talking about?!" It's a horror film. He's possessed.

Wriggling like a fish on a hook and trying to get his hands off me, I dangle like a doll. Jewellery judders on my dresser. A scarf slithers to the ground. All I can hear are my gasps and his grunts. He has eyes only for me. Hands only for me.

Finding a footing on the edge of the little drawer in the bottom of my standing mirror helps me find balance. I use it to half-stand up, face him and go limp. His hands are squeezing and he is grinding his teeth in hate. I look him straight in the eye but am so frightened by his face, I close my eyes for 8, maybe 10 seconds. Taking a last breath, I inhale his familiar scent and nearly gag with pain. Then the anger seeps in again.

"Go for it, you fucking bastard. You think this'll hurt more than what you've already done?!" He stops. Something changes in his face. It relaxes. I feel his grip loosen. He almost looks like my Jonathan again. The strong arms I've caressed and kissed. The face I love to stroke.

He lets me go suddenly and I stagger backwards, nearly knocking the mirror over. I grab it and watch him lurch off towards the toilet. Breathless and devastated, I sit on the floor and weep.

He's asleep again so I'm running a bath to stop me shaking all over. I feel so fucking cold. My neck is red where he held it but I don't think it will bruise. My backside is sore from how I landed and I have a graze on my elbow from knocking it against the window ledge. I'll be stiff tomorrow. I'd rather he had beaten me black and blue than have seen those messages in his phone. I'll never ever forget what I saw.

Lying in the bath for more than 2 hours, I let it go cold, top it up. Let it go cold and top it up. This fucking urine infection is getting worse- it's my own fault; little sleep and even less fluids can't be helping.

Crying quietly, in all types of pain, I realise only a couple of days ago we were talking about our next holiday. Giggling and kissing, walking through the town centre holding hands like a normal, happy couple.

Denial seeps through me... The oldest messages seem to be to the Jen Cruise Conference woman and start around early September. That's not so bad. He's obviously been drinking for longer than I thought- that's when he has been doing it. Pissed as a fart and missing me and reaching for any sort of distraction from his mad exes messing with our lives. Yes- that makes sense.

Thank goodness, it's only been messaging for a few weeks and no longer!

I must try harder to stop making mistakes. Have I not helped him stay sober? Should I have just let Sinead blow hot air over us like the pointless annoyance she really is? Trust she would disappear soon enough? Should I maybe not work these funny hours? He always says when he misses me, he is more likely to "do something stupid". Maybe this is my fault? Trying to work and handle the kids has me away from him most of the day and we're only seeing each other 3 or 4 nights a week right now.

Shit! I haven't got Harry's number out of the effing phone because I was in such a state earlier.

Drying my hands on a towel, I reach over the edge of the bath and pick Jonathan's phone up. Seeing the messages again only serves to solidify my determination to take control of whatever is going on and fix it. On instinct, I open his Gmail. He isn't an emailer and doesn't use it for work but a little voice suggests I do it anyway.

I scroll past crap about computer games he's bought online and emails about loans he's trying to bump. There are even a couple from me from when he's been in one of his huffs. Pleading with him to stop ignoring me, hurting me and to please call me or let me in the flat.

I stop. My eye catches something. There are emails back and forth between him and someone calling herself "Lady Joy"- I know immediately it is some sort of professional sexual service.

In them he's been asking her to meet him. No, begging. There are 6 emails, one after the other. It's cringe-worthy. Not to mention the whopper taking him from lowly lifeguard to a whole different job! "I'm an instructor in the spa gym. Come in and see me. I'll get you in for free" he pleads. "I would need your credit card details first" she replies.

The emails stop at this point. It was January. This January. Months after we met. Days after our first Christmas together. Ok, well at least it stops and I don't see any attachments of images or videos. I'm sure it was a one-off. Just a sort of tease or test- he didn't give her money and obviously was just messing about. Yeah- I can let this go.

I wonder how he found her? So, opting to check his google history, my gut drops when it shows dozens and dozens of visits to a porn site. Funny name it has- don't think it's really about Hamsters.

He's visited the site repeatedly for months! Hundreds and hundreds of times. Looking at the sort of stuff on there shatters the strange numbness that was settling in.

Again, I retch but there is nothing left. My heart actually hurts. I want to scream and tear my eyes out.

He's been watching porn and messaging these women saying he is "lonely" and "needs sex" while I'm half a dozen feet away, singing along to the radio. In bed next to him, naked and dozing. Three foot away in the kitchen making him food specially designed for after the gym.

Some of the messages were sent while I was discarded too. A lot of the messages, especially the picture ones, have been sent while he's been on shift at work. I can see his uniform and the distinctive tiles of the health suite and toilets in the background.

Oh my God.

Standing in the doorway to our bedroom, I'm watching a stranger sleep. Jonathan's stopped snoring but seems restless and keeps changing position in bed and making an odd tutting sound as though disgusted with me even in sleep. I can smell the sweet, sickly smell of stale alcohol and something else. Something unfamiliar, bitter and almost chalky.

I daren't help him take his clothes off, so choosing to sit on the floor, I wait. At some point I drift off, damp, straggly hair spread across my bare knees. I am a child again- lost and alone, just needing a cuddle from my mum and someone to tell me they can fix this for me.

About 5.00am, he starts rolling about and groaning loudly. I wonder if the hangover is kicking in, so I slide out of bed and crawl on my hands and knees towards the door just in case he wakes up and goes for me again. Deciding it's safer in a different room and the smell in the bedroom is just too vile, I creep away to sit in the living room again.

I am half-way through my 1st coffee at 5.30am and hear a commotion from the bedroom. It makes me jump. My nerves are shredded.... It's Jonathan shouting. The first word I understand is my name. I don't go in. I'm scared. "Lucy- where is ma Lucy?" I hear. My insides clench like a vice but I don't move.

Then I hear "Ellen!"- the name of the woman he lived with 10 years ago, who he has his eldest child, Leo with. He is still delirious, I realise. What the fuck was he on last night?!

Then I catch a word that makes me sit bolt upright. My ears prick and I hear the word again, "Valium".

He stops shouting suddenly but I can hear him grumbling and complaining to himself. I've placed two painkillers and some water by the bed. He goes quiet and I wonder if he has taken them. He will feel better soon. Harry will fix this, then we can talk. Sort this all out.

The shouting has frightened me. With shaking fingers, I fumble with the notepaper I wrote his number on and text Harry, even though it's not yet 8 am.

Relief soars through me when he texts me back within only a few minutes. Thank God! Hunched in the corner of my sofa with the lights still off, I wrap a cardigan around me, wishing desperately I wasn't so fucking cold. Stage-whispering what's happened as best I can, I talk and talk, but towards the end of this hellish story, start to cry. Keening like an animal, Harry listens to me and lets me release as much pain as he can bear.

"Lucy, calm down. I'll take Jonathan to a meeting. A small meet with older people- he'll be ok, Lucy," his smooth, mature voice lifts my soul up with hope. "You've done the right thing. Let him sleep as long as he needs. I'll be there before 10."

I've held back the stuff about the sexting. Jonathan will be furious if I tell his "business" to someone he respects as much as he does Harry. Keeping it to myself for now feeds the fantasy that I imagined it all. A disgusting nightmare. None of it ever happened.

Harry needs to go. He has to get dressed himself and wake his wife to tell her he has an emergency. "We'll get him there again, Lucy. It will be easier this time because he has you. You are a stable influence. You're not involved in anything that triggers him like his exes."

I just don't have the strength to ask him what he means. I can't explore this right now. I have 3 little boys who need me. I need to put a brave face on and focus on them and focus on

Jonathan. Focus on getting him better. My feelings don't matter right now.

Harry will be here in a few hours so this gives me time to have a wash and prepare some breakfast for the boys. I do dishes and put some washing on. Cleaning my teeth, I stare at myself and see a woman broken. I look away from the mirror quickly and resolve not to worry too much if all of this is actually ageing me abnormally.

I go about tasks robotically, pretending it's just a normal Saturday morning with my family. The mundane activity of moving bread, butter and jams here and there, looking for the porridge he always has before work, makes me heave. I choke it back. Hands steadying me on the counter, I let my head drop. Fast, unrelenting tears fall onto my black marble worktop. Oily and slick. I don't make a sound.

"Jonny's not well, boys- get yourselves dressed. Teeth and faces quietly, please!" I whisper into the gloom of my children's bedroom. I can't bear to see their faces, so when I hear a muffled "yes mummy," I back out into the hall and quietly click their bedroom door shut. For a few seconds, all I can manage is to stand there with my forehead against the cool of their bedroom door and pant like a dying animal in a trap.

Sitting on the bed in the dark I force myself to look at Jonathan. The room stinks. He's sweating and holding his stomach and rolling around as though in pain. I wonder if he ate something bad yesterday.

Reaching across to stroke his head, I whisper "Harry is on his way." At the smell of him, I almost lean back in disgust.

Working hard to maintain some calm, I don't recoil and try to smile for him. Reassure him. Stay in control. "Everything will be ok. We'll get you sorted today, baby."

At the mention of Harry, he wakes up a little and pushes himself back into the pillows as though away from me. His face is grotesque. One eye open, then the other. Then a long, slow gurning of his jaw. He's trying to work out what's happened between party time and now, here in my bed. He doesn't know where he is.

He gives up the effort and slides back down to cover his face with the duvet. Eyes closed, he shouts again through the fabric, strangely clear: "Valium. Gimme Valium".

It hits me like a train. Valium?! What? All I know is it's something American housewives took because the stress of microwaving meals and caring for 1.2 spoiled kids was just too much fucking stress for them.

"Sinead is a Valium nut. She drove me mad with it. I tried to help her but she's too far gone. She orders it online and fucking stock-piles it," he said once when I wanted to know why she acted so nuts.

I sit on the end of the bed and desperately claw through everything he has ever said about Valium. It was always Sinead he said was into it- not him. I don't understand!

I stare at him. Who is this creature in my bed? In the last 12 hours, he has almost completely been replaced with someone I would avoid in the street. He has been sexting people, watching porn, emailing a hooker, taking drugs and drinking with people even worse off than him. He has violently attacked me and I've far seen too many unfamiliar looks of loathing and hatred. "Get me Valium. I want Valium. Need it!" he says again. Louder now. I ignore him and hope he will fall asleep.

Harry arrives around 9.30 and I leave him and Jonathan in the living room. In the kitchen, I quietly say a prayer.

As I put a bowl of porridge in front of Jonathan, Harry says "We've agreed to go to a meeting at The Rooms, Lucy. Jonathan understands this is what he must do now." He's looking at Jonathan and I catch a whiff of fear. I realise with a thud that Harry is out of his depth. He doesn't have the confidence or skills for this. Surely, he is an AA sponsor so he can sort out an AA member who's relapsed once? For God sakes, how hard can it be?

Jonathan is smiling inanely and playing with his hands. He is still incredibly high. "Yeah, Harry- we'll go to The Rooms. Get a coffee. Do a share. Get me back on track." He still isn't looking at me. He is talking to Harry. Smiling, he pats Harry on the back. Old buddies. In this together. Sort this silly mess out.

My hands curl into fists and I want to race across the room and punch him repeatedly. I want to kick him like he kicked me.

"Jonny, this isn't funny. Do you know what you've done?" I say carefully. "Have you told Harry what you have done to me? To us?" The last words are broken, cracked. Higher-pitched. I'm losing it.

Jonathan lifts his head, turns it slightly like a predatory animal readying for the kill. There are 2, maybe 3 heartbeats of heavy silence as he stares at me venomously. He has absolutely no intention of talking about the Valium and certainly no intention of telling Harry about the other drugs or the vile sex addiction symptoms he is displaying.

This is a standoff. Guns drawn. "Jonny, you need to tell Harry the truth. This is not one night of drinking. You need to be honest with him about EVERYTHING!" I say the last word with more emphasis and set my jaw. I have to be strong. I have to be firm. I can't lose control here.

He stares back at me & I watch a shark smile open up his face. "Och, it's just a laugh. A few messages that's all. Just daft messages." My head hurts. Everything hurts.

"It's not funny to cheat on me, Jonny. It's not funny to sexually use and abuse women the way you have been." On saying the word women, I remember them all. Every message. Every image. Each one so different. Each one a stranger to me, but some sort of lover or fantasy or goddamn game to him. I swallow back bile and dig my nails into my knees to try and come to.

I look up to stare at Harry. "Well, are you going to sort him out or not?" my glare says.

"What've you been doing? What is Lucy talking about?" he asks. I am a little unsettled. Something isn't quite right here.

Jonathan manages to look slightly embarrassed now. He shuffles his feet and he yet again is refusing to look at me. He looks at the door again. He wants to escape.

I fire another shot. Let's get this over with. "Jonny, you need to tell Harry about the drugs."

Harry is still as stone. He's looking at the floor, then at Jonathan, then at me. Back to Jonathan. Why is he not recoiling in horror and shock at all of this? I don't understand.

Now he's speaking. I try to focus on him fully but I am
struggling to stop rocking. When did I start rocking?

"Lucy, this is not Jonny's first relapse. He's only just 2 years
clean and sober." 2 years, not 8 or 9 years? What? My living room
sways a little and I can hear that awful whooshing sound that
precludes the wave of reality hitting me.

I look blankly at Jonathan. He is an addict. A proper one.
Like you see on telly. Like you walk past in the street. Harry's
voice again. I want him to stop talking.

"In my time supporting him, he has relapsed twice before this
and before that, he had a couple of other sponsors who had the
same struggles with him."

I flash to the puzzled faces of colleagues and AA members
when I proudly refer to his 8-year abstinence- they all know it's
less. A lot less. Shame and embarrassment roar through me. In
front of two silent men I trusted more than my own father, I hunch
forward and wail like an animal. They sit there quiet and listen
until I stop.

In the distance, Harry is using his special "AA chat" to try
and get through to Jonathan. I hear quotes from the AA "Big
Book". Familiar words about hope and recovery and love. My
chest hurts. I remember writing a long love letter to Jonathan just
before a discard and hiding it in his Big Book ready for him to find
if he decided to seek advice from it. Advice to help him love me
better and be kinder. He said the letter made him cry. That was
only 3 weeks ago. I want to scream.

Jonathan's nodding away, smiling stupidly at Harry. Wrapped
up in AA crap, Harry chatters away, talking. Harry thinks he's
winning. I don't.

"Does Jonathan have a Valium problem. Like a proper one?
Worse than the booze one?" I say suddenly. He stops talking and
looks at me. It takes Jonathan an extra 2 seconds to catch up and
he slowly mirrors Harry. 4 eyes bore holes into me but I steadfastly
refuse to back down.

Harry looks uncomfortable. He darts a look at my beloved
who's found something fascinating to look at behind me.

Harry nudges Jonathan. I catch him muttering something benign about how honesty will help him get sober and stay sober and that he must be honest with me.

My bowels loosen as I hear these words; "Jonathan, have you not been going to the NA meetings we agreed?"

Jonathan is supposed to attend Narcotics Anonymous meetings as well as AA meetings? What?

"What do you mean? He's in AA. He's an alcoholic. No?" The blood has rushed from my face and I almost pity Harry for being here. "Tell me what you mean. I don't understand. Drugs? What drugs?" I'm shaking and wringing my hands. Jonathan has now decided to look out of the window. He looks bored.

Over the next few minutes, Harry, not looking at Jonathan, explains to me that drugs, especially cocaine and Valium, have peppered my partner's life since he was in his early teens. At this point, I just want him clean and sober. I can't take all this in. It's too much. I say nothing but I look at Jonathan throughout Harry's explanation and he avoids eye contact with me the whole time.

"I want my car keys," Jonathan says suddenly, looking at the door. Harry stops talking and looks at him, mouth wide open. Finally, some real emotion. I'm not the only one shocked here!

My heart skips a beat. Sweat prickles my neck. I remember he drove to the house he was found in last night. I am in no doubt he has driven there under the influence. I'm disgusted and shocked that now (still out of his tree) he wants to drive.

Harry has his car so I am immediately conscious Jonathan has no interest in going to a meeting. He's planning on getting in his car and going on a bender.

I tell him I don't know where his keys are and he gets agitated. He is wringing his hands and making beseeching faces at his comrade. "I'm fine, Harry. I will meet you at the meeting. I just want my keys." Neither Harry nor I seem to be moving fast enough for him.

"Where's my fucking car?" he shouts, running big hands through greasy hair and over his stubbly face in panic. I sense a disaster. "I don't know. I brought you home in a taxi. You were pissed and away with the fairies on something."

"You, you, you! You took my car!" he shouts. He is so out of it he's forgotten that I can't drive.

Suddenly Jonathan's eyes twinkle and darken into pools of oily water. He is calm in a split second. He has an idea. I feel my stomach tighten and my mouth go dry. I watch him and wait. Slowly I stand up, ready for the fight.

He slaps Harry on the back. "No probs. Let's go to The Rooms. I'll get the car later. I don't need it now. Harry can drive us. So, you need to give me the keys, Lucy. You know, for later"- Harry relaxes (the fool!!) and smiles stupidly at me.

I look at the pair of them and wonder if I'm the one who is bonkers.

With a plummeting sense of foreboding, I go and get the keys from inside a shoe I put under my side of the bed. Ironically, it's the lovely red stilettos I bought to wear for my birthday a few months before. I stifle a sob as I lean forward, face first, into the side of the bed.

When I stand up, I feel like an old woman. Tired and sad, I walk back into the hall, and not taking my eyes off Harry, hand over the keys to Jonathan. He grabs them so fast he catches my fingers. He cut's one with his fingernail. He doesn't apologise and I don't even wince. I still have a little scar on my right pinkie now. It is the shape of a crescent moon.

As they move for the door, I start to beg. "Please, please go to the meeting, Jonny. Please." Holding his hands in mine, I'm almost bent over pleading. I can't do another night like that one. I can't cope with any more stress and shocks. I am on a knife edge as it is and feel like I will lose it completely if this carries on.

Jonathan hugs and kisses me as I stand limp in his arms then anxious to leave he shakes me like a broken mannequin. "I swear on my dad's grave I'll be back in an hour or so. I promise." He has his dad on a pedestal, so I believe him. He would never make such a promise in this way and betray not only me but the memory of his dad. Never. I relax significantly. Opening the door, I say nothing & watch them go.

I literally lie face down on my bed, holding my phone and staring into space for the next 2 hours. Then 3 hours. At some point, I fall asleep. I wake up to see 4 hours have passed. It's past lunchtime. It all crashes in as I open my eyes so immediately I want to sleep and forget again.

He's not coming home and he's not going to do the right thing. This is only the beginning, I realise, as I sit up. I can't even cry. Numb and determined, I know I need to do everything possible to fix this because he is my man and I chose this. It is not in my nature to give up.

A Few Hours Later

I've run all over the city looking for him. In and out of pubs with pool tables, in and out of the shop where he buys his e-cig oil and even to his flat. Finding it empty and exhausted, I wander home like a lost animal. Surely, he will be home tomorrow?

I decide to run a bath to centre my nerves. I don't eat and I don't have an alcoholic drink of any kind. I need a clear head and my mouth has a funny metallic in it taste anyway.

In my hand-painted, slightly dusty, bathroom mirror, my face traumatised. Big, dark, wide eyes stare back at me & my lips are tight & papery. I haven't drunk enough this last day or so, running around in a panic. My skin is a strange bluey-grey colour.

Numbly I wonder if this bout of cystitis is something more sinister and he has infected me with something from cheating.

The images in his phone and the words they use and the strange huffs and discards are all coming together. Has he been cheating literally this whole time? Have I been broken hearted while he has been ball-deep in some manky, fat slut?

I can't stop retching and crying and curl up in a ball on my bathroom floor. I lie there for an hour until the need to sleep overwhelms me and my survival instinct kicks in. I will not break. I will not let this break me. I am made of stronger stuff. I will fight.

Strangely, I do manage 4 hours sleep and come alive. Today is Sunday & I will try again to get my man back.

I put on black dungarees, my green and white Converse trainers (in case there's more running) and an off-the-shoulder

127

striped "French style" top. I even put make-up on. The first time in 2 days. These acts of normality help make me feel like this is all going to be ok after all. In reality I'm numbing out.

In a taxi on the way to Jonathan's flat, I message Harry, checking when he will be there. The reply sends me cold. "It's best Jonathan works this out for himself- if he wants to attend a meeting, he will take himself there. He needs to help himself."

I nearly drop the phone. Surprise turns to shock, turns to dismay and yes, almost disgust.

Stood on that doorstep all alone in this hellish situation, I have a sudden sensory overload that actually, no one cares. No one cares about him or me. I am friends with these people. They know I love him, that my kids love him. That we have a life! Why is no one in this fucking fellowship helping us? He is not in the right mind to help himself! We need an intervention. If they don't help, I am losing him to skanky females, drugs, drink, dealers and worse. I know for sure that he will lose his job. When this all comes out, he will absolutely never get to see his kids again. He could hurt or kill someone and not just himself or me. He's drink-driving and he's already harmed me and absolutely is escalating.

If all these things happen and he sobers up to realise what he has done.... he will want to kill himself. If he loses everything, he will want to end his own life. The sense of panic and fear is overwhelming and when I run across the road to the car park he favours, I sit on the ground in dismay to see the car missing.

Twenty or thirty seconds pass and I am still sitting on the wall in the car park. I can see more clearly now. I don't feel anything but a desperate need to fix this. Almost fully numb to my own wellbeing and entirely focused on my beloved, my survival instinct is kicking in. A plan starts to form.

Suddenly it strikes me that if he is in his car, he is not alone. I believe he's partying with Ratty Paul.

Jonathan would never show this true self to anyone in his false life. No colleagues and no one in AA would see him like this. No way.

Standing in the street looking up at his flat, dark and unwelcoming, I decide I am not letting this go easily. I can see my red heart fairy lights hanging loosely & a little uneven in the window.

The next few hours are similar to the day before. I try pretty much every pub in the city centre and punctuate this running around with sitting in doorways, crying and sobbing. On one occasion, a fucking homeless man gives me a pound coin.

Then out of nowhere late in the afternoon my phone pips. Three texts, one after the other, from Jonathan. Happiness surges through me like lava. I come alive. "Come get me. In toilet. Love yu." A fourth message is the name of the pool bar we were in on my birthday.

What if he's overdosed or been attacked? Texting from a toilet cubicle in a pub can't be a good sign. If you get a toilet-text from a nut job partner or friend, they are either dying on a dirty tiled floor or cheating on who's out in the bar, let's be honest.

My heart skips and bile rises in my throat as the taxi I flagged down 10 minutes ago pulls up outside the familiar double doors.

Unfastening my seatbelt, I can't help but throw the door open before the taxi's even fully stopped. I try and walk "normally" into the pub, because any commotion will draw attention to me and the last thing we need is the police being called. Almost staggering with adrenalin, shock and a lack of food and sleep this last few days, I want to kneel on the floor when I see the scarred back of Jonathan's head (fast becoming a common sight) and opposite him is seated Ratty Paul. To Jonathan's right is a woman I am not at all happy to see.

Moira, Jaydee's on-off partner is talking to Jonathan and turns pale as she sees me. It takes one look at my face for her to click I'm raging. She is heavier and taller than me and yet looks absolutely terrified to see skinny little me marching towards her. I feel a rush of pleasure- it's about time someone has some consideration for how fucked off I am right now. I could get a hold of her hair and ram her face straight down into the grubby bar table without so much as a Bonjour right now.

Pauls' reaction is different but expected. His mean, tanned face falls, and he looks away with what looks almost like a hint of shame. Again, that feeling almost like pleasure lifts me up. I could get used to this. Anger and spite...yeah, I like it.

I wonder if perhaps Moira's managed to convince Paul that Jonathan really is ill and that he should not be feeding his addictions with quite such vigour. Two angry, sober women probably is a bit too much for the wee bastard and I stifle a smile as he scans the floor for something really exciting to concentrate on instead of me. He stares at a forgotten chip & fiddles with his drink. The vile little wimp.

Standing by the table I can see that Jonathan has a drink in front of him and a half-eaten plate of food.

I look at it, frown and slowly look round to glare at Moira; she's been stupid enough to feed him.

I sit down between her and my beloved and hiss, "You stupid idiot- why did you feed him in here for god-sakes?"

"Everyone knows the best way to get anyone out of the pub and home is to make sure they have the fucking munchies!"

"He said he was hungry," she says weakly, gesturing a pale pink fake fingernail at the plate. "I thought it would sober him up so we could talk." She shrugs like a teenage girl caught sticking gum under a table. I want to slap her ridiculous, cosmetically-enhanced face. Slap it hard. Twice. No, three times.

"He's a fucking alcoholic, Moira. They don't talk when they are on a binge. They drink and drink and drink and lie and drink some more. Now he's got food in his belly, he'll get a fucking second wind and off we go again, you idiot". Desperate to keep my voice down and not alert the bar staff, I hiss at her like a trapped cat but don't feel one ounce of pity when she flinches and goes red.

Feeling the urge to wriggle on the sticky leather couch I bite my lip in pain. In all the drama I'd forgotten I was pissing glass and suffering one hell of a temperature. I am not well. Not well at all.

The sofa squeals in protest as Jonathan half-turns to look at me. He smiles at me but his eyes miss my face. He's virtually cross-eyed with whatever he's been taking and I sense the gradual spread of a carb coma creeping in.

I tug him backwards, forcing him to fully face me. "Jonny-Can we go home?" I attempt a smile but fail. I don't have it in me. I smell his familiar aftershave and the bitter tang of stale alcohol and want to lean forward and bury myself in his chest and scream at the wrongness of all of this.

Out of the corner of my eye, I catch Moira taking me in. We haven't met before, as she is apparently very close to Sinead. Like most women around Jonathan, I am sure she has Facebook-perved on me and observed my life just as intently as her pal has. She won't have been able to resist. Jaydee and her don't live together although they share a young child. Jonathan had often remarked that both Jaydee and her were jealous of us and that was why they caused so many issues for us.

"Erm. I don't want to be in the way...soooo..." She mumbles and starts to stand, pretend-stretches to buy herself some time then awkwardly rubs Jonathan's shoulder. I shoot her a look that would make a fresh turd go white and crispy in an instant.

Jonathan is now slumped down into the sofa. I notice Moira has a full face of fresh make-up and has ensured her shiny white designer bag matches her shoes. She's come here ready for something- likely a celebration of our downfall. The party they've all planned since he chose me over Sinead.

As Moira hovers nearby looking uncomfortable, it grabs me that Jonathan secretly contacted me, didn't tell her and for some twisted reason brought us both together right now in this fucking nightmare. Deliberately in public.

Besides us, he laughs and coughs as the last of his drink goes down wrong. He thinks this is hilarious. With a pique of sudden creativity, he blurts "I want you to make friends. To meet and be friends." He almost whines like a child. "I thought this would be a good idea. Drinks together."

I watch Moira reach for her coat. Over her shoulder she tosses her unconvincing hair extensions and says, "call me later Jonathan". She's trying to be confident and sassy. The slight shake in her hands and unsteady walk betrays her. She scuttles out and I smile nastily as she gets her sleeve caught in the door. She's desperate to get this new story off the press and over to Sinead. My humiliation and his relapse. Read all about it!

A silence settles between Ratty Paul & my chap beside me. I can't give up now. I betrayed my marriage for this man. Lost my business and my dignity. I owe it to myself, my children and Niall to prove I wrecked everything for someone who is worth it. I have to believe Jonathan is worth it and the life we have built is worth it. I am not letting my relationship end today. Not like this.

Jonathan's staggered to the pub doorway and his face is angry. I've been sitting thinking and forgotten he's the focus right now. I've been too slow to follow him. Paul walks past me and starts to talk to him closely. They lean together and are both slightly weaving. It is an ugly dance and I curl my lip in distaste.

I see something get passed to Jonathan and he reaches behind him to put it in his back pocket.

As I am following them outside and reach for Jonathan's hand, he turns away from me, opens his flies and starts to urinate in the glass doorway of the pub, in full view of a table of customers just inside.

"Jonny. Jonny. Fucking stop. You'll get arrested!" I try uselessly to pull at his free arm and he roughly pushes me away without even turning around. I stumble backwards and almost fall onto the street.

Ten minutes of drunken Jonathan lurching left and right, back and forward up Sauchiehall Street brings us to the car which is (ironically) parked a few yards down the road from the community centre we nearly booked for his birthday.

I see the janitor stood outside, smoking, and I feel a surge of relief.

Jonathan and the janitor get on very well and I often sit in the sun and chat with him about recipes and other mundane topics if Jonathan is at a meeting or if I'm passing on my way to the shops. He's a big guy & a friend so I feel safe suddenly.

Jonathan is all over the shop, staggering up the hill behind me. The incline is clearly a challenge for this 7 day a week gym-goer and he's comically almost tipping backwards as he doggedly walks upwards. I honestly would not recognise this man walking past

132

him in the street. The thought hurts my heart. There's that sharp, stinging pain in my chest again & it makes me breathless.

The janitor looks genuinely sorry for me as I run up to him, breathless and half crying. Over my shoulder, he sees Jonathan and frowns in surprise. "Need a hand, hen?" he says simply. Four words that give such warmth to my soul that it's almost painful. I knew he would help. He likes us. He likes me. He likes Jonathan. He is a good person. Not one member of AA has helped us, and yet the janitor for the place they have meetings in is all about helping us.

"Thank you," I say, hoarse with stress. Jonathan is suddenly beside me, prickling with rage. He's reeking of alcohol and urine and his stubbly jaw is gurning with the drugs he has consumed. He is also very grubby and I suspect he hasn't washed for a few days. He has various crusty leftovers on his black jumper and trousers. He looks like a bad person. A person who doesn't care. For once he looks like what he is.

Scanning the car park, the trees, the play park, I realise Ratty Paul is gone. He's wandered off to likely find another party with that girl elsewhere. This has got boring now for him. It's not fun now there are more tears than jokes.

While Jonathan talks to the janitor, I half-walk, half-stagger to a stone bollard on the other side of the road. Sitting down here, out of his orbit, I can watch what's happening and try to get some sort of sense of what's next. In the relative peace and quiet, things go all blurry.

The ground's throbbing and pulsing beneath my feet and there's a strange taste in my mouth- like when you lick a battery. Someone's shouting in the distance- far, far away. Feeling sick, I slide off the bollard to sit on the ground like a forgotten doll. Suddenly, he's in my face. "She. Her. Her! Is stopping me enjoying myself. I deserve some laughs, mate," Jonathans yells echo round the quad. "She's a fucking psycho. I just want a life for fuck sakes!" He staggers a little and steadies himself against the bollard and looks down at me. He laughs at his drunkenness and claps his hands like a child.

His face twists and folds into something monstrous again. "You! You've got my keys" and as he pushes away from the bollard to step back and point at me, he loses balance a little and weaves on his feet. I slipped the keys off the table and into the front pocket of my dungarees when Jonathan stood up to leave. I didn't think he would ask for them again. I had hope we were going home. Stupid, stupid hope!

Crouching down to make eye contact, he wafts poisonous breath on my face. "Gimme the keys, Lucy. I fucking mean it!" he says- an angry, deep-throated growl.

The janitor's hovering nearby waiting to see what to do. The commotion's attracted a few neighbours now and I can see more and more people opening windows and starting to peer out. There are a couple of people stood across the other side of the road, watching. A woman with long dark hair and a striped top is watching me in particular. She looks worried. I look away, my face burning. It's not my car... I just help pay for it.

The janitor motions to me with a sort of weird sign-language that he will keep them out of the way while Jonathan sobers up. I slowly reach into my dungaree pocket, but in a blur, Jonathan grabs at them. He is like a raging ape. Snatch! and they are gone and before I can stop him, he is lurching away towards his car like a zombie chasing a kill.

I start to cry again and shout and beg and plead with him. "Jonny no! Please no! You'll hurt someone! Please calm down. Please come home!" I'm ashamed of my whining. My snotty, scared begging. But I still don't stop.

Eyes glittering with hate, he turns to look at me. He's backing towards the car waving the keys at me and smiling nastily. I continue to beg. I don't even know what I'm saying. At some point, I fall to my knees on the cold, jaggy tarmac and shout "please, please, please," over and over. Someone strokes my head and tries to lift me up. I don't see them. Staring at me, he puts the key in the lock and opens the door.

On impulse, I leap up to run towards the car. I'm going to try and get in. He's grabbing at me and grunting. In my desperation, I am stronger than he is. I manage to squeeze past him and climb over to get into my seat in the front.

If I am in the car, he won't risk my life. He loves me. He won't drive with me in it.

He grabs at me, trying to get me out of the car. We are all arms and legs and grunts and yelling. It is disgusting. I feel him tear at my clothes and my hands. He wants me out of here.

I'm not letting this person drive this car in this state. He will hurt someone. He might kill someone. He might kill himself.

The janitor's run over to help. He is leaning in the driver's door, trying to talk sensibly to Jonathan. Trying to calm the situation down. Jonathan grabs my arm and is trying to half-push, half-pull me away out onto the ground. He is pulling at me mercilessly. "Bitch. Get OUT!" I'm shouting "No. No. No, you can't drive! Please, Jonny. Please!" over and over. There's movement to my left, behind the car. It's the woman with the stripy top. She's walked closer. She looks terrified.

She looks nice, normal and kind. Gesturing a phone sign to her with my left hand I mouth the words "phone the police" and nod madly. "Police," I mouth again.

Jonathan is too busy grunting and snarling, "Fucking cow. Fucking leave me alone". Now he's grabbing at the waistline of my denims and trying to drag me out. He has a good hold now and it hurts as he pulls me back and forth, trying to loosen my grip on the door handle and make me let go of the steering wheel.

God, I hope she understood. I'm being pulled all over the place but all I see is her. She nods back at me. Thank God.

I loosen my grip with relief but go limp, so suddenly I'm on the ground. Snot and hair all over my face, the janitor helps me up. "Jonny! Come on, man. You can't do this. Look at your wee Lucy. Look what you've done. What the fuck are you playing at? She's gutted, man!"

Jonathan stops moving and looks at him. I can see his phone poking out of his back pocket. I have no idea why, but I grab the phone and start to back away, not taking my eyes off him.

He turns to look at me with a hatred I hope I never see in anyone's face ever again. "You cunt. Give me my phone back!" he roars. The janitor moves a little to stand nearer to me.

I lean forward a little and wipe my face with my sleeve. "You can take a fuck to yourself, you stupid, cheating arsehole. I'm done!" The look of shock on his face is really pleasurable.

He is deadly still. God, it feels good. So, so, so good to be in control. I want to hurt him and his tool of hate is the grubby Apple iPhone in my hand. If I take it, I can at least stop him cheating, even for one night. It's a ridiculous pathetic idea but I don't care.

I don't have time to enjoy his fear about losing his precious phone. Ramming the phone into my back pocket I turn away & not looking back, start to run.

Twenty minutes later, the police arrive, take my statement and his phone and assure me that he will now be in cells until Tuesday when he will be up in court on a charge of Domestic Fear and Alarm. I've gone through his phone again and found more messages sent last night-even after being caught by me, he was still creeping on the women in his contacts list. I don't know why I'm not even shocked.

The police didn't tell me about his previous convictions for violence. It would have been incredibly useful if they had because I might not have taken him back if I knew I was the 4th partner he was known to have traumatised and harmed.

They said he caused quite a fuss on arrest and failed the breathalyser test significantly, but because he was only sat in the car talking to the janitor and shouting at me, he'd not been charged for drink-driving alongside the domestic.

I haven't slept. I haven't eaten. Doped up on pain relief my social work neighbour slipped me, I drink pint after pint of water, desperate to not be in pain. Whatever this is, it isn't a bog-standard urine infection.

Jemma Hotel is niggling me- there were a lot of messages to her. Very sexual and, heart-rendingly, also some which were very chatty. "I'm lonely"; "she's demanding"; "I need comfort and sex"; "She just sits there and does nothing". Lie after lie. She first favoured him with extreme sexual images within 2 days of them encountering as far back as May... I'm sickened, livid and broken. I waited 6 months for this... man-creature. 6 fucking months!

She fell for his grooming hook, line and sinker and sent true filth! and for me (a right old sext addict slut, apparently) to say that, you can imagine the content.

136

Locating her was difficult as I only had a first name and a mobile number- she ignored most of my messages although replied later that night with some abuse telling me to "fuck off" and she had "nothing to do with anything" that was going on.

I called and got to speak to most of the other females. Polite and calm explaining about his evil behaviour, I think they thought I was a total oddball.

The one I struggled to get any info on was the outward call person. I saved the number in my phone as "Who September 2015".

Cold inside and out, I wonder, is this what shock feels like? I'm grieving and miss my partner yet hate him and feel shock and disgust. My stomach hurts with all the anger and loss inside me. The feelings fight each other and sit deep and determined. Little voices whisper that nothing, no one can fix this. By morning I come to realise only he can fix this and I need it fixed.

He's not a bad person. He's an addict. He's a kind, funny, charismatic loving man who desperately wanted me to be with him. Show him love. Build a life with him. We can get through this. It's just a blip. We are perfect together. We just need peace from our enemies and time to heal. I can help him.

It's useful to stop my story here and explain why Narcs and their manky cousins, Casanova Psychopaths, struggle with maintaining relationships and staying faithful, even when they "have it all". These personality disorders are all about greed, selfishness, a lack of morality and most importantly, a sense of entitlement complemented by complete lack of empathy. The people around a Narc and feeding their constant hunger for attention and power are "Supplies of Fuel". There is a lot of information on Supplies across the internet, but for ease of understanding, I have sectioned them up here for your own interest.

Hot Supply: This is the person who provides the Narc with regular sexual encounters, advice, support, guidance and makes them "look good". This is usually the "serious partner" they have on show in life and online. Those of us who play this role are not aware (usually) that we are only there as a food source for these vampires until it is too late. We are blessed with the Narc's charm most of the time because the Narc enjoys us, due to the wide variety of ways we make the Narc feel and look good. Lucky us.

Warm Supply: This is the close friend, close family member, eldest (adult) child who is devoted to the Narc. They are always in the background but for everything other than sex. Money, advice, guidance, a roof over their head, adulation, defence in times of crisis, the Plan B if the Hot supply can't hold the Narc's hand at a party, work event, gym etc. These are held on to tightly by the Narc as they are a useful ally when the Hot Supply isn't around or eventually gets fed up and fucks off. They will see Hot Supplies come and go, but never quite be Plan A for the Narc, and are happy to be Plan B because the relationship is superficial and the lack of sex means they are never hurt in the heart enough to walk away.

Tepid Supply: These are the semi-sexual relationships (sexting, occasional 1-nighters, flirtations) and long-term ex-partners usually. Or in some cases, the ex-colleague with good contacts or wealthy family member the Narc sometimes taps up for cash. These people are held at arm's length, but the Narc still has one finger digging into their wrist keeping them around. These people also believe the Narc "wants" and "needs" them, even though they are rarely given anything in return for their attention. These people are also fervent supporters of the Narc when he/she is in contact with them and often very bitter and nasty when the Narc is away enjoying their Hot and Warm supplies. They always "make up" with the Narc though, because they have self-esteem issues and miss their presence (no matter how toxic or selfish) far too much.

Cold Supply: These are the hangers-on- random colleagues, customers, friends of friends and group members from hobbies or memberships the Narc belongs to. The "Hi" people that the Narc doesn't actually like who they say "Hi" and "bye" to so they can appear friendly, popular and jovial. These are the 500+ Facebook friends the Narc has but doesn't really do anything with or communicate properly with. These people are the ones who sympathise with the Narc when they claim you (the victim) have hurt them in some way. They come out from under their stones and play flying monkey then disappear again. Narcs need these people desperately to validate their behaviour. Because they have no potential at all for seeing the real Narc underneath the mask, they are a good easy way for the Narc to spread news, get info (about victims) and gain a wee ego boost from. Sometimes the Narc may also hunt for victims in this group and promote the members up the ranks to Warm Supply. I found Jonathan did this regularly and still does, I believe.

Monday, September Weekend 2015

Jittery, stiff and emotionless, like a wind-up toy robot, I make a coffee and sit down with a pen and paper to list what needs done now. Dry-eyed and doped up on painkillers, I sit there for an hour until it's time to leave the house to visit the police station where the love of my life is in cells.

On the train into town, I texted his solicitor to tell him I will be there in court tomorrow. Next, I google where I'm supposed to go to get checked out for whatever is making me so sore and unwell.

In A and E, I sit there with a temperature, bent over and trying not to sob in pain. Now I'm here, it's suddenly so much more painful. Closing my eyes while the waves of pain and hot flushes flow over me, I'm a sad figure in the corner of the waiting room, clutching a plastic carrier bag with a freshly ironed T-Shirt and black denims for Jonathan's court appearance. Every few minutes, I grimace and suck air in through my teeth at the waves of pain searing across my cervix.

In the appointment with the doctor a few hours later, I explain what's happened. I don't even cry. "I think my partner has given me something. He is in relapse and because of it, he's been cheating on me. He denies physical contact with anyone, but I definitely have some sort of bad infection. There is something wrong. I know my body."

The GP looks at me with concern. He's clearly worried that I am not acting normally. Why am I not freaking out? Why am I even still referring to him as my partner? I sit and stare at the wall while the doctor makes some notes.

With shaking hands, I hand him a urine sample and describe my symptoms. The GP agrees with me that yes, it sounds like Chlamydia as my usual cystitis medication hasn't worked at all. He gives me a script for infection-specific antibiotics. Thanking him politely, I nearly crumble, so quickly walk out the room and leave.

Walking out of the hospital into weak sunlight, I feel so unbearably alone and ashamed suddenly. I catch sight of a woman waddling into the maternity area and my knees buckle. "I want to have a baby with you. Make a family," he'd said only last month making up with me after a discard. He'd kissed me fervently before wrapping a blanket around me and pulling me onto his lap. I'd decided to come off my pill and he was delighted.

My next stop is the police station to give in the items for Jonathan. I've brought the clothes, 2 books and at the last minute, put in some of his medicated skin cream.

Placing the items on the reception desk in the station in Cowcaddens, I turn to leave. "You need to wait and take his other clothes home," the officer on reception says to me. What colour was in my face quickly vanishes. I want to leave here- I can't hold his clothes. I can't have anything from him that smells of him. I'll fall apart.

It's killing me knowing he's just a few metres away already. I start to shake. "Please- can you not keep his old clothes and give them to him when he's released?"

"No. We can't do that. It's not what we do. Sorry," she says without pity.

I must look such a fool. She knows why he's here. A domestic-against me. This tiny, snivelling wreck in front of her. I must disgust her. Fuck, I disgust myself, to be honest. "Did anyone else bring anything? Clothes or......anything at all"? My voice is as weak as I am. "Nope" is her one-word answer as she stares straight through me. No one wanted to help him- only me, the person he's hurt most of all.

Ten minutes later, the officer comes back with a bundle of clothes and roughly hands them to me. They are still warm from his body and I gasp. Holding the clothes to my face, I breathe in the smell of him. The warmth of him. I slump into the plastic chair in the empty reception area and sit there crying, my face in his clothes, for nearly 20 minutes in the stark reception, with its pamphlets and posters about hate crime, addictions and police complaints.

To me, it was like he was dead and I'd just picked up personal items from a morgue. That feeling of bereavement was true and deep and agonising. For many months after that Hellish September weekend, I cried every day for the person who was there one day and gone the next.

Fortunately, that Monday night, I managed a couple of hours' pain-free sleep, so the next day I managed summon the energy to dress and prepare for court. I was convinced that if my beloved saw me there, waiting for him, we would be able to talk and fix everything.

Tuesday, Sept Weekend 2015

In the court basement waiting area, I sit for 3 hours watching people come and go. The "guess the crime game" wore thin after 40 minutes.

Something isn't right. I've a strange feeling of foreboding. Around lunchtime, I start to really panic. Something isn't right. It shouldn't be this long to wait, surely?

Then through the crowd I see him. The sunken eyes, moon face and mean mouth of Jaydee, Jonathan's best friend are trained right on me. He's staring and smiling. I feel such a surge of hate; I have to sit down again and swallow spit. Spit I would happily launch into that vile bastards' visage, a hundred times. God, the hate! What is wrong with me- so much hate!

Fast and angry, I walk over to him, not caring that my stride and manner is attracting attention. "What the fuck are you doing here? Jonny's my partner. This is our business -not yours!" I hiss.

Forced to look up to avoid my eyes, he juts his greasy chin up and I can see he's uncomfortable now.

"I mean it! You lot need to leave us alone! It's me who's his partner. It's not your place to be here. I looked after him. Got him away to get sober. Took his shit to the station! You stirred it with Sinead and Moira all this time. You pushed him to this!" .... Overwhelmed & faint suddenly, I step back and reach for his arms to steady myself which he pulls away like a petulant child.

Slowly Jaydee pins small, dark eyes on me. "You're too late. He was up in court 2 hours ago. I'm taking him to a meeting then I'm taking him home. He's my friend so Fuck you". Apparently, I've lost whatever game this is.

A slow, evil smile spreads his mouth wide. "He says he doesn't want to see you anyway. This is all your own fault. You shouldn't have got the police involved" Then carefully he leans down & I recoil from his vile breath on my face. "You're fucked. He's done with you! Just... like... all the others! He's mine now" He says this so quietly, people nearby don't hear.

Somehow, I make it outside to sit on the wall. Banged to rights. Convicted of being a heart-broken loser.

"This was all you!". Someone's shouting. Jerking up, I see Jonathan 20 yards away, spitting with rage and jerking around like a marionette. His friends are trying to pull him back by his arms. "You did this, you bitch!" he shouts again.

The 3 days in a cell have not done anything to calm him. Red with fury, his eyes are just tiny black holes in his face. He has long stubble and the smart T-shirt I left at the station for him is crumpled and sweat-stained.

He stops shouting when he sees a police officer peer out of the court doors and turns abruptly away from me, straightening himself. I watch, transfixed, at this display of cool as he fixes his collar and flattens the thing he pretends is a fringe. He even pats his friends on the back.

They smile nastily at me over his shoulder, pat him hard on the back in return and guide him away out of sight. The last thing

I see is Jaydee looking back around the corner to me and flipping a "fuck off" sign.

The leftover Merlot smells like a hug. Warm, rounded and comforting. It's strangely familiar, and I realise I used it to make my darling beloved a lamb puff pastry pie a few days before our world shattered like stomped on ice.

Washing down day two of the antibiotics with the wine, I tug a blanket over my knees. A friendly thud and creak signify the heating kicking in & I close my eyes in pure sorrow before taking another mouthful of wine. No longer grimacing in pain from pissing glass, I realise the antibiotics are working. Looks like it was Chlamydia he gave me after all.

For the next 4 hours, all 3 of my girlfriends give me the same telephonic advice- "let him go unless you get the full story. A proper apology," alongside "He's a cunt", "He's a loser", "You deserve better"- same old, same old. Even I'm bored of my own voice analysing every move he makes. As the wine goes down, I stop crying and start planning.

Yes, tomorrow I can start again. It's tragic and tangled this ending, but it's for the best; it's finished. The police have said social services will want to visit to assess me as a parent now I've been a victim of a domestic- they hinted I could lose my boys if I choose to take him back and there are more issues.

My phone buzzes over and over for almost half an hour just before midnight. The timing and the messages, one by one, say -it's him. I nearly drop the last of the wine in surprise. For all I know, it's the usual discard chat- "Go find someone better", "I love you but can't have you", "Leave me be- I deserve to be alone". Yadda yadda.

"I am so sorry, baby. I don't know what happened. I love you. I need you. I feel so ill. I promise I didn't do anything. Those tramps were just a laugh when I was lonely without you. Please forgive me. You are my everything. You are my love. I'm sorry about court today. It was all their idea to leave you. I didn't want to. I need you."

Variations of the same message come through 5 times. Misspelt apologies and platitudes. Compliments and promises. He talks about how happy I make him. How he's relapsed and how he's different when he's high. How he's scared to be loved. Scared to be loved by someone amazing like me.

I read and reread, eating them up. I drink another glass of wine far too fast and without thinking, wipe my mouth on my pyjama top. The stain looks like blood.

I'm weak, tired and desperately in need of his nourishment. This language is all I've ever hoped for. This is the Jonny I met. Mr Nice Guy who makes mistakes every now and then. This is ok. I can handle it as long as he's sorry and he's honest. We all make mistakes.

"You need to see a counsellor for what happened to you when you were a teenager. All that danger and drama and then your dad dying. I think you need proper counselling. I've looked into it and I think you have either manic depression or borderline personality disorder. You might even be an empath like me?! You've all the symptoms. You're such a lovely person and yet you do these stupid, crazy things!" I think I'm helping him with my support. This seems like such a good plan; I can't help but be enthused now he's being so honest and open with me.

All any abuse victim needs and wants are words like Jonathan showered me with after each incident or discard. The ice packs on the bruises. The kisses on the scabs. The firm hand caressing tugged, broken hair.

He seems distraught. Begging for my love and forgiveness to "help" him. I'm thrilled. This is my lover, friend, partner. I don't have the strength to ignore his pleading and walk away. I lost everything in taking him into my life. I have to try.

Thirty minutes later, he's back in my home, my heart and my head. An hour after that and he's inside me in my bed.

He doesn't talk about what's gone on and I don't dare ask. He is too high and I'm too low to start to open the wounds this night. There is no in-between. We hover together over a gaping black abyss of distress and suspicion. The only bindings we have are made of lust and hope. We have sex through the night and when he finally sleeps, I cry quietly in the dark.

Listen to: Kiss: "I Was Made for Loving You Baby"

Red Flags

- _You will find yourself analysing your Narc's bad behaviour._ In worse cases feeding them what you believe has made them behave the ways that hurt you. It's a sort of pro-active denial. You become their counsellor, doctor and psychologist. You diagnose anxiety or depression or a daddy complex and tell them how they can help themselves be happier/kinder/more faithful/clean and sober. They nod away but don't take the advice- of course!

- _Narcs are determined to keep the false image of respectability and good behaviour as far as possible._ They will leave gaps in stories, gloss over bits and use vagueness to fog the sharp edges of bad behaviour they don't want to admit to. In telling the truth about bad behaviours, most normal people can then use this sense of shame and guilt to fix things. Narcs have no desire to face up to the hurt they cause and they certainly have no interest in fixing any mistakes they have made. This is why they struggle with rehabilitation. This is why they keep making the same mistakes and keep relapsing in behaviours they are well aware are harmful and cruel to others.

- Narcs can't bear to have you there as a reflection of who they are. Once you start to get upset, cry and show anger, you are reminding them of what they have done. The result of their abuse pisses them off. They don't feel guilt! Its despicable to them that you dare show them up for what they really are. They don't want reminded of their failings as a human being.

- _Narcs don't like direct questions._ They don't like demands or accusations. The only way you are likely to discover your Narc's secrets is by mistake. By observing them. By joining the dots. By waiting and watching. Asking for honesty will piss them off so whatever they do say will be them turning it on you & demanding you stop "pressuring" them.

- _Intense confusion that is never resolved._ We simply can't understand what's happening and why. Our long-held beliefs about fairness, true love and equality simply make it worse.

The Narc has us doubting everything other people tell us and everything we thought we knew about people & relationships.

- *Dangerous Schema's form. Roller-Coaster Love or "Star-Crossed Lovers" The victim's sense of reality and sense of self is lost. The relationship is not "bad" or "stressful"; it is PASSIONATE & THRILLING and born of two people fighting to be together against all odds! It is meant to be because nothing worthwhile is easy etc. This also a type of....*

- *Trauma Bonding. This is what keeps Victims and Abusers together for so long. It can even develop into Stockholm Syndrome.*

- *Social Set Ups/Street Theatre designed to humiliate you and entertain the Narc/Flying Monkeys. They invite enemies to the same party. They share secrets they know will cause trouble. They give out your new phone number to old enemies. They try it on with your ex-best friend. They try anything that creates situations that may test & embarrass you and certainly entertain them. Watch out for these little games. They may seem small but they can cause people huge upset and problems.*

- *Forgiving the unforgivable. With Co-Dependent relationships, the victim of a Narc will simply put up and shut up with the most awful betrayals and harm. In "normal" healthy relationships, both parties will see that things can't go on, and it will be an honest and gentle parting of ways. Narcs can't let you go until they want to make you go. True Co-deps simply can't bear to be without their abuser so will take hit after hit. Malignant Co-Deps will join in with the Narc (and possibly even some flying monkeys) to fight/attack anyone they see as a possible threat to their precious & toxic coupling.*

October 2015

Over October 2015, I ran around like a headless chicken after Jonathan, helping him detox. The sweats, cramps, lack of sleep and poor appetite I watched him endure were horrific. I became a nursemaid to him. I had a role. I felt of value. I felt needed.

In the first 3 weeks of this medical nightmare, we danced around the cheating. I occasionally took a quick furtive step towards the truth with small benign questions about what I saw or read. In response, he would take two steps back with black fire in his eyes and fists tightly clenched. "I don't remember", "I was high", I wasn't well". The apologetic, begging Jonny had gone and I was too tired to search him out. "You need to move on," he'd say and leave the room clutching his phone like it was a fucking Fabergé egg.

None of it was real. I imagined it all. I was talking rubbish. In fact, I was apparently making him more ill by seeking closure.

"Please stop, baby, or I'll relapse again. I might die this time" treating me to big sad eyes. "You are making me ill. Please leave it be," he says as he puts my hand on his crotch and leans in to kiss me. "Ok, let's forget what happened. I'm ok" my lies are lost in his neck as I do it exactly the way he likes.

Skin to skin every few hours, I'm convinced we're together now, forever. In bed, I do things I've never done before and his eyes glitter. I think he's happy.

When he's not brooding or playing on his phone, he's desperate to distract me from my own phone & laptop. He's terrified I'm looking for the women he's been messaging, charming me with surprise kisses on my neck, my favourite flowers, big shiny cookery books I've coveted for months. Once he brings me a pair of earrings I admired in a nearby antiques shop- emerald. My favourite precious stone.

Sometimes I get so anxious I cry and sleep with the earrings under my pillow in case he changes his mind and takes them away again. Money had gone missing from his birthday collections box and I had come to accept that he'd taken it himself to buy drugs.

In my worst nightmares, I see the earrings on another woman, dripping from her ears and sparkling in candle-light as she rides him and he kisses her. I stand in the corner of the room in the dark and watch them writhe in my bed. I have this dream more often than anyone normal or mentally well should.

Once he wakes up when I'm in this nightmare. Half-asleep, I cry & beg him not to leave me for her and he shushes me.

"Of course not, baby-there is no one else. I will never leave you," he says as he pulls my nightdress over my head.

As things settled down towards the end of October, I started to see glimmers of "My Jonny". He'd whisper "I love you. I'm proud of you. I need you" into my ear as I fell asleep. He started to send me love songs again, played with the children and even told Jaydee & Moira to leave us alone.

The night he did this, I listened to them argue and call each other names and felt a warmth spread through me like hot tar. Dark and vengeful, it felt like I was back in the game again.

He even messaged Sinead one morning and told her to leave us alone so he could "get on with his life with me". He told his mother I "saved" him and insisted she apologise for screaming at me the weekend I was searching for him.

With all these gestures, I felt myself come back to life. Scarred and bruised, yes, but I felt a change in the air. Starting to feel hope and faith, I dared to wonder if we could get to be happy again.

By late October, he even seemed physically less affected by the detox. No more sweats or cramps or shouting about pain, it seemed my Jonny was nearly home.

It's Halloween season and I'm back at work and managing to concentrate enough to get by. Customers have noticed I'm different. I smile less often and avoid chatting with customers as best I can. There are rumours circulating in the pub something's happened, but no one asks what and I'm glad for it.

Jonathan's still on the sick leave that I requested from his boss. They still believe the story we created that he fell off the wagon with booze. Only booze.

As I recover slightly from the state of shock I fell into, I can't help but wonder again who Jemma Hotel really was. How he met her and what really happened between them.

While Jonathan naps in the early evenings, I secretly set about social media searching for the more elusive women he cheated on me with, trying to piece together the tiny scraps of truth he's allowed me.

I'm unashamedly hunting for them. I want to tell them what they've done to me. I think I want to humiliate them. Make it clear

148

they weren't special. Just more fannies and tits and filth to feed his chemically-driven hunger for sexual control. My poor, addicted partner was so sick, he needed them to make him feel important. I'm starting to twist into not a very nice person but I don't care.

Guessing Jemma was associated with our holiday in Tunisia, I have somewhere to start.

Instinct tells me there will be something on Facebook because much of the filth I found in his phone relates to that platforms messenger app.

Finding the Facebook page for the Tunisian hotel we stayed in, I search through its feed and wonder if this page or even google maps will find a female staying there the same time we did. I'm expecting someone pretty, young and slim. I've only seen her fanny mind, and that wasn't great, but you can't judge a book by its... labia. For him to be sexting someone behind my back and lying about me, she fucking better be hot, or at least hotter than me.

It's a long shot, but I'm getting good at this investigative work. It's the only thing keeping me sane right now. I feel in control when I'm searching for answers and judging the women he's cheated on me with. This is my time now and while he sleeps, it's my own dirty little secret.

I look up the last week of April 2015 and scroll down. My eyes catch on a picture of two large, middle-aged women in kaftans. My vision blurs and I have to take a breath and try again. I feel my stomach grab as I read the tags. The younger one -she's called Jemma. Jemma McMoore. Oh God- I really didn't want to be right.

A bead of sweat prickles my neck and my gut rumbles in fear of what I'm going to discover next.

I want to see if she is on his friends list. Surely, he isn't that stupid? Or cruel? To have her there in plain sight? Surely not?!

I scroll down his list slowly, not wanting to miss her and not wanting to see her either.

I beg to God. Please don't let her be here. I almost miss her. Maybe I wanted to. Tapping the keyboard, I go back, up, one two, three pics.

She's there on his list. Her profile picture shows a big, fat face. Ridiculous faux fur hat on. Long pink fake nails a match to the ones I saw clasping her (not very designer) vagina. She looks stoned r on high level meds- she's certainly a partaker of something benzo and funky. I open her profile.

My heart stops. I remember them now. The two hefty, rough women from Ferguslie Park, who exchanged familiar banter with Jonathan in the restaurant on the first morning of our holiday. It's definitely her. He's met her on that holiday. The holiday I paid for.

The filth has continued long after we got home. Our anniversary. His birthday. Mine. His daughter's 1st. Various discards... Nights of tears and vomiting and begging him to be kind to me. To not discard me. To speak to me. I need space, he said. He's used that time away from me to do this! To sext this... thing in front of me.

I run to the toilet and throw up. My ears are buzzing and I can't see properly. Is this what it feels like when you start to go mad?

Kneeling on my bathroom floor panting, staring at the turquoise bath mat which stupidly perfectly matches the toilet mat, I'm thrown back into hell all over again. I only climbed out recently. Now I'm back there again.

I envisage taking pills and just falling away to forget. I want to feel nothing. Jonathan's been lazy with pissing again and in a blur, I get some anti-bacterial wipes and clean the floor. I notice one of his usual skid marks as well and clean the toilet fully, getting rid of his filth. Crying quietly to avoid waking him up, I wail & keen into a towel until I'm all dried out.

Its late now. Nearly 4 am, so I run a bath, furtively watching the bathroom door. I can't see him right now. He'll know immediately that I'm upset. I am not ready for the anger or looks of disgust at my mistake of breaking the rules. No emotion except for adoration and lust is allowed. No emotion apart from the ones he likes.

In searing hot water, I feel calmer. I look at our loving, funny shared posts on my page. The Tunisia tart has had the cheek to comment on some of our pictures together and even on a video he posted of us dancing in a sweet shop on one of our date nights a month before. "Typical Jonny. Lol!" and a variety of laughing, kissing emojis. In the picture, I'm in the background flushed with love, gazing at my Jonny as he hurls himself about, most likely in a Valium haze.

I see her mother has commented with laughing emojis. Shaking with humiliation, I just can't get warm.

Hunched in the bath, I cry and rant to myself for 2 hours. When I'm ready, I tiptoe into the bedroom. He's now fully spread-eagled across my bed. Mouth wide open and snoring gently. While I've been gone, he's taken over the bed. I feel a rush of anger.

I slap his face hard. A wide Dynasty-style sweep that satisfyingly hits his clammy cheek just the way I want. In slow motion, I see his face wobble then as my breath catches in fright, his eyes dart open.

Like a beast, he rises up and looks right at me as though he's been waiting for this. His jaw is pulsing.

"What the fuck!" he roars, sitting up and swinging his legs off the bed and not towards me for a change. "Don't you fucking dare touch me, you cheating, filthy bastard," I hiss. I grab the shoulder of his T-shirt. It's one I bought him for our holiday.

"Fucking come here!" With almost superhuman strength, I pull all 12 stone of stinking lying arsehole up to stand face to face with me. I glare at him. I know my face is twisted in rage and I'm ugly with it. I really don't care.

"Let's go and see Jemma Hotel. She's waiting for you." Stalking into the living room, knowing he's behind me most likely panicking about what I've uncovered, I feel good. Wet and completely naked, I'm standing next to my laptop and pointing a shaking finger at the screen. I smile a nasty "explain this, you cunt" smile at him and watch him try to focus.

Her big daft face is staring out at us. She looks totally gormless. She has a fur hat on even though she's clearly lying back on a bed. Attempting to pout and look sexy, she fails significantly. If you have to try that hard, you ain't never going to be sexy. Just a tip. It's also rude to wear a hat indoors. My mum told me that.

He stands unsteadily in front of me, holding the top of a dining chair and shaking a little.

I watch him lean forward to stare more closely at the computer. I'm disgusted. He looks like effing Mr McGoo. He's trying to decide what face or words to use next.

His mind's racing so fast I can almost smell smoke. How's she found out? What can I do? Should I run? Should I stay and shout. Maybe argue my point? Should I tell her half the truth and hope she accepts it?

Jonathan opts for confused and forgetful "ohhhhh...erm... don't know who this is?!" He actually manages to look nonplussed!

I lean over, click her picture away and open the image of her comments on our video. "She seems to know you. She thinks you're absolutely hilarious." I prod each word out, poking on the high def flat screen and making her big fat face wobble like blancmange - I take minor satisfaction from this. I want to reach into the image and tear her pigging eyes out.

"No, she doesn't, fuck sakes. She's just a random. Dunno who it is." He starts the Facebook hacked shit again. "I bet Sinead did it again. Yeah, that's what's happened. Yeah. I'm so sick of her ruining my life" I listen and smile as he rambles on with varying theories and ideas to get me back on side and make this terrible mistake go away. "Sinead 's done this. She wants us to break up. You know that."

He stops talking and looks at me. He doesn't like this silent smiling Lucy. He likes begging, crying, meek Lucy.

Wordlessly, I pick my phone up, look at him and open my WhatsApp. I almost hear his heart beating. From the scrap of paper, I slide out from under the table mat next to the laptop, I type in the number for Jemma Hotel and save it as McMoore The Hoor, a play on her second name I thought was rather clever.

The tension's building like a storm swelling on the horizon. He knows what's coming next. Oh my God, I'm really enjoying watching the gathering fear snake around him. It's almost a turn-on actually.

This is the first time in 2 years I've felt a semblance of control. The pride & success at answering my own questions is immeasurable right now. I feel bizarrely lit up. Where the hell have I been all this time?

Taking my time, I scroll down my WhatsApp contacts list alphabetically to J and watch as he shuffles his feet and glances at the door.

Opening up the WhatsApp profile I already know is associated with Jemma Hotel, my face curls into a snarl of disgust at her big, daft face again, this time with long, stringy yellow hair extensions. Again, a pic of her lying on her back (no surprise there) facing upwards to the camera. For a second, I have an image of her underneath Jonathan. I close my eyes and swallow. Stay strong, Luce, stay strong.

I turn the phone round and put it close up to Jonathan's face. I want to smash his face with it. Flatten that big, ugly nose and hear him yelp in pain.

"Oh, wow! She's here again. So, let's get this fucking straight, Jonny. Let's really clear all this fucking confusion up. You look a wee bit lost, mate." I put one hand on my damp, cooling hip and glare at him. He's gone a strange green grey and his eyes are bloodshot. I want him to cry. Badly.

"Ok- so she's in your phone as Jemma Hotel. You begging to see her only a month ago. I believe you wanted her to want you to fuck her on... oh... the Thursday night before you went mental and ruined my life. Remember that?" he winces.

"So, she's there in your phone. Yeah?! Then I get fucking clever and find her on Facebook at our hotel when we were there in Tunisia. Then I find her & her daft mother on your Facebook on your friends list. So, what's the story, you fucking, cheating, lying cretin!" I don't care that I'm literally frothing at the mouth.

"I don't know. I don't understand," he mutters, looking at his feet. He fiddles with his fringe. Chin. Shorts. The cushions on my dining chair. "I didn't do anything. I swear on ma weans' lives ah never touched her. I'm sorry. It was just messages when I was bored."

"FUCKING SORRY!!!" I screech. I've lost it now. I admit. From within the hell he has put me through all this time and the lie after lie I have discovered, I've become a monster myself. Incoherent with loss and rage. I repeat back all the filthy things I read. I describe the vile things I saw. The videos and images.

He flinches at every sentence in what appears to be shame and embarrassment. I love every second of the hate I fire at him. The first seeds of the new me are being sown. I like the feeling of rage and hate and power. I like it better than vulnerability, loss and grief. "Those females were fucking minging! What the fucking hell were you doing?"

He starts to plead now; "Luce, please stop. Baby, please stop…you're going to knock me sick. I didn't do anything. It was just messages. I don't even remember half of what you just said! I was aff ma nut"- he has his hands clasped in front of him and is stooped to make eye contact with me. He's begging and I adore it.

Somehow, we've ended up in the boys' room & I'm ranting and shouting, throwing duvets and sheets about like a woman possessed. His begging fuels me. I don't care if he's sweating, crying and begging. It feels fucking good and I want more of it.

He stands in the doorway, hanging his head and wringing his hands like a naughty schoolboy. "I don't know what you are talking about. I don't remember any of it. I was high. We never even met after the holiday. Genuinely! It was just messages, baby!" I stare at him. A challenge to not dare defend his abuse of my trust.

"She was easy. I never even fancied her! I used to send the other guys from AA all her messages and pictures. It was just a laugh."- this one works. I like this sentence. It's disgusting, but for a few seconds, I feel a little better. She saw how I adored him! Everyone did!

"Let's pretend you're telling me the truth, Jonny. Let's just kid on it really was just messages between you and the other fucking 8 women. Do you really think I deserve this? That I should put up with that shite like some complete fucktard?"

"No, baby. No. But I swear to you, there was no one else. I never touched anyone. I haven't been well. You're the only person I have touched since November 2014. That was mad Sinead. You know that. She's sent me mental playing mind games with me and the baby. I just wanted a distraction. A way of forgetting I'm not allowed to be a dad to ma weans. There will be no one else for me ever. I swear to God, baby. Please stop!" Satisfyingly, he gets on his knees in the boys' bedroom doorway. "Please, baby. I will fix it and make it up to you forever!" He looks at the front door again and my spidey-senses tingle.

I point a very pretty, blue-painted finger-nail at him; "if you fucking walk out that door without giving me more details, I'm done with you! Walk out that door and you will never see me or my boys again!" He lowers his head even further and starts to sob- I'm surprised at this. I've never seen or heard him cry properly before.

Resigned now that he's sufficiently sorry, I sigh and drop the bedding, preparing to hug him. Tired suddenly, I close my eyes and put my face in my hands.

Sensing movement, I realise what's going to happen next. He is going to bolt now he has been faced with more truth. He is going to discard me, yet again. Ten seconds later, I hear my door downstairs slam and watch out the window as he runs to his car.

My poor boys must be sick to death of hearing my muffled cries in the bathroom in the early hours of the morning. They go to bed to it and they wake to it. My poor, poor boys.

Jonathan's blocked me as usual on social media and is ignoring my attempts at contact to, at the very least, get answers.

I called his mother who (yesterday adored me) treated me to a barrage of slurred abuse. "You've thrown him out in the street, you bitch. You've made him ill. He is fucking ill because of you." She screeches at me as I cry and beg for time to tell her the truth.

"He's staying with me you psycho!" she shouts into the phone. It is on speaker phone to entertain her other two daughters and I can hear them throwing insults & laughing freely. I was a selfish whore who had no business going in his phone or demanding fidelity.

I felt like I was going crazy- everything I knew to be true, was not true and when I tried to make sense of things or reach out for help, there were more doors closing and more lies being told. I just wanted it to stop.

At some point in the early hours, I sat and made a plan of what would happen if I ended my own life. My boys could stay with their dads. I had £250,000 life insurance that would cover my mortgage and they would be well off.

They would grow to be men and understand Mummy did her best, but her choices meant she was struggling to be a good parent and was best away from them. My boys would have nourishing, calm, happy lives without me. I was convinced of this, enough to make a plan using an old Ikea pencil & the back of an envelope.

Last month I was angry, a fighter. Only a few weeks later, I'm now fantasising about ending it all with a tub of pills when the kids are safely at school.

Listen To: Meghan Trainor: "No Excuses"

Red Flags:

- *Allergy to shame/embarrassment. The instinct to run when this happens is very common in Narcs. They feel it more strongly than us normals certainly. They feel it for themselves, not the people they've wronged and not even the people they've used to create wrongs. They loathe confrontation and fear the mask being removed intensely.*

- *Cognitive Dissonance. Narc victims can have periods of emotional and psychological numbness in times of severe trauma with their abusers. Victims use and then need these cold, strange emotional blackouts to cope with intense stress and trauma. Narcs specialise in emotional abuse, so a common coping strategy is to simply teach yourself not to feel or to feel other emotions instead of fear, pain and anxiety. It can lead to and be a part of the Narc-Infection.*

- *Toxic friends or family members abusing you in times of crisis. The Narc will have had dramas many, many times (especially with partners) over the years and family members will take it out on you as you are just "another one" who brings trouble. You will also be blamed because let's face it, Narcs raise more Narcs and it's likely the mother or father will have the same lack of empathy their child has. The lack of support from your Narc's family and friends circle will be shocking and in stark contrast to "healthy" relationships you've had or will have- trust me!*

- *Narcissistic Virus and Co-dependency symptoms. Hatred for the person we love who has hurt us, a growing lack of respect and empathy at inappropriate moments. Turning "stalkerish" and being obsessive about getting answers. A desperate need for the truth because we know we are being lied to and will get answers at any cost. Grieving for our lover yet loathing them and not trusting them at the same time. Staying in the relationship even though it is unhealthy. Fighting anyone who comes near it....*

November 2015

Tunisia Tart, aka McMoore The Hoor, wasn't answering my messages or calls and Jonathan was still stone-walling me and refusing any knowledge of what he had been doing with her.

I was determined to find my closure and I suspected she had blocked me in a panic. Like most side chicks, she shat it, basically and wanted to pretend it had all never happened and had blocked me. So, like all psycho-girlfriends, I set about looking for an address. I knew her full name and that she was from the Paisley area so I had a closer look at her Facebook page to see places she visited a lot. This would help me narrow down the likely town or area in Paisley she stayed. She liked and commented on her "favourite ever" takeaway shop and also frequently went to a hot tanning salon, both in a part of Paisley. I spotted a pub as well that she had some selfies in, and decided this particular part was going to be my main target area. I searched in the council rolls for an address for a Jemma McMoore in her 40s, staying there and tickety-boo, came up with a postcode that matched to a Harris Crescent. I've always wanted to go to Harris. I don't like Skye.

The bus twists and turns along unfamiliar roads towards the town where Jemma McMoore lives. I'm not nervous- I feel angry and bitter and highly proud of my investigative work. The one decent thing this female will do for me is speak to me.

Getting off the bus in the centre of Linwood, I pat my pocket to check I have all my friendly little notes for her. I'm going to leave these messages in the places she goes, to get her to contact me and talk, purely so I can then reward her with being left alone. "Hi, Tunisia! Can you give me a call please? Lucy xx" I have written on all 4 of them. Three for the places her Facebook says she goes to a lot and one for her doormat.

One by one, I deliver them and feel rather empowered. The sense that I am doing something that Jonathan would fear genuinely makes me feel good. This is not what a victim would do- this is what a survivor would do. I don't want to crawl into a ditch and sob, I want to know what has been going on and recover from it. Why should these people cause so much harm and get away with it without explaining themselves?!

The gaps he wants to leave in my understanding are filled with the most awful imaginings of what he has been doing to me behind my back. I would rather know the full painful truth, then I can try and rebuild myself, maybe rebuild my relationship. It all depends on what McMoore The Hoor has to say.

Listening to music while I trot through the town and playing postal-predator, I drop all 3 notes off. Her takeaway, the chemist her mum gets her meds from and the sunbed. Coldly cheerful, I head up the hill towards where google maps says her house is, occasionally singing along to favourite songs when I know the words. Creepy? yes- but I don't care.

Reaching a small, slightly shabby council estate, I remember I don't have a house number so need to look for the car that was pictured in her Facebook selfies.

Disappointed to find the car isn't there I sit on a kerb to think. It's my own fault- I've visited in the middle of the day and she is most likely out having an extra-large vajazzle, or getting her moustache bleached.

Someone walking towards me catches my eye, so I jauntily jog over; "Excuse me. I work in Paisley and a lady visited where I work but left her purse. I managed to work out through checking Facebook that she lives in this terrace, but I don't know what number." I open my phone to a screenshot of McMoore "That's her. She's called Jemma or Jem McMoore. Do you recognise her?"

"Oh, aye, hen. She stays at this one here,"- I feel a surge of joy but start to shake with the adrenaline rush "Really?! Thank you.

This one, the one at the end?" I'm already backing away and getting ready to ring the doorbell. "Yes, hen. She stays here with her 2 kids and her man."

I stop. "She has kids?" I right myself "Oh, I'm glad I brought her purse back then. Kids are expensive. I've three myself!" I force a laugh. I hadn't seen children on her Facebook, nor a husband.... I feel sick now and in a film reel, see the disgusting images all over again and almost fall to sit on her doorstep.

Suddenly this feels wrong. I should be at home watching a film with the boys and planning a date night with Jonathan. I should be smelling lasagne cook in the oven and laughing at Charlie's impersonations of teachers at school. I should be telling Rufus to stop talking over us all and cuddling him when he gets angry for being told off.

Not for the first time in the last month, I put my head in my hands and weep. I don't know what's happening! One minute I feel strong and the next like the world is ending! Why has he done this to me, to us, to my boys? This woman! The others! The drugs...The pointless passivism with Sinead. It's all come down to this point. Me, crying on a kerb in a scummy council estate, somewhere I had never even heard of, looking for a woman whose vagina is more familiar to me than her face.

Suddenly I feel it again- that disgust and hate. "Fuck it," I say to myself through gritted teeth. "I need to know the truth," I say to myself as I stand up. Feeling dizzy, I lean a hand on the door to steady myself and remember I haven't eaten for 3 days again.

It's a small, slightly grubby-looking pebble-dashed house and I feel a pang of pity for her. It's not what I imagined this smutty, cocky female to have. The net curtains need a wash and there are old-fashioned ceramic ornaments of fruit in the window. I wait a few seconds, trying to decide if this is the right thing to do. I imagine myself walking away. Back to his lies and "I don't remembers". Back to lying in bed at night, crying for him, imagining him inside her. Underneath her. Giving her oral sex.

Before I know it, I've rattled the letterbox and posted the note through. Crouching down, I can see inside and it's neatly lying right in the middle of the doormat.

A dog starts yapping and I remember she had small dogs on her Facebook page. This is definitely the right house but there's no one in. Quickly, I walk away. My heart is beating fast and I know she will get that note, contact Jonathan and all hell will break loose. "I had no other choice," I say to myself, "If he won't speak to you about it- she has to."

Back at home, I try and act normal with the boys and we make a quick visit to our corner shop for some treats. One of our songs comes on over the shop's sound system and my chest feels like it's on fire. I release a strange half sob and slide down to a sitting position on the floor. The pretty young woman who works in the shop puts an arm around me and comforts me while the boys stand at the end of the aisle watching.

My phone pips and I see a text from an unfamiliar number. Its 2 messages from Jemma.

I ignore them. "Right, boys. We need to get up the road and get some dinner on. Mummy has a wee job she has to do."

"Is Jonny still not well?" Charlie asks, his wee face crumpled in worry. "Yes, baby- he's still not well. His mum's looking after him" I say, as I take his hand and hand the money to the cashier. "He'll be fine, I'm sure". I'm not sure. I swallow the lump that seems to sit permanently in my throat these days and blink back tears.

WhatsApping Jemma before I call her, I know she'll open my profile picture before calling me. I want her to see my face so she can't help but imagine how broken I am. My message reads simply "Jonny and I were a solid couple. We loved each other. I met you on holiday. That's where it started, isn't it? I've 3 little boys who love him very much; you have blown my life apart. We are all absolutely devastated. I need you to tell me what's gone on but I want to speak to you. No texting."

Within a few minutes my phone rings- I breathe in and out a few times before answering. This conversation is going to be the deciding factor on what happens next with Jonathan and me.

I was flooded with relief when she mirrored him staying adamant that they'd not touched each other. Laughing bitterly when she admitted they had never even spoken on the phone.

"Wow- you're classy. You send that gross stuff. Say those things to a guy in a relationship and yet you haven't even had any phone conversations!"

"Yeah, well. I was flattered by the attention," she bleated.

Much like the others, it appeared it had been all purely cyber-based contact. I started to consider allowing Jonathan back into my life, yet again.

My laughing sets something off in her and she gets nasty; "I know things that would kill you. Destroy your relationship." My vision blurs.

"Tell me then! If you know so much, what's the hold-up?! You're just some female who has degraded herself for absolutely nothing. Betrayed your kids and husband for some dick pics off a guy messaging 7 other people. It's insanity!"

I'm getting angry myself now. This is all such a disgusting, smutty, filthy mess. Lives blown apart and hearts shattered for some cyber filth and mind games. These women took advantage of my poor Jonathan. It's clear now- he was drunk and high and lonely and these females were getting more out of it than him- they fancied him and needed him in their lives to feel better about themselves.

"Jonny is an addict. If you offer him anything that takes him up a level, gives him a thrill or a high, he will grab at it. If you offer him a pint of Toilet Duck and tell him he will get an up off it, the dafty will ask for a bib & straw!"

"I couldn't sleep with him even if I wanted to anyway. I have a disability that affects my back. Jonny knew that." I can't help but laugh nastily. "It didn't affect your hand actions or exotic selfie positions love & you managed to travel thousands of miles to North Africa as I remember!"

Towards the end of the call, Jemma starts to panic. "Please don't come here again. My husband knows about your note; my daughter told him. She's disgusted with me. He's left me," she wails. I realise that she actually thought I was going to slide off into the shadows and lick my wounds and let her get away with this. "He said you were a psycho and he was lonely. He said he liked talking to me because it made him feel better. He invited me to his birthday... But I decided not to go at the last minute."

161

Something crashes into my sternum at the mention of his birthday. A picture I saw in one of the message streams. A memory of his red shorts and his hand around his penis....the timing of his shift in mood this summer... she's talking again. She's read my mind.

"He wanked for me on his birthday. While you served his mates in your sad little apron, he had his cock out his red shorts for me and sent me the video before going back to the party."

I only just reach the bathroom and vomit on the tiled floor. Virtually crawling back to my bedroom, I'm met with silence. She's hung up.

Those few weeks across November 2015 were classic trauma-bonding. The horror of what had taken place in such a condensed period of time drew me even closer to Jonathan. I believed we were unique in what we had gone through and in who we were. I believed the way he "loved" me was unique out of all his past relationships. I decided we were star-crossed lovers. True soul mates.

"Look what we've come through. It's proof this is our destiny," he'd talk over me when I tried to talk more about how I felt. "Don't keep bringing it up. You're ruining it. What we have is good now. Please don't ruin it." The last sentence was always said more firmly.... a warning for me to stay silent and move on.

At other times he was verbally gentler. "We're stronger now. I'm so proud you got through this, baby," he would say as we undressed for bed. "I know I'm complicated, but I love you more than you know," he'd murmur as we started to have sex. "Stay with me. I need you," he'd growl as he came inside me.

I became obsessed with us staying together. Proving the haters wrong and getting us "back to where it started".

Listen To: Britney Spears: "Toxic"

Red Flags:

- _Trauma-bonding._ _This is like an addiction to the "rollercoaster" of an abusive or toxic relationship. The downs are terrible but the up phases, where you reconnect with your partner, create these amazing memories and feelings you cling_ *to. It's deeply unhealthy but extremely addictive. It is a key part of toxic relationships like I'm describing. Narcs thrive on trauma because it is a perfect test of your adoration for them. Watching you desperately attempt to recover from their attacks on your confidence and sense of self is delicious for them. The more you try, the greater the ego boost.... This is why the attacks on your sense of self get worse and the Narc escalates.*

- *<u>Shutting you down.</u> When you try to talk to a Narc about anything they do/have done that hurts you, you will be told it's "nonsense" or "history" or "not relevant". You will be told to move on and the Narc will say you are hurting them and dragging them backwards when really, you're just trying to understand what's happened, get to the truth, feel and see that they are sorry and move forward together. You will never have space to learn and heal with a Narc.*

December 2015

We are on a public "high" with our new fresh and fabulous bad-romance. Social media is our stage and he has the leading part of stable yet recovering alcoholic, champion of honesty and of course, extremely sheepish yet "proud" partner to me.... we are having more sex than ever before and I'm deliberately more and more adventurous and creative. In my twisted mind, I believed that he watched porn, masturbated constantly and sexted strangers out of some sort of sex addiction that I could now treat. I did things I didn't want to do, thinking that these physical sacrifices would feed the voracious appetite he seemed to have for anything that distracted him from his problems and in particular drugs. He had successfully addled my mind with his rules- his problems were his exes, and drugs were what gave him the need for other stimuli.

"Lucy, I want to be with you forever. You're my soulmate. You'll be who I grow old with" As we sweat and twist and curl together in bed, he tells me again he wants me to have his baby. "We can make a family and get married. I want to marry you!" I don't say yes and I don't say no.

One day he drags me, laughing his head off, into a ring shop in town, but I'm too embarrassed to choose one. He's manic and acting oddly and it just doesn't feel right. Later, when we're walking back home, we bump into one of his friends from AA and I tell them Jonathan's proposed. My face virtually falls off my skull when he denies this and walks away with the friend, leaving me stood in the street alone.

A week later, I went straight back on my pill. After my period arrived, I wasn't remotely disappointed to not be pregnant. I started to directly lie to my lover just like he did with me. Lying to protect myself and because it felt kinda good...

All that winter, he happily pumped away on top of me thinking yet again he would spread his seed and forever have a reason to have contact, and probably sex, with me. Like the others.

My phone buzzes. I stop peeling potatoes and grab at it. He's been quiet today and stayed at home last night, citing "stress and pressure"- it's been a mini discard but I'm almost used to them now. They are horrific, true. I almost always want to die when I'm in one-true, but they are less often and I thank the devil for that. I've crawled into work looking like death warmed up, but at least I'm here.

I've felt something coming for the last couple of days.... something sneaking and swirling around us like a suspicious rotting smell from the end of the garden. It's been too long since a drama. I've been waiting for one.

"You are so stunning, baby. I love you. Can't wait to see you later." Reading these words, my knees buckle with relief. It's ok, he's just been busy. I curse my paranoia. How silly! He's fine. I start to type a lovey-dovey reply. He doesn't like me not replying straight away these days.

Before I'm finished, another message comes in. A picture of me. I frown, unsure of what this means. It's a picture of me in my red bikini in Tunisia. Alongside the pic is a repeat of his earlier words "you're my stunning baby".

In closer inspection of the image, I noticed it is not a picture, it is a screenshot of a picture.

At the bottom it has text. It's the name "Victoria" and is butted by 3 emojis with heart eyes and one laughing emoji.

It looks as though someone called Victoria has sent him the picture of me, commented on it with some sort of jokey emoji stream and he's mistakenly forwarded the pic to me in his rush to break the silence and hoover me in as usual.

Of course, I make a mistake and message back "Who's Victoria"? Feeling a cramping in my chest, I recognise my old best friends, Fear and Shock straight away. They've been missing for more than a fortnight, but now they're back.

"What do you mean?" he replies with a cluster of laughing emojis. "Dunno whit ur talking about, baby. I'm having problems with my phone again…". Now that metallic taste in my mouth and white noise again.

I stare at the picture. I know I can see the name Victoria. I know I can see it's a screenshot. I know it's me. I know there are emojis on it. It looks like he's sent it to her or her to him and in some way, they are discussing me, laughing at me…. I'm pretty sure laughing about what I look like.

Before I can stop myself, I dare to go there. He answers the phone after far too many rings. He's been working out what to say, knowing why I'm calling. "There- there's the name Victoria, Jonny. Can't you see it?" My voice is high-pitched yet emotionless. I'm cold all over. "It's there. I can see it." My voice wobbles now. I cough as my throat tightens with the promise of tears. I don't know what's happening here.

"No, baby. I can't see anything. Not at my end. It's just a picture of you. I sent it to you because I think you are stunning……. Look," I hear him sigh then a grunt. That sandpaper sound as he rubs his stubble close to the phone. Suddenly, he's angry. "Don't start. I can't handle this. You'll knock me ill again. Stop being paranoid!" another grunt and I hear him pull on his e-cig. A long pull, then another. It crackles and hisses under the pressure. He's worried.

Yeah, maybe it's just a glitch in the phone. Maybe it's sending screenshots as pictures. Maybe water got in the battery. Yes. That must be it. My heart still doesn't slow and now I feel sick. I drop down to sit on the floor of my little kitchen away from the drinkers' eyes that are now on me, sensing an atmosphere emanating from the chef pale as snow only a few feet away. I don't care that I look weird. I'm way past being ashamed of what he makes me do or how I look when he causes me pain.

"Ok- I'm sorry. Let's forget about it. I'm making your favourite aubergine fritters and that tomato and mint salsa you like." As I say this, I delete the picture. Maybe it never even happened. He's gone quiet. He makes me wait for more than a minute. Not moving from the floor, I sit there waiting to hear his voice. A reassurance is all I need. I can forget about the picture. It's nothing. I hope no one orders anything. I don't think I can stand up.

"Love you, baby- see you later," he says suddenly out of nowhere, to reward me for ending the conversation about who "Victoria" is.

I never did find out who she was, although Jonathan had a habit of keeping females in his phone recorded by where he met (and often fucked) them. Armed with knowledge about how he (and other Narcs work) now, 2 years later I found out she is a girl he creeped to. She worked in the sunbed shop we often used- on Victoria Road. I realised it was her when months and months of wracking my brains resulted in a shock memory of a tall, rangy girl with long black extensions. Pretty and a mum like me, I remembered her because one of her sons had Asperger's, like my Rufus. In a rush, I realised she mysteriously stopped working there a few days after I caught him going in without me.... even though he lived 6 miles away.

She and I exchanged some banter about the girl code when he was there stood awkwardly alongside us. I thought it was odd she raised that and I remember noticing him go pale when she did. Funny how those little memories surface months, even years, after you escape the mind fog a Narc has you suffering with.

If you are reading this Victoria, and you think you are her, please do get in touch!

A few days after the Victoria thing, Jonathan surprised me at dinner time by turning up to collect me from work.

He'd been AWOL all that day, not answering messages and calls. Riddled with anxiety and in a severe panic believing it was possible he was on a binge again; I'd refused customers and simply sat at the bar watching my phone like it was a rattlesnake.

"Where are you. Please call me. I'm freaking out!" I texted a minute ago. My 14th message so far. I'm not blocked so I don't think it's a discard, so this must mean it's a relapse! Omg! He's not replying because he's drunk in a ditch or in some female's stinking bed! I've called and left messages and even tried his friends.... well the few that still speak to me since his last relapse.

All of this signals something bad- something serious. His mothers' response is vile- "If he's away drinking again it's all your fault, you crackpot!" This is her version of empathy. This is her sisterhood. This is how she mothers him. It's no wonder he's the way he is.

There's a loud bang and I jump nearly falling off the bar stool. It's the thunderous sound of the bar's double doors being swung open together and hitting the wall behind them. Frozen, I watch Jonathan march round the bar towards me. He looks pleased as punch. He isn't angry. I haven't done anything wrong. My stomach gurgles and my mouth falls open in shock. He's fine. We're fine. It's fine. He looks.... happy... Why's he so happy?

"Why haven't you replied to my messages! Oh my god! I've been freaking out!" Relief makes me confident enough to berate him for getting me so upset.

"Look at this, baby. Look what I got!" he shouts. He's rather drunk. I don't think he is high but he's been drinking for sure. I can smell it.... he's all flushed & sweaty too.

"Where have you been?" Asking him carefully is best. Gently probe what's going on. I mustn't seem upset or angry. "In fact, forget it. It doesn't matter where you've been. Do you want something to eat? I've some Singapore noodles here," I turn my back to him to faff about in the kitchen, Grabbing a bowl and a napkin. I can't let him see how freaked out I am. Kneeling down, I lean into the cold of the fridge, close my eyes and enjoy a second of blissful peace and relief that he's here, which can only be a good thing. Drunk is ok. Drunk away from me, on a rampage and during a discard is not. I can take him home, dry him out and sort a meeting later or tomorrow. Most important thing is he's happy.

Suddenly I'm up in the air. Jonathan is pulling me to my feet over the little kitchen gate and onto the bar floor. He thrusts a huge bunch of beautiful flowers at me like a gorilla on a date and starts to take his t-shirt off. I don't know what's happening. Where did the flowers come from? "Look at this, baby! I love you!!" he crows, flinging his T-shirt onto the bar behind him. I get a waft of fresh sweat as he does this and without thinking, step back.

Then I see it. In shock, I almost can't work out what it is. Has he had an accident? Is that a bandage? No, it's cling film. Why is he wrapped in cling film? I don't get it.

I reach out to touch the huge red rose tattoo above his pectoral muscle. It's still bleeding slightly. Only hours old. A red rose and black writing. It's maybe 5 inches wide...no 6. It's enormous! Way bigger than the tiny, 10p-sized J on my lower back!

It has a name, my name.... drawn across it in black in a romantic, italic style. "What the fuck have you done?"- I start to cry with shock then relief then shock again. "Oh, my God. You're mad!" He grabs me and kisses me. "I wanted to show you how much I love you. Show everyone!" and he swings me round, laughing, as he carries me across the bar to show the punters. "I love my Lucy!" he yells at a group of drinkers nearby.

I make the effort and laugh along as, hand on hip, he parades himself round the bar topless and pointing at his chest like a camp Neanderthal. People are clapping. It's all in slow motion.... I feel sick so slink away to sit in a booth in a corner to watch.

One of the older customers is in the same booth with me. She's seen me fall apart this last few weeks and catches my eye. "What's he done now?!" she says and laughs. I bark a broken cackle at the heart-breaking joke. She sees I am in pain and behind his back places a warm, wrinkled hand over mine and squeezes. A fat tear falls on to our hands and she squeezes harder

Listen To: Sugababes: "Denial"

Red Flags:

- *Ownership.* Narcs will use behaviours (as well as language) to own you. Tattoos, assurances of fidelity "forever", living together, engagements/marriages, starting a business together, shared investments, children and so on. Be aware of this language, false promises of "forever" and babies. A key NPD Abuse symptom is never genuinely letting you go.

- *Egocentric Legacies.* This is my term for when Narcs create trails of children to exes behind them. The idea that they have "created life" is an incredible supply to them. It's a God Complex that goes unnoticed until you see how the Narc treats their children. There will often be a lack of true attention/love/interest in the child and they will be picked up and dropped (metaphorically!) on a whim. You may see that the Narc is actually fine with no contact with the child ...but likes to play the part of doting dad and devastated dad when it suits.

- *Grand Gestures.* These are rewards for your sustained addiction to the relationship. They form a part of the common Hoovering that the Narc will indulge in, but are often also extremely attention-seeking acts of "kindness" or romance. It's also worth mentioning that these immensely public shows of commitment to you are designed to harm anyone watching who the Narc wants to hurt/humiliate or.... make jealous. These are messages, not for you, really for someone or some people watching. In my case he enjoyed hurting Sinead and other exes by posting things about how much he adored me on social media. It fuelled their hate of me and yet made me feel spitefully "clever" to have him all to myself. Its toxic.

- *Other people start to notice your decline.* NPD Abuse will absolutely make you ill. In extreme cases, it will affect your body as well as your mind. Your previously bubbly or outgoing personality is long gone and you will be openly unhappy, quiet and sad. Now you are becoming almost completely devalued by this point and it will be so obvious that relative strangers will comment on it and ask if you're ok. Extremely empathic *people will have attempted contact like this long ago but you will have brushed it away- madly in love! Now you are madly in pain, you are more readily showing symptoms of the abuse and more open to receiving support.*

January 2016

"This year, Sinead, you and I are going to set a proper contact plan for our baby. I am going to see a solicitor, but if you wish to set out some contact days and times now, we can avoid the legal route. I am paying child maintenance and I am on the birth certificate. Please let Lucy and I be now and just let me be a father." I watch avidly & sigh in relief as he hits send.

We wrote the text together, sitting in bed, waiting for our too hot coffees to cool. Absolutely thrilled I smiled widely at him. This was it. This really was a new start and my Jonny was back. New year and new relationship! I hadn't been discarded at all through the rest of December and Christmas was fun, yet quiet.

Sinead called him within seconds of the message being delivered. She wanted to see who it was who sent the message. I found this a little odd but he did tell me she was strange. Sat next to me, he speaks to her, and putting a finger to his lips, shushes me from speaking. I sit quietly and sip my coffee, listening to my man finally stand up for us.

"She isn't happy she can't manipulate us or use the child as a weapon anymore," I mouth to him. "I know," he mouths back and kisses me. Tinny and screeching, I can hear her voice but not the words clearly enough. She's irate. She should get together with Niall; they could form a band. The Howlers. The thought makes me giggle. At the noise, Jonathan shoots me a frown so I get out of bed to make fresh coffees and laugh more openly in the kitchen.

Just so delighted that things are going so well, we have sex until the sun starts to set. When I go for a bath, he sits in the kitchen singing loudly along to the radio and playing on his phone. At one point, he throws himself into the bathroom to kiss me again and we end up together in the water. Things are going to be alright.

As promised, he has started to do the right things and I thank God. And guess what, when Sinead stopped him seeing the baby again the very next day, this time he brushed it off without blaming or discarding me. I was amazed!

Listen to: Loryn: "Stand By" (lyrics) ft Rudimental

Red Flags:

* _Suddenly acting "right"_. Narcs do not act right unless they have an agenda. They have no interest in making life easier for you or them as a couple, so when (out of nowhere almost) they suddenly take advice or behave absolutely NORMALLY, they are up to something. They have a plan of some type and you are not privy to it.

February 2016

It's early morning in mid-February and I've not slept one minute. He's displaying all the tells of drug use and cheating again. The sleep-eating, the long naps, the hyper-sexuality, the obsession with his phone. It lies face down even when it's on charge or between us in the car. Transfixed by his behaviour over and over these days, I don't fail to miss the dark, glittering eyes and satisfied smile of someone stuffed full to the gunnels with too many secrets.

Before I chicken out, I slide out of bed sideways like a centipede, crawl round the bed, low to the ground, and reach for his phone. Its poking up out of the space between the mattress and the bed frame itself. As usual, it's closer to him than I am. The bedroom is dark. It's the middle of the night and he's sound asleep, gently snoring.

Carefully, I open the screen using the new password he chose at Christmas. 1888. There's nothing there. I sit in complete relief at finding nothing. My eyes blur and I let out a long-held breath. I've been worried sick for 2, maybe 3 weeks now. I'm just so fucking thankful he's not up to anything. Flooded with shame at not trusting him, I close my eyes and rest my forehead on the phone which is now face up between my knees. Everything really is fine. It's all in my imagination, like he says. Thank God. Thank everything, ever!

I open my eyes again. Shit, I've pressed the message app again.

Frowning in almost comedic puzzlement, I read the title of a message that came in last night. "Know anyone looking to buy a range rover xx?" How odd. It's from someone he has in his phone as "Guy from Chillies". He hasn't mentioned anything about a new car and there's no way he can afford a Range Rover. All he does is moan about money. I know the guy he's chatting to though- he's the manager of a tandoori and ice-cream place near his flat. He took me there on our second date. Eating pistachio ice-cream and kissing in the middle of the road, we stopped traffic. We didn't care.

Trembling, I open the message stream fully, out of a mixture of instinct and nosiness. I don't expect anything bad. It just feels out of place and strange. Life is moving in slow motion and I see the kisses before I read the message. The room tilts. "I miss you so fucking much xxxx"

I lean forward in a sudden reaction to a stab in the stomach. This is not the guy from Chillies. This is a woman. I push up on my knees and scroll up to older messages past the shite about a fucking Range Rover. It's happening again. I start to hyperventilate and pant to try to get air into my lungs, lungs which right now are trying to claw their way out of my bony chest.

There's another message, this time a video. The screen is suddenly filled with a blonde woman (about my age, maybe younger) completely naked. She is astride whoever is holding the camera phone upwards to capture her full frame. A frame very like mine- sporty but curvy -she could be me. She holds a paddle, like a ping pong bat, and she is rhythmically slapping the man's engorged balls which are wrapped so tightly with a rubber band that they are huge. Purple and engorged, she goes slap, slap, slap. She should be in the fucking Japanese table tennis team. This is gold medal stuff.

I can't help myself and shout in agony. A burnt hand on a searing hot hob. That awful shot of almost unbearable pain. This time it's not for seconds though. It's forever.

172

Dropping the phone and roaring over and over, I hold my head in my hands and start to rock back and forth keening. "No, no, no! Not again!!!! No, no, no!". I start to head-butt the wall behind me. Once, twice, three times...I need to feel physical pain, not what's inside me.

The commotion wakes Jonathan up- he sees me on the floor first, then catches sight of his phone lying beside me. The screen is lit up. Of course, he knows what I've seen.

Without a word he is up, grabbing at his clothes. "You are a fucking psycho!" he shouts. I can see he is panicking.

I stand up so he pushes me backwards into the wall. How dare I find out about his filth again. "You are ruining my life!" he screeches in my face, and storms past me looking for his clothes. "You're disgusting!" I splutter. "How could you do this to me again! You're going to kill me! What is WRONG with you! Why can't you be normal? Just normal!" My head in my hands, I think he's left the room to get his backpack but then I hear breathing. Before I can open my eyes, I feel the full force of a slap to the side of my head. My ears are ringing.

"This is all you, Lucy. All you! You want, want, want. Just like Sinead. Just like the rest of those bitches. Take, take, take. That's just some joke that the guy from Chillies sent me. It's nothing!" He's shouting in my face. "It's just a joke! You imagine problems and make them real because you're sick and twisted!" I stand there holding my face where he hit it- he's been clever aiming for my head because my hair will cover any mark. "Ok. Ok. Ok. It's nothing. Ok. Ok," I chant. I can't let him leave. I can't be left alone here, with this inside me now. He's putting his shoes on and grabbing his hoodie off the door. "No- I'm done with you. This is it. It's over forever now! You ruined it!"

I don't even bother to challenge him and lie there sobbing and begging for someone to help me. I can't stop seeing that message with the video of the girl who so dreadfully looks like me. I see how her hair is like mine, a short, light-blonde bob with blunt straight fringe, and how the man's penis was almost black with the abuse she gave it. It was grotesque.

"I'm away up the road!" he shouts 2 minutes later from the hall. He hesitates a second, waiting for my pleas and shouts for him to stay, but I'm bent over and can't speak. "Not again. I can't do it again. I can't handle this again," I whisper over and over. There's a scuffling in the hall. He's trying to decide what to do. Then suddenly I hear the door slam. He's gone.

For the next 36 hours, he refuses to speak to me. I'm blocked in all avenues. I call his mum to ask her for help and am told I'm a "nosey fucking crack-pot. It's your fault for going looking". I decide it was my fault. I don't even know if it was him in the video. Maybe it really was the guy from Chillies and they send each other gross porn as a sort of joke. Slowly I convinced myself it was indeed just a joke and I've insulted my poor partner by not trusting him. I don't even consider that he hit me. It's my fault for scaring him up out of a deep sleep with my bonkers reaction to something so…. trivial.

At least I could just lie in bed and cry this time because by now I had no job. Work was just untenable when I was with Jonathan. My concentration and memory issues were terrible and I either looked like death, OR acted manic with anxiety and false positivity. All I could think about was him. Keeping him right and keeping me in his favour. As long as I was with him, he was behaving.

So now, with no income and no perceived "escape" from the life wrapped tightly around us, I became very physically unwell. My weight at this point was only about 7.5 stone. I hadn't had a period for 3 months and I knew in my heart of hearts I was letting my children down very badly. My hair was, by this point, very fine and only ear-lobe length. I'd lost 6 or 7 inches out of sheer stress and lack of true nutrition. My sense of taste had almost completely gone too and I often had a strange sense of foreboding, similar to depression but wrapped up in a constant fear of "what next". I kept walking away from cash machines and leaving precious cash to blow away in the wind or be snatched up by passers-by. Several times I flooded the kitchen, having wandered away from the sink to sit and stare into space. I stopped reading books because I'd forget each page as soon as I turned it. Watching television became impossible, again because my focus and memory were shattered. One of the worst symptoms was being so jumpy that any sudden movements or loud noises made me react in an extreme way. Changes in routine or surprises would make me angry and even aggressive at times and I began to avoid contact with the outside world unless Jonathan was with me. This was partly my choice, and was because when he wasn't with me, I was so anxious that he was misbehaving, that I couldn't converse with other people or behave normally and, ashamed of this, I just gave up on it. The other reason was Jonathan reacted with paranoia and accusations if I went to a different gym or posted on social media that I was out anywhere that I hadn't pre-advised him of.

Later That Month

It's Friday, so I've brought the children to Jonathan's house. It's late and after a big Chinese they have easily sloped off to sleep in Jonathan's bed while we grab an hour of peace together.

Walking back in from finishing the washing up, I see Jonathan is now on his 3rd can of beer and seems manic rather than sleepy after the takeaway. Nervously, I sit next to him on the sofa and pick up the television magazine to pretend to choose something for us to watch. He nudges me. "I want a life, Lucy," he's slurring his words a bit- that lager isn't even strong...what's wrong with him now? "You're boring. I want a life," he repeats. The words are a slap to the face. Boring? I plan and pay for every single day out, mini-breaks, holiday. He gets sex several times a day wherever he wants it, however he wants it. Only yesterday, he reiterated his desire to get married once my divorce comes through.

"I don't understand what you mean. That's unkind!" I say weakly and my eyes fill with tears. "Oh, forget it. You're not listening to me" he grumbles and lurches into the kitchen to fetch another beer. He starts to take his phone out of his pocket as he disappears around the corner.

My anxiety skyrockets from "sad and OK" to "oh shit, here we go again" in 5 seconds. I feel extremely sick and hyper-aware of something coming like a tsunami, yet I'm stuck knee-deep in mud and can't run.

I dream about that even to this day. Nightmares about being stuck, trapped and unable to run as a gargantuan wave curves up behind me. I feel the mist of spray on the back of my neck and frantically try to wade through the cement-like sand, crying soundlessly and unable to move or make a noise and attract help. I wake up as the wave pummels me to my death.

He's muttering to himself in the kitchen and a few seconds later shouts "Darren and Mary Anne are coming over. They are on their way. Make sure you fucking cheer up!"

Fuck! It's past 11 o'clock. This means trouble. More booze, 2 people who aren't that keen on me, him on the edge of an abusive rage and (most likely) they will bring drugs.

"Jonny, please. It's late. The kids are sleeping. Let's just go to bed. Please," I whine. I hate the way I sound but by God I'm afraid.

"They are on their way and I want to fucking have some fun. They are my fucking mates and it's Friday. Stop being booooooriiiiiing!" He sings this like a petulant child. I hover in the doorway of the kitchen, visibly shaking, and watch as he pulls out glasses and slams down an ashtray. It makes me jump and he grins at me like a drunken clown. "We're having a party!" he declares and lurches to the bathroom. I hear him pissing fast and hard and want to scream and shout NO, NO, NO! Instead, I set about putting away the washing up and tidying the living room.

Ten minutes later they arrive with a case of 24 Fosters, some vodka, cola, weed and cocaine.

"Guys, the kids are in Jonny's room so we need to kind of keep it low key," I stage-whisper to three flushed and slightly sweaty faces. "We didn't know you were coming.... Sorry!"

Creeping around them picking up empty cans and wiping ash off the table, I'm pathetic. I try to join in the conversation, but I'm sober and polite. I don't fit.

"You're English!" Darren incorrectly states in reference to my nicer accent than his. "You're a fucking snob. I can tell!" He laughs at his own joke and rocks back on the kitchen chair, smiling at his not very attractive, dumpy girlfriend. "Yeah- you're an English bastard. That's why your kids have got stupid posh names," he declares.

Gritting my teeth and taking a breath, I stop myself from hitting him on the head with the ashtray I just washed- again. "Actually Darren, I'm not. I was born in Dumbarton not that fucking far from here and if I was a snob, I wouldn't be hanging about with you manky folk, would I?" This is my partner's home. My children are asleep and apparently paying for holidays abroad, wearing size 6 red lace lingerie, cooking amazing food and giving my partner blow-jobs whenever he likes, makes me boring. I'm gold standard boring! Anger and rage are replacing my fear now.

"Aye well. If a kid called Rufus stayed on my street, he'd get beaten up!" Darren laughs again at his hilariously disgusting joke at my 5-year-old son's expense.

I stare daggers at Jonathan. Biting my lip to stop a retort, I taste iron. I swallow, raise my eyebrows at Jonathan. He looks down at the table and starts to play with some strands of tobacco.

"Okay. Okay. Leave it, mate. She'll go fucking mental if you don't cool it." He slaps Darren on the shoulder and stands up to go to the toilet yet again. He tries to kiss me as he staggers past, but catches my ear instead of my mouth. "Fucking get them out of here!" I hiss but he pretends not to hear me.

Now he's out of ear-shot, I can try to manage this situation somewhat. "Don't give him any drugs. I mean it. He's not well. A few drinks is ok, but he's in a weird mood and I'm begging you, please don't." Speaking to them both leaning forward over the kitchen table, I'm trying to appeal to whatever decency is in there. "Please, guys. I have the kids here and he's horrible when he drinks as it is. Don't give him anything when I'm not looking."

I'm actually desperate for the toilet myself but held it in to avoid leaving them alone. As Jonathan comes back into the kitchen, I risk it and slide away for no more than two minutes.

As I walk out of the bathroom, I stop dead just before reaching the kitchen door. Sidling away back into the dark, I lean against the wall and my hands curl into fists as I hear them. "She's a bitch. A snobby cow," Darren says. "Yeah, man. She controls me. She's fucking my life up," Jonathan says next. "Get her dumped!" Mary Anne says. They all laugh. This has gone too far. I don't feel safe. I'm going to get my sons and leave.

Creeping towards the bed in the dark, I lean down to wake the boys but feel a presence in the room. Hot fag ash breath is suddenly on my face. "What the fuck do you think you're doing?" she says. The smell of sweat & and cheap perfume. It's Mary Anne.

"I just think it's best I get the boys up the road- it's getting quite noisy and I'm shattered," I whisper.

"Fucking leave them and stop making a fuss," she hisses and grabs my arm. I don't like this. I don't like her. Something inside me rears up. Glancing at the sleeping forms of my two older sons, I stiffen and stand eye to eye with her. "It's best we go home, Mary Anne. I want to take them home, please. Let go of my arm."

"You're embarrassing Jonny. Stop being a selfish bitch!" she spits. I don't want an argument here over my sons sleeping, so I step back and walk past her; "No problem. You guys have a great night,"

Sitting on the sofa, I try to think how to handle this. For god sakes! She's followed me in. She stands over me, hands on ample hips, and I look straight ahead, eye line to her chubby, grubby, denim-clad knees. God, she's vile. There's a faint scent of something fishy.... it's those plastic chairs in the kitchen. Sitting on them too long in too-tight, size 14 jeans has soured her (assumed) traditional floral freshness.

I'm not afraid of her, but I'm afraid of what she might do next. My sons are here and I'm on my own. My partner has gone feral again and worst of all, I'm outnumbered three to one. Looking up, and pointlessly trying to make contact, I open my mouth to speak.

"Who the fuck do you think you are, you snobby bitch?" Then a sharp thud before pain as she hits me in the side of my face. She's swung wide, standing over me and the force moves me to the left. Staying sitting upright, and not being thrown out of position, I don't react. Things have gone quiet in the kitchen, but no one comes to my aid.

Lifting my hand to my face, I touch it where it's now roaring hot and stinging. Ugly, fat women always go for my face- I wonder why? It's a wonder I don't look like a patchwork doll, all scarred and pitted from the number of unsolicited attacks to my cute little dial.

With steely green eyes, I slowly look up to stare at her and smile. She looks a little unsettled at my lack of response and I smile wider. I think she expected a screech or for me to cry. Yes, ideally, she wants me to cry. To ruin my pretty face with streams of mascara. To shrink back and cower. Wither and beg for her to leave me alone. That isn't going to happen tonight. I don't beg anymore. I ran out of begging weeks ago. This is just another monster he's brought into my life. Another monster in my boys' orbit.

She reels back and staggers into the kitchen to share her win. I hear them laughing and high-fiving each other and the clink of cans and glasses. "Gave her what she wanted, English bitch," she says and they cackle together. "Who's got the lighter?" I hear Jonathan ask. "Me. It's here" says Darren.

Sitting on the sofa where I gave him hundreds of "Cheer me up, baby" hand jobs, I have an epiphany. I'm leaving him. It won't be immediate, but I need to escape this relationship. He won't know it's even happening, but I will go down fighting.

Between the living room and the kitchen is a small mini hallway- a sort of walk-through area. Quietly standing up and wincing at the squeak of the fucking sofa from hell, I slink to press myself against the wall. I can see through into the kitchen, but they can't see me.

I know she is going to come back for round two- I took that hit far too easily and my lack of reaction has not just unsettled her, it's given her an appetite for one. Bullies like to get a response and she, by Jove, is a classic bully.

A minute passes; maybe two, and I hear the squeak of a chair as someone stands up. Instinctively I know it's her. She is hoping to strut in and find me sitting on the sofa, weeping and afraid.

As her first foot passes across the threshold, I swiftly reach out to grab her long, greasy ponytail and yank back hard. Very hard.

With a big grunt, I pull all 10 stone of her to the floor. "Get off me. Get her off me!" she starts to screech. I am grunting and pulling and I really don't want to let go. I have her face in one hand and her hair in the other. Somehow, I've dragged her 4 feet across the living room and now I'm lying face up on the lazy-boy with her lying backwards between my legs. Wrapping my legs around her hips like a vice, I use the position to get traction and pull her hair even harder. "You didn't expect this, did you?" I hiss in her ear. She stops moving, then kicks and bucks to try and get me away. She's frightened. I'm not what she expected- not at all. She's heavy, so unless she gets up, I can't move and to be honest I don't really want to.

Actually, I'm quite enjoying this. It's about time this bully bitch got reminded that Posh Bitches can fight too. These skinny legs are strong, thanks to Jonathan pressuring me into the gym. My insecurities at trying to keep him faithful with a perfect arse and pretty good six-pack are proving helpful now. I'm strong as an ox.

Darren and Jonathan lurch in. She's openly screaming for help and for a heartbeat, they stand staring. They expected it to be me getting a doing. I think I see Jonathan smile before they both leap forward and start to try and prise my hands and legs of her.

"Lucy, baby, leave her! Get off her!" He shouts. "Stop, stop, stop!" Darren chimes in. It takes both men at least 15 seconds to peel me off her. Well, to be honest, I just decided to let go.

Lying back on the lazy-boy, I slowly smooth my hair and smile. Sitting up and smoothing my own (fresh-smelling) denims, I point at her. "Don't fucking touch me again. Next time they won't be able to get me off you!" I say it in my very best snobby English bitch voice. Walking past my beloved like a cat, I whisper "Still boring Jonny?" He says nothing but I enjoy his wince.

Ten minutes later they were gone, taking their cheap vodka and soggy tobacco with them. Sheepish and tired, they spoke very little as they gathered their things together. Jonathan and I found more cans they had brought and threw them out of the window, trying to hit them as they scuttled to their car. Sadly, we didn't hit any targets but it was fun at the time.

Jonathan was paralytic, so once he rolled onto the bed, I took the boys out. Half-asleep, they let me usher them into the living room and tuck them up on the sofa. My plan is to wait an hour or two then leave.

At 9 am, the boys and I quietly let ourselves out of the flat and walk the 5 miles to my friend, Annie's house. I'm not ready to go home to be faced with my nice, normal flat and the shame of what has happened.

I also need someone to see me, see the scratches on my hands and bruise on my face. Annie won't tell me it never happened or say it's my fault.

Her pretty, puzzled face goes pale as she listens to what happened in my beloved's flat last night. "Why are you messing about? You need to just end it and never talk to him ever again honey!" she whispers, furtively looking at my overly quiet sons playing on the floor nearby. "He's a psycho and what happened to you is sick!"

"I need to fall out of love with him first, A. I need to move slowly because I'm going to suffer when it's over. I think he's done this before.... I think he did stuff like this to women before.... Cherry Anne and maybe even Sinead. The things he said about me sound just like what he says about his exes!"

Suddenly the shock of it all and the finality of my plan hit me hard and fast and I start to cry. She ushers me away from the kids and into her kitchen and puts the kettle on while I try to convince her. "Look, let me explain it better. If I end it right now, I'm gonna go nuts with all the gaps in his stories. The questions about why he did all this. Why he lied about such seemingly stupid things. Why stuff kept getting weird and going wrong. Why the fuck he cheated, and with such mingers! It makes no sense and I have too many questions to walk away and not look back." My little friend isn't impressed, but I can see in her lovely eyes that she respects my logic.

We spend the day drinking tea and talking over how I would detach from Jonathan safely. We come up with a loose plan, but the most important part is that he will have no idea it's happening. I know I'm a victim of domestic abuse and the advice is always to make a plan and don't tell your abuser- I'm going to follow that advice.

"Boys, come on! Annie has to get the wee one from her pal's and we need to go!" I yell up the stairs to be met with thundering feet and 4 little faces appearing on the landing. "Good stuff. Don't forget anything," I say more gently with a wobbly smile. I don't want to go home, but I have to.

As I start to gather my things together and pick up my phone, I see there's a WhatsApp. I haven't chased him today and only sent a voice note telling him what happened the night before so he had no room to say he didn't know what took place.

For the first time in a long time, I'm not happy that he's resurfaced. This means going back.

"Baby, I've no memory of last night!" crying emojis and green love hearts. He is starting out with the old denial trick. Standard Jonathan, I think bitterly to myself. Tut, tut, he's getting over-confident in how weak he's made me.

"I left you a WhatsApp voice note saying, in detail, exactly what happened. I recorded it after I tidied the kitchen up and left." Broken hearts and an angry face for good measure.

"Yeah, I listened to it. I don't remember any of that. Fuck sakes, I'm never talking to Darren or that nutter Mary Anne again. I'm so ill today, baby, I am so ill," more crying emojis.

I lay the first of my traps "Ok- if you ever speak to either one of them again, I'm done. What happened last night was a dangerous, disgusting mess. I told you I didn't want them there and you ignored me. They are no longer to have contact with us. You'll be fine with a pint of water, some food and a sleep. I'll see you tomorrow," a green heart and punching fist to seal the deal.

I've put a rule down now- those people are to stay gone from our lives. "Ok, baby. I'll do that. Call you later. Going to see what you've left me in the freezer. Love you!" a dozen green hearts; he goes offline all jolly and chuffed with how easily he's won me over.

At this point, I still believe I am dealing with a nasty, selfish, sext-addict junkie. I have no idea how this is going to play out. I just think it's going to be a bad break up with a lot of gross revelations about his time with me and I believe I can survive it

relatively unscathed. Gutted, embarrassed and humiliated yeah....
but I have no idea at this point that it's going to be far, far worse
than that. I did not know he had NPD Disorder however, he did.

That night, Jonathan sent song after song and WhatsApp after
WhatsApp, describing his love for me and his plans to give up
drinking again and be more careful, kind and thoughtful. He
apologised profusely, which was interesting, and told me both
Darren and Mary Anne had apologised but he wasn't going to have
contact with them anymore because they were "pricks" and she was
"jealous" of me, so it would never work the four of us being friends.

I let him think everything was fine and reacted on script just
the way he liked.

Listen to: Katy Perry: "Roar"

Red Flags:

- *Your Narc lets you be bullied and even attacked. As already
  displayed, Narcs love a drama and putting you in positions
  where you squirm and cringe either in embarrassment, shame
  or fear of what next. If your Narc escalates, as mine both did,
  you will find they stand by when you are the focus of bullies
  in your circle. The Narc will wind them up and watch
  them go like venomous toys. The Narc will observe them "go
  for" you.*
- *Strangely Extreme Language and violence will happen to and
  around you. People will act unusually around a Narc (and
  FOR a Narc!). I don't believe the two friends here really are
  naturally violent or vicious, but Narcs have a way of getting
  their flying monkeys and exes to act out in extreme ways.
  They are masters of stage management and puppetry.*

March 2016

"Let me read your tarot cards, baby." Rolling over to kiss him, I
stifle a smile as I feel him tense up. We are in bed even though it's
late in the afternoon. I let him carry me here after some passionate

kissing got out of hand in the kitchen after lunch. Sliding out of bed, and slipping on my pink cotton kimono, I can feel his eyes on me. He doesn't want his future read- he fears things like this and these days I get great dark pleasure out of winding him up.

Even star signs give him the jitters. They represent an other-worldly knowledge, the universe watching him and a deep understanding open to others that he finds stressful and intrusive. Now I despise and love him, I'm growing in understanding of what is really going on inside his head. It's only a little insight, but my own skills in manipulation and his training of me are making this clearer and clearer by the day.

Bending down to gather up the silk scarf I use and the box of tarot cards, I almost feel something slither, snake-like, around my ankle. I love this feeling of control and power. It's like I've a really naughty comforting friend with me. She's around more and more often now and her dark comfort feels right.

I don't realise at this point that I am deeply affected by the Narcissistic Virus. Lying to Jonathan, manipulating him sexually to keep him believing, I'm still totally in love with him, pretending I trust him and enjoying little games that unsettle him- I'm acting like him. I believe I am simply an angry partner, making her escape just a little more fun. Co-dependant and still obsessed with him, I should have left instead of partaking in this toxic game. I'm also not aware that although I am winning little battles, he is actually overseeing a war....

With shaking hands, he chooses 5 cards for me to read. I've deliberately chosen the "5-card horseshoe Reading." The cards form an arc, left to right, like a rainbow. 1. Present position. 2.Present expectations. 3. What's not expected. 4. Immediate Future and 5. The Long-Term Future.

As I lay out my green silk scarf on the bed and make it all neat, I can see out of the corner of my eye that he goes a cute shade of terrified white.

Pausing for dramatic effect, I start to turn the first card over. The ten of swords. "Betrayal.... hmmmmm, bit late for that!" I joke, and he struggles to smile. Rushing past this- I don't want to trigger a discard, just have a little fun with him- I move on.

"Right, second card!" I declare jollily. "Oh! The Hanged Man," he swallows hard. "This is about secrets or information coming out! Let's hope it's something about how you can get to see the baby! I told you seeing the solicitor next week will help!" I kiss him quickly and he doesn't move. Turning over the third card, I almost laugh out loud. It's the two of swords and the character holding them is blindfolded. "Ok, so this is your 'what you least expect' kinda card. It represents a surprise, but don't worry! It can be a good one!" I smile at him but he doesn't smile back. "Come on baby, cheer up!" I say as I turn over the 4th card- "Ah! the Joker. Perfect for you, Jonny. This means you wear a lot of masks and often play different characters ..." He shuffles backwards onto the pillows of my bed like he wants to get away. "The cards say that you need to be honest. Step out of your shadows." He swallows.

"Now the last card is interesting, and actually doesn't mean you're going to die, for fuck sakes, but more that it's a time for change or that you need to change, perhaps." Tapping the Death card deftly with a chipped green fingernail, I see he's actually sweating now. He licks his lips and I smile nastily. "Oh well, it's a load of nonsense isn't it, babe?"

I stroke his face and tidy my cards away fast. He's out of the bedroom and into the toilet as fast as I can say "Mystic Meg".

The last few days, even the last 2 weeks have been relatively quiet, so I dared put my plan to end the relationship away to the back of my mind and started to settle down my little games.

Jonathan seemed quieter in himself. He was again being permitted to see his daughter and Sinead wasn't causing us much trouble. About half-way through the month, the air warmed up with the promise of a good summer, and on impulse, I booked and paid for two mini-breaks away, 1 to Amsterdam and 1 to a spa hotel in the borders.

With this strange phase of relative peace, I started to soften and warm to him again. He wasn't intensely hoovering me and seemed almost.... normal. I wondered if perhaps the attack in February and my extreme confidence and sexuality in "managing" him had taught him a lesson-that I wasn't a pushover and we really were meant to be together.

What a fucking dangerous mistake it was to let the anger go and start to feel happier....

Today was Lyall's sentencing. It's been 4 years coming. My friend, Mona, comes with me because she worked for him and lost money and her job too.

Lyall was found guilty, ordered not to mention me on social media or make any contact for 2 years. Of course, he breached it almost immediately but I didn't care. Jonathan was my focus.

"Let's get a glass of wine and some lunch to celebrate honey," she says as she hugs me as we walk over the bridge away from the court. Unsteady and shaky but delighted at the verdict, I can't believe it's finally over.

"Ok- but I can't stay long. Jonny and I have a night out planned. We've been looking forward to it for weeks!" I'm gesturing a ten-pound note at the barman. "It's been a nice, quiet wee while and we want to celebrate that. Celebrate him getting to see his baby really. It's a nicer thing to celebrate rather than that wanker back there in court."

She grabs my money and shoves it back in my coat pocket, so I kiss her cheek and we laugh. I love her.

Settled in a leather booth with drinks and steaming food before us, I excitedly share my plans for the evening.

"I've bought this gorgeous caramel off-the-shoulder mini dress. It's a sort of jersey material but looks velvety. Jonny's going to love it." Mona and I clink glasses; she has her usual big Pinot and I've got a small Merlot.

"Jonny says he's going to take me to Crab Shak- that place in the west end that I have been ogling for more than a year now. He knows I love, love, love shellfish. If it's in the sea, I'll eat it. Even a floating jobby!"

Mona laughs uproariously at my filthy joke and we continue to banter back and forth about how I have such a potty mouth and she can be such a prude. She has another glass of wine but mine isn't finished yet, so I refuse a second.

"I know what I forgot to tell you! Fuck sakes, how could I forget! He proposed again! On one knee a few days ago. In the morning. Totally bollock-naked, with his daft Rolling Stones on too loud in the living room!" I put my hand over my mouth at how loud my voice is, unashamedly excited and bursting to share the good news with my friend. An older couple at the bar turn around, but I'm relieved to see them smile at me.

Warmth spreads through me. This is what it's like to be normal. A drink with a friend. Exciting plans to share. Jokes to laugh at. This is what I've waited for. This is what I've been waiting for. It's been 2 weeks since the last "drama" and there haven't even been any discards at all since that awful night in February.

"Just be careful. Don't rush into anything. You know what he's like. He's put you through a lot," she says, not breaking eye contact. "I don't want you hurt again"- she takes a sip of wine and eats a chip. She is still looking at me. This is why I trust her- she cares.

"Mon, he's been better recently. Happier, more positive. Now he's getting to see the baby and Sinead's left us alone, things are quiet and calm. He thrives on the peace! Mind you, we both do! It makes sense, no?" I take a sip of wine and reach for a chip.

"Hmmmmmm." She's unconvinced. "Let's just wait and see. You need longer than a couple of weeks peace before you can decide to totally trust him again." I feel a prickle of unease. I know she's right but I don't want to hear it. So few people seem happy for us. We have had such a nightmare getting him settled and getting some peace. My instinct flickers and I've lost my appetite. I push the plate away and put my fork down. Looking over at the door, I feel the pang of missing him. He was supposed to be here 10 minutes ago.

"I'll be careful M, I promise. He's my soul mate. When it's good...its fucking good!" I wink at her and finish my wine. Placing the glass back on the table, I push it away and my eye catches the door again. Jonny's stood there. He's been watching us.

When he sees me, he juts forward, trying to pretend he was in motion & walking towards us all the time. His smile fades as he gets closer and he looks at Mona who's flushed and yes, looking a little tipsy.

"Hi, baby. Do you want a munch? Put you on until dinner later?" I say, but falter as he doesn't make a move to sit down.

"I had something in work. I'm shattered," he says. He looks odd. He looks angry. I don't understand why. Something isn't right. He still hasn't asked me about today's verdict and he seems distant and off. My chest prickles with that old sense of impending doom and unease.

"I'm going up the road for a sleep. Talk to you later," he says as he puts his e-cig in his mouth and spins on his heels.

He doesn't say goodbye to Mona and walks out of the bar fast. In shock, I watch him walk past the windows to where he will have parked the car on the road by the Clyde. He's parked there knowing he was going to be in then out fast. He never had any intention of joining us for any period of time. In the last 60 seconds, my life has crumbled, again.

My phone pings "You're drunk- go home tonight. I'll speak to you tomorrow," with one kiss.

"Why are you doing this?" I reply. Then a second message; "Jonny, he got convicted and we were just happy it's over. Please don't do this!" I'm starting to beg. I can't help myself. Mona is quiet next to me. She's seen this many, many times before.

"Leave me be, Lucy. I'm going home to sleep. I said I'll call you tomorrow." This time no kisses. Nothing. The discard is in full flow. The train is hurtling on and I can't stop it.

I start to cry openly and the couple who smiled at me earlier look uncomfortable. They turn away and whisper to each other. I scrabble at my bag and coat. I want to get away from here. Fix this. Each time it happens, it's more agonising. It's harder to recover. I shouldn't have cancelled my plan. I should have left weeks ago. How could I be so stupid to feel hope!?

I ended up virtually running up-town to Jonathan's flat to find he had locked me out, left his keys in the door and was now sitting in there silently stewing over whatever it was I or Sinead had apparently done now.

Sitting on the top step outside his door, I cry and text him over and over to please tell me what I've done wrong. "Please open the door and let me in so we can have our night out and get back to normal." I send the same message, worded differently, over and over. He's inside the flat waiting for me to leave. I can hear his phone pinging with my texts, one by one, over and over...

Finally, my phone pings with one from him and I fold over in relief. It's going to be ok. We can pull this back. Make up. Have sex. Be together on our night out. It's going to be fine. If he replies, it means he is open to talking.

"If you don't leave, I'm calling the police. I want you to leave me alone NOW!" the message reads. The stone walls of his stairwell echo with my sobs.

I don't reply, but I know he hears me click-clack down the stairs in the heels he says are his favourite.

Having got into bed as soon as I got home, I fell asleep on damp pillows, clutching my phone. I awoke about 7 pm to no messages. Determined to end the discord as soon as possible, I wash and change, but without make-up, head across town to the pub at the bottom of Jonathan's road to sit and drink and wait this out.

My saddo levels go up a notch as I buy a magazine to read while I wait. Sitting in a corner where I can see both entrances, I catch the barman watching me and burn with shame. I'm the epitome of the lonely girl suffering a bad relationship. Red-rimmed eyes, puffy lips and her phone grasped tightly in her hand while she watches the door... How many other women have done this for him? For people like him?

In the pub, I got rather drunk and soon made friends with a nice couple my age and some other people they knew. We ended up sitting in a big group, drinking and laughing for the rest of the evening. As the alcohol soothed me and people managed to make me laugh, I almost felt calm, and looking at the handsome fireman sitting too close to me, I dared to revisit the idea I could survive a break up from Jonathan and perhaps be normal again.

The fireman is looking at me like I am the only woman in this room. He is tall, muscular and polite. Ok, not the brightest machine in the arcade but he seems kind and sweet. My new friends keep nudging us together, changing seats and giggling as we keep blushing to find our long legs pressed together around the now very crowded, sticky table.

It's been more than 3 hours since I've messaged Jonathan to tell him where I am and plead with him to please not let this roll into a new day. I have been distracted by this fun (normal!) evening and he's had radio silence, partly by accident. Blurry and giddy, the edges around me disappear. The lights are dim and people are funny even when they're not funny. The drinks all taste great. I'm thirsty.

I take a selfie of us all and tag it with "missing you- not!" all laughing emojis and our usual green hearts. The message goes through immediately. In the time my begging and pleading have been absent, he's unblocked me. I hadn't noticed his picture reappear on the WhatsApp account, signalling him opening up communication lines yet again.

Fast to come online, he responds to my picture message with "please don't do anything, Lucy! I'll speak to you tomorrow. Please don't do anything, baby."

Now he's the one afraid of humiliation and loss, I feel a surge of dark, oily satisfaction spread through my chest and up and over my shoulders like a set of big, black wings. Remembering how this power felt 6 weeks ago, I sit up straighter and smile at the fireman. With my head tilted on one side, I consider what to send back.

My finger hovers over the screen. I want to tell him to fuck off. Tell him on another special night he's ruined, yet again, I've pulled a guy far hotter than him. I want to delete Jonathan's number and escape this nasty, complicated and harmful situation. I want to end this, here and now. "Lucy, I love you. I'm coming to find you. I miss you," comes another message. "Come on! We're getting married. I've been stupid today," all broken hearts and crying faces. He's coming to find me and I don't try to stop him.

The pub's saloon doors explode open 14 minutes later and Jonathan flies in like something out of a spaghetti western- the hero coming to the rescue of his distressed maiden. Wild-eyed and sweaty, the white T-shirt I bought him for our Tunisia holiday is stained with something dark, maybe cola, and it's twisted slightly and stretched across his ample belly. His dark hair is plastered to his forehead. He looks like a middle-aged ned looking for trouble. I feel a twitch of shame in my gut. My new friends will be disappointed that this is the reason I have been so distraught. My eyes widen in shock as I recognise who is with him. It's Darren. Yes, THAT Darren.

He still hasn't seen me. He's scanning the bar like a lighthouse. His eyes wont alight on me easily because I'm not alone and hunched in a corner like usual. My heart jumps as he double-takes and fixates on the fireman now reaching down to hand me a drink. Jonathan gets redder and redder and clenches his fist open and closed like an angry toddler ready to demand his plastic truck back.

For sure, he's picturing me enjoying a hot, fast, doggy-style fuck in the disabled toilet with the best-looking guy at this table.

A harsh little whisper shocks me. It's my little snake friend. The one who enjoyed the Tarot teasing. She's my new internal voice. "I don't want him here. Get rid of him." There she goes again. I don't know what's different but I feel like I'm in some sort of transition. Hearing that little shimmery voice, the voice who hides in pillowcases, under beds and behind my ear when he hurts my soul.

Jonathan is cutting through the warm, throbbing crowd and I see he's switched masks already. He looks softer and welcoming. I relax a little and shoot a look at the fireman. Poor guy is still watching me. "What are you doing after this?" he says as he sips his drink, not losing eye contact. He's been waiting to ask me this all night and his timing is like Jonathan's- the stuff of the devil. For Fuck sakes!!!!!

In a heartbeat, Jonathan is stood beside the table. "Baby, I've been looking for you everywhere. Fuck sakes we were worried about you!" he says and reaches down to my shoulder, not to stroke it, to hold it. Feeling the pressure of the squeeze, I know he's marking his territory. I like the fact he's jealous. I like it a lot.

Darren's hovering behind him, looking like he wants to be anywhere but here. "Darren can buy me a drink to apologise for his girlfriend attacking me and you can buy me some crisps to apologise for "losing me," I say using my fingers as quote marks. Smiling sweetly at him, I stand up to go to the toilet.

I squeeze past the fireman, who now is trying to look anywhere that is not Jonathan or me. He can't help but look at my backside as it slides past his eye line. I don't blame him. I have a wonderful backside.

"No problem, baby. You left the flat without making plans with me. I just met Darren to fill time 'til I worked out where you were," the lies slither smoothly out of his mouth as he catches the eye of everyone at the table. Slowly, they relax. This person is charming. I don't bother correcting his shite.

In the toilet, I gather myself and wash my face, re-do my ponytail and stare at myself in the mirror. "Here we go again,"

The girl in the mirror looks tired but angry. Trying a smile, I make a good job of it. Her eyes glitter and there's something about her I recognise.

Three hours later & we are home. Darren passes out on the sofa and Jonathan and I go to bed. I fall asleep almost immediately, but about 4 am I'm woken up by the ominous sound of Jonathan unzipping his flies far too close for comfort.

Opening one eye, I can't see in the dark but realise what's happening too late- he's urinating up against his bedroom wall, only a metre or so away from me. "Jonny! Jonny! Stop! That's not the toilet!!!" I grapple for him but he shoves me off. I fall onto the floor, hitting my hip off the hard plastic of his shitty, futon-style bed. I lie there and watch as he simply carries on. "Fuck off" he grunts. He finishes and falls back into bed with his penis poking out of his flies. I can smell the tang of his piss and want to cry.

When I hear him start snoring gently again, I creep out of bed and go into the kitchen to boil a kettle and look for the non-bleach spray. Quietly, I kneel on the floor in my pyjamas and scrub at the carpet and wipe the walls gently. Cleaning up his mess, I hope he stays asleep now. Drunk, high and bad-tempered, he frightens me.

At about 7 am, I hear Darren get up and leave. He manages to be quiet but the bang of the door rouses Jonathan and he rolls over to face me. His penis hardens as he feels for my buttocks and pushes against me to try and kiss my neck. He smells of urine, alcohol and cocaine and I recoil away from him. He's still half asleep so I'm able to slide slowly away across the bed and onto the floor, where I sit for a moment deciding what to do.

Last night was an indicator he's up to something again. I've realised he acts out dramatically when he's cheating on me.

Without the slightest guilt, I check Jonathan's phone again-the first time since I found the gross ping pong S and M video. I'd promised Jonathan I would trust him in not checking his phone. I kept to it until last night. I've followed his rules but he's broken mine.

"She broke into my phone and sent those messages about my contact with the baby. She's a fucking nut job," a rainbow of heart emojis peppered with kisses. Shock isn't a word that would actually fit the emotion that's currently roaring through every cell in my body. The messages, hundreds of them, are to Sinead.

"She wants to be there when I have contact. She is controlling me," angry faces and broken hearts accompany this cracker.

Sinead helpfully replies "Get a second phone- she's psycho. Totally bonkers xxxx". Every part of my body turns to cement- all I can move are my fingers which are doing a fine job of discovering quite how evil these two people are.

"Yeah. I think I might do that" he agrees. "She's not well. I've tried everything with her to get her to stop upsetting you. I really appreciate you putting up with her," he whinges.

I want to throw the phone at the wall. I want to throw it and stamp on the pieces until they are dust. I want to force these people to eat that dust and watch and clap as they choke on it.

Messages from yesterday. "She won't let me visit the baby. That's why I keep missing contact visits," he complains. "Don't tell her when you have one arranged with me and then she can't stop you," she smartly replies.

These people are perfect for each other. Sitting there on the floor with his urine staining my knees, I really don't want any part of this.

The messages to Darren the night before are also shocking, hurtful and unkind. "She's nuts, man. I just wanted a lads' night and she totally fucking kicked off. She's jealous of us!" Laughing emojis and punching hands. "Come over. I've been looking forward to this and she fucking knew I was meeting you, planned for ages," angry faces and pint glasses.

"Aye, pal. On way. Knew you'd get it sorted. What's she all about?!" Darren replies. "Trying to fuck your night up is crazy business. You said that was what she was like when we were over at yours last month!"

I'm grinding my teeth so hard it's a wonder I don't chip them. My knuckles are white on the phone and something bites me on the heart. I feel the sharp, searing pain and wonder again if I am having some sort of attack. There's a strange tingling in my legs and my hands seize up. It's a panic attack- I haven't had a "full body" one since I was 15 years old.

Dropping the phone, I lean forward trying to get a rhythm back. I count to 10, forwards then backwards, to try and calm myself. Remembering the panic attack resolution training I had when I was learning how to help people who had suicidal thoughts, I stare at a pebble we collected off the beach, sitting innocently on the TV stand. Focus on that one thing and simply count. Breathe and count. Take your time. Breathe and count. Prayer-like, I crouch on the floor for what seems like hours but is probably only 10 minutes.

Leaning back against the wall, close to the door, I re-open his phone. Sinead will think she's special, but I know my man! He never just cheats with just one creature; he likes a whole zoo.

A message from early yesterday, when I was in court, catches my eye. It's from a guy in his work. A nice, big, handsome fitness instructor we have worked out many times with. Privately, I call him Hot John. Unoriginal, but apt. He's called John and he's hot. "Can I buy some C off you?" the message reads.

He was planning to upset me and discard me to go partying long before he even saw Mona and I giggling in the pub. The realisation makes me let out a small sound like an animal trapped. Putting my cold, shaking hands over my mouth, I wince in fear. I don't want to wake him up.

Reaching across the floor, I tug the red throw I bought him off the sofa and wrap it around me. I'm still slightly rocking back and forth and in desperate need of a drink and a cigarette. Anything to numb the pain and help me breathe. This isn't a relapse again- it's just how he wants to live. It's his real personality and his real life.

"Do you want to go for a coffee?" reads another recent message. It's to "Cowboy Colin". I recognise this nickname we have given to a terrifically handsome older chap who swims regularly alongside me. He often does extras work on films and loves Westerns.

I wince at the funny memory of Jonathan and I giggling about Colin's enormous bulge and teeny, tiny, pale blue speedos. A tear escapes and I wipe it away with a corner of the throw. I read on through the messages, hoping that this will in some way remind me of who my lover really is. A kind person who wants to help and support lonely people like Colin.

"Don't message me when I'm driving! I've got Bluetooth and sometimes my husband's in the car". It's not Cowboy Colin. It's a woman. A married woman.

Jonathan sends laughing emojis to hide his discomfort at being put in his place. "Whatever. So, when am I taking you for a coffee?" he persists. I hit my head on the wall just to feel something else. It makes a dull thud and for a second I want him to wake up so I can confront him like last time, but I remember how he kicked and throttled me and again so decide I want him to stay asleep. Leave me in peace to watch my life shatter. Again. "Did you get the vitamin tablets I got you? I left them at the reception." She's bought him those?! I buy him those…. fucking bastards!

"Oh, and I'm off Friday," she goes on. "Me too! Lucky me!" he flatters her. She doesn't reply again and I notice that this conversation also took place the morning before. Wednesday morning. Just before he messaged me to suggest he does an extra shift on Friday and that he would be tired and want to go home after it. "We can do something special on Saturday, baby," he'd said.

I agreed, thrilled he was planning time together. It was lies; he was just booking himself time away from me in case this woman, like the others, would be retarded enough to get sexual with him.

The blessed rage and hate kick in suddenly. Thank God. "Right. Let's see who's turned his head this time! Mind you, I'm not expecting much after the mingers last September, but maybe he will surprise me and for once will have some taste,". Grabbing paper and a pen to note down her number off a note-pad on the top of the fridge I mutter away to myself like a lunatic. "He's going to regret this and so is she," I hiss, scuttling back down the hall to bed.

I tuck the scrap inside my pyjama trousers and slide into bed. We always slept naked up until recently. For some reason, I've started wearing pyjamas. Maybe deep down I wanted some sort of barrier between us. Some protection from whatever it was that lived under his skin.

My resolve nearly cracks and shatters when he rolls over at about 8 am and puts his arm over my hip, brushes my belly button ring with his finger and kisses my neck roughly, making his usual encouraging noises. I used to love it when he did this- morning sex was a solid agreement, every single time we spent the night together.

He snuffles my neck. A mix of groans and grunts I used to find endearing. Now I realise they disgust me and fill me with tension. I nearly start crying again at the realisation that the last thing I had for him has gone. I had lost my respect and trust weeks ago, but now I no longer find him attractive. I no longer want to be intimate. It's gone.

As he pumps away on top of me, holding my face in his hand and pulling at my mouth, I fake, every single sigh, moan and gasp. Every. Single. One.

Over the next week I gently needled Jonathan about tiny little things I knew would lead to him lying to me. I started to lay these little traps for him again and he desperately tried to step around them.

"I haven't seen Cowboy John for ages," I say, as we sit together sipping matching black coffees in his kitchen. It's a few days after I went through his phone.

"He's good- saw him yesterday," Jonathan replies, making full eye contact with me. His mouth is full with the cinnamon pastries I just warmed for him in the oven. He spits some crumbs onto the table as he blethers away about leg day at the gym and I wipe them away with the tea towel I have hanging casually on my shoulder. I am preparing Persian lamb for dinner later. I rub a paste of cinnamon, cumin, paprika, garlic, salt, olive oil and harissa over the meat and roast it slowly in pomegranate juice and halved lemons. I serve it with saffron rice and warm pittas. It's one of his favourites.

"Do you want a vitamin drink?" I ask suddenly and stand up. He has stopped talking but is still chewing. I cup his cheek with my palm and stroke it lovingly before walking towards the cupboard where I usually keep these. I need to act the way I always have. Affectionate and helpful. It's my turn to wear a mask.

"Yeah, ok," he says as he throws back the rest of the coffee and points the empty mug at me. I take it from his hand and smile. Inside I am clenching and unclenching. Hit him. Don't hit him. Hit him. Don't hit him. Would the mug do too much damage? Maybe his false teeth would fly out. That would be funny. I nearly laugh.

I checked his bag after I last checked his phone and of course, found a brown envelope holding a tube of the exact same soluble vitamins I've been buying him the last 2 years. "Hope these work Jonny. See you at the pool xxxx" her scrawl on the envelope.

I reach up to the cupboard and gasp. Ready for my Oscar-winning show of "Oh dear- none left!" Hand to mouth, frown and sad face in his direction as I pretend to take one from the batch in my cupboard. I am successful. "Oh, baby. There aren't any. I forgot to get some more. I'm sorry. But you have spares, don't you? I'm sure I saw some in your gym bag." I am saying the last sentence as I walk fast past him, out of the kitchen and through to the living room.

As I walk back in, jauntily waving the tablets and grinning, I note with satisfaction that he looks confused.

"Ummm. Erm. I didn't know I had those," he stutters. He is a shade of pale green and searching my face for any emotion other than perfectly happy. I plop the vitamins into two-pint glasses of water. One each. I do this never taking my eyes off his face.

There is a silence. He is weighing this up. I am pretty sure (99%) sure he is stoned on Valium so is confident enough to think I don't know a thing. He thinks I genuinely believe every word he says.

He gathers himself and slurps half his coffee in one gulp while he thinks. "Oh yeah- Cowboy Colin gave me those yesterday!" he almost shouts. He is delighted with his cover story. The fake name in his phone and the fact I know this person and will believe the lie. I laugh. Sharp and quick. It's almost a bark and it's a little too loud. "I'll thank him when I see him next- he swims a lot the same time as me." I hand him the drink and sit down on his knee. As I take a drink, I sneak a look at him.

I feel him squirming in his seat like he is shitting a hedgehog. "Oh, don't do that- you'll embarrass him. I thanked him already," he croons at me while he strokes my hair back behind my ear. I smile sweetly. He misses the cold, glittering eyes because he is looking at my lips. He likes my lips. "No bother, love. You're the boss!" I say and lean over and kiss him before taking an unladylike slurp of his vitamin drink. He relaxes and kisses the tip of my nose.

There is a moment where I want to burp in his face- remind him of how unpalatable his lies are, but I'm not that far gone, yet.

We have our DVD day fairly uneventfully and I play the part of His Lucy very well. Loving, kind, trusting, stupid Lucy. She lets him have sex with her on the sofa and she checks on the lamb dutifully so it's just right for him. Lucy tidies the living room and the kitchen while he naps and she runs a bath to wash every piece of him off her body, knowing he will want to enter it again later. Lucy sits in the living room and hears him tap, tap, tapping away on his phone, messaging Sinead and "the others" while he thinks that she thinks, he is asleep.

Over dinner the next night, I ask Jonathan if he minds if I join the running team at his work. The woman listed in his phone as Cowboy Colin is in the hotel staff running team. Smiling, I watch as he nearly chokes on the crispy beef and spinach salad I've "lovingly" dressed in his favourite lime and soy dressing. I've added extra, extra, extra chilli-it hurts his arse the next day. I smile as he wafts frantically at his mouth and his eyes fill with tears. Poor diddums. Yup, a sore one tomorrow after his first bowel-loosening coffee, I think to myself.

I entered her phone number into WhatsApp and did a reverse image search on google yesterday. Found her on Facebook as well as Kik. Sickened to discover she was in her 60's and a grandmother, I numbed out for a bit, but luckily the anger seared in again when I saw a picture of her standing with her daughter; she's closer to my age and has tats like me too. They were in swimming costumes and I felt almost nothing when I spotted myself in the background talking to Jonny.

Grab A Granny's page showed regular visits to the hotel spa and her membership to the running team. A little memory is niggling at me but I'll work it out- I'm sure.

"Oh baby, I'm not sure you're fit enough. I'd miss you if you joined it and were at the gym less," – his eyes slide away from my face as he says this. "I like running though and the summer's coming, Jonny…" Reaching for his hand across the table, I squeeze it and he doesn't move. "Oh well, just know I'm definitely thinking about it and you can't stop me… I'm too fast. Hah!" He's a little pale now. I almost feel sorry for him.

As he eats, something scratches my subconscious. Running team…running team. A mother and a daughter…. oh my God.

"You know the woman you said fancied you…way back in December? You were kidding on that she was chasing you round the pool, all old and wrinkly? Isn't she in the running team?" Holding my breath, I laser him with my eyes. I think I hear his arse creak.

Staring at the salad and twirling the delicious long strands of crispy beef, he doesn't want eye contact. He needs to think about how to get out of this one. "Oh, I think she left. I heard she had cancer or something. Real shame."

I imagine myself leaning across the table, flicking the fork out of his hand and ninja-style rotating it back and over my wrist so I can stab it, dagger-like, into his right eye- the one above his gross Coco Pop mole. I let the fantasy go. I can't let him see my anger and hate.

A Few Days Later

Today I started gathering my clothes from all over his flat. Sexy knickers, shoes, coats, gym gear. You name it, we were such a close, solid couple I had an entire wardrobe here so I didn't have to have an overnight bag every time I stayed over. We shared our bodies, homes and lives… I thought we were in love.

He wanders around after me like a fart I can't escape, talking crap about his sore legs from the gym and wittering about the next date night we can have. Muttering assurances that we'll arrange something soon, I occasionally let him grab me and accept a kiss. "I need to take all this home and wash it, sweetheart. It's just not getting done here and I can't do your washing and mine, so it's best we separate the clothes for a bit" toneless, but a good excuse to move out without him knowing.

Sensing something different about me, he's trying to gain my attention and calm whatever it is that rumbles away in the atmosphere between us. "I love you, baby, you know that," he says as I tie the last bin bag with a rubber band. "Yes, love"- I don't look at him. "Of course you do! I'm amazing. You won't ever get any better!" Sounding a little bitter, I sweeten it with a giggle and a kiss. He grins at me, assured now.

To solidify my determination, I laid another trap a few days later. The vitamin tablet farce had been a success, so as we lay in bed together that afternoon, I dropped a little bomb. Attempting to be generous, I decided to give him an opportunity to be honest with me.... in particular about those messages to Sinead.

"Jonny, you know you can talk to me about anything don't you? Is there anything you need to tell me?" I look at him earnestly and bite my lip sexily for good measure. "You know I love you. I adore you and have always said if you're honest I won't ever be angry. Is there anything I need to know about Sinead ... for example?"

"No, baby. There's nothing at all. Why, what do you mean?" Trying to look confused and innocent, he knows I know something now. I'm not going to correct him and reassure him though. It's time he started to feel unease and I want to see him off kilter and uneasy. A heavy silence settles between us.

"Ok. As long as you're sure." I wink and throw a long leg over his ample waist and deftly roll on top of him. "No problem at all!" I say and kiss him full on the lips. Sliding my tongue inside his mouth without closing my eyes, I note that he looks unsure. Confused and maybe a little afraid. None of this is in his rule book. None of this is planned or expected. I rock back and slide his cock inside me and watch his eyes roll back in pleasure. As long as I smile and have sex with him, we are all good. Briefly, I wonder if other women ended up this calculating and hollow... as I rock back and forth the thought falls away into the sounds of his pleasure.

I feel nothing as he cums quickly inside me. No, that's a lie; I feel hate and I feel power.

It's about a week later and I'm well into my escape plan. We are out for dinner at a new Turkish place on Sauchiehall Street. We 've dutifully posted happy, kissy selfies on Facebook. Winter hats and rosy cheeks, we look proud & happy, waiting for delicious food before going home to cuddle up, kiss, make love and fall asleep together.

Emboldened by a few lagers and the knowledge I'm only a few days away from leaving him. I flick open trap number 3 and "Baby, when is your birthday thing, you know, anniversary of your new sobriety again?" If he says September 28th he's lying. That's the day after he was arrested and there should have been no drug use at all since that day if I'm to believe his lies.

Spooning big piles of lemon couscous into my mouth, I don't make eye contact. I need to act dumb. Keep him confident. If he's not looking at me, he lies easier and talks more.

"Well, the last time I used Valium was last September and the last time I used coke was the same time. Coke's not my thing, you know that.... Valium's bad for me and makes me do things.... things that hurt you." He's stuttering over his words a little. He should just have stuck to a date and not all this waffle. Liars waffle. "I'm never taking it again, baby," he says, not quite looking at me.

I know he is lying. While I was looking for knickers under the bed and packing my things up, I found a little empty plastic pill-shaped vial that even an idiot knows holds powder, probably Molly or coke. It was quite big, maybe three times the size of a normal pill and I could unscrew one end from the other and when I tasted the powder inside, my tongue went a little tingly then numb.

"Ok. Well, we need to celebrate it, baby. It's coming up for 6 months! You've done so well and I'm incredibly proud of you.

Your so determined to be clean and sober, I love you more every day." Leaning over the table to kiss him, bile rises in my throat and I stifle the urge to slap him.

One of his pupils is bigger than the other. It's a tell-tale sign of more Valium abuse too.... I realise the napping never stopped but, as normal when he's up to no good, it's got out of control.

He's gaining weight from night-time bingeing on sweet things while I sleep. His skin condition & prostatitis are in flare. He's brazen, cocky and confident. Sexually, he's aggressive and controlling.

At my compliments and affection, he beams at me and takes a large bite of his kebab. I wish he would choke on it. Mind you, the kebab deserves a better ending than finishing off this horrible bastard, to be honest.

We needed to get out of the stifling atmosphere festering away between us the flat. He knows something's afoot. In the last week or so, I have asked 3 trigger questions that have unsettled him and pointed at lies. He's getting ready for a discard- but for me, it's too soon.

It is grey and dank outside and freezing mist is snaking itself around all the buildings we walk past. It must be below zero today. A cold snap's taken the city by surprise, so I'm wrapped up tightly in a long, bright scarf, hat and winter coat. He's moody and on edge...our secrets hover between us, crouched and whispering.

"There's something I need to tell you," he's not looking at me. I keep walking but almost trip as adrenaline and panic flood me head to toe. Oh God, what now?

"You know how Jaydee told you that we visited a prostitute in Ibiza a few years ago... before I met you.... and I said I wasn't even there.... that I was back at the hotel?" I knew he was going to tell me something, but I wasn't expecting this. I was actually kinda hoping for the truth about the young girl who's popped up twice. The one only about 16 or maybe younger, that two people have told me he had sex with in his work's changing rooms.... she's niggled away at me for ages. Damn her.

I stop. Drop his hand. "Yes, I remember. It came out in October when you argued with Jaydee and he said it happened. You said he was just trying to hurt me and it was all crap and he went alone to the prostitute."

"Well... I didn't actually go to the hotel. I stayed at the prostitute place. I pretended to go in & have sex with her but really, we just talked. I swear on my life, Lucy". He reaches for my hand again but can't quite make eye-contact. Ahhhhhhh...he thinks I'm worrying about that! Hah! He's gifting me this half-lie to keep me sweet... he fucked the prostitute same as his mate did. I know that like I know my own face.

"Oh well. It's in the past now, baby. Come on, let's go home. It's too cold to be wandering about out here talking shite. You're my guy now and you love me!" Grabbing his hand, I tippy toe to kiss him passionately. He responds and sags in relief. I want to bite his lying tongue off.

2 Hours Later

Jonathan is stretched out on the lazy-boy. He's fallen asleep and his mouth is slowly sagging open. I stand and watch him in disgust.

He's always slept like a man with no conscience. But he's simply a man who does not care about the people he has used and hurt. When he does complain of shame, guilt, or remorse he's just saying what needs to be heard by others around him, not what is inside him.

He's confessed about the prostitute to gesture me a gift. To show me he can confess to errors and is not always simply found out. He is trying to show a different, better, honest side. I know him too well now.

Later, while he's still asleep, I lie in the bath and think. There's something annoying me about Grab a Granny.... the daughter keeps surfacing and I can't stop thinking about it.

"Can I ask you if your daughter ever met Jonny?" I send the message fast, not wanting to change my mind. She reads the

WhatsApp and starts to type without pause. That shard of glass in my chest again- pure fear.

"We were going to make a complaint. She's married. Has young kids. He touched her hip and shoulder...her tattoos and complimented them. Trotted around after us a few times, right up until February. She was really angry that I didn't want to make a fuss. He's lucky she hasn't told her husband. He's a creep." I read the words and can't quite make sense of the horror.

Getting out of the bath slowly, I gently lie my phone on the side and reach for a towel as if in slow motion. If I move too fast, I think I'm going to lose it. Explode with rage. Catapulted by adrenalin into that dingy living room, I'll smother him with one of the fucking red and grey throw cushions I bought him.

Watch his fat, scabby legs flail and feel his big scarred hands scratch at my own slim ones trying to get me off him. With the strength of 10 angry, humiliated women, I'll push down and grunt with the effort. I won't let go. Shouting, I'll tell him this is for all the women he's hurt. All the women I know he'll go on to hurt if he gets to stay alive. I'll watch his movements slow. His limbs twitch. Watch as he falls limp. Panting, I'll lift off the cushion, close his eyes with gentle fingers and sit on the sofa with the cushion on my lap. Then I'll go to eat my dinner in the kitchen and not throw up for the first time in 2 years. While his body cools and stiffens, I can maybe make a New York cheesecake. Or perhaps a caramel apple crumble.

I enjoy this lovely fantasy sitting on the toilet with a mascara-stained towel wrapped around me. It's soothing and I feel calmer now. He's done me a favour being so vile. It's time I end this. I can't kill him but I can leave.

Listen to: Carrie Underwood: "I'll Think Before He Cheats"

Red Flags:

- _Sexual Secrets_. Extensive porn, masturbation and sexual needs. Nothing works to "settle" the Narcs needs. They promise to get help and/or stop, but don't.

- *Not fussy. Anyone and anything can be a target and you won't be able to make sense of it. The Narc will make the most unlikely people feel "the one" while you think you are. It is not "traditional cheating". It is pretty darn filthy and dark.*
- *Hate for your beloved. Murder fantasies and loathing that feel unhealthy yet delicious. I'm sorry.... you're in a toxic relationship.*

PART 3.
The Ultimate Discard

It's the last Wednesday of March 2016. Jonathan is expecting me to message him and ask when he wants me to be ready for him to pick me up. Being at home last night allowed me to form a final trap for Jonathan. I've decided on an ultimatum. I haven't messaged him all day and pleasingly, he started to get frantic around our usual meeting time.

5.12 pm - message number 6; "Baby, where are you? Have you lost your phone? Why aren't you replying? You didn't come to the pool today!" crying emojis and broken hearts.

Sitting alone in a darkening living room, I'm glad the boys are at their fathers'. I don't want to move and put any lights on or turn the heating on. If I make the house feel cosy and welcoming... I'll change my mind and want him here. How ridiculous that anyone else "normal" has become so potentially heart-breaking?

Around 7 pm, I finally reply to his several messages "Jonny, you know I love you and you know I have done everything possible to show you this, including taking you back in September. I believe you haven't touched another human being since Sinead in November 2013, but the sexting and other stuff absolutely broke me. I nearly died with pain and shame and I still took you back. I believe you love me but I have to ask you to get clean and sober again, maybe go to a rehab to PROVE you mean it? I also need you to be totally honest with me about everything before, during and since you have met me. Everything. If you do these 2 things, I am yours. If you don't, I'm seriously done."

He blue ticks the message and immediately goes offline. He wasn't expecting this.

I sit and I wait. He is taking his time.... I've gone rogue. He won't be happy. A big part of me is hoping that he'll reply the way any decent person would. The way a loving partner would....

"You're right, baby. You deserve the truth and yes, I need help. I've used drugs again. I'm back on the Valium and I'm lying to Sinead about you.... and this behaviour is wrong. I will call the GP tomorrow and we can talk tonight. I love you and will do anything to keep you."

I shouldn't fantasise about him messaging me like that. It hurts. It makes me shake with regret. I want to message him again.

Tell him I'm stupid and selfish and that I'm sorry. This feels so final….

As I start typing a new apologetic, whining message- he replies. "Are you fucking serious? Are you actually kidding me on? You are a fucking nutter! You've sent me sick. I'm ill and it's all your fault. You couldn't just let things go and let me be! I told you I never touched no one. I'm not taking nothing. It was all just September and just a joke! Just daft messages. Months ago, crackpot! Leave me alone. It's over and for good this time!"

Interesting. Very interesting. I'm stone and start to numb out. It's my fault that he has a secret cocaine and Valium addiction, yet I'm anti-drugs. It's my fault he has sex with pretty much anything, anyway, here, there and everywhere and has no respect for me, them or his workplace. It's my fault that his addictions and criminality span 30 years. It's my fault he doesn't see all 3 of his kids in any sort of real pattern. It's my fault that he has exes going back 17 years that loathe and despise him.

Well, I'm glad! If I'm out of his life he can be a great person. He can be sober, clean, honest, loyal and faithful.

"No problem. I'm gone." I reply.

I cry, but it's not for him. I'm crying for who I used to be. I cry for the loss of all that time and hope and trust. I cry for the disgusting way he threw away my offer of support, even when he didn't deserve it.

Within two hours, I'm teetering on the edge of changing my mind & going to his flat. With a big glass fizzing on the table filled with 3 shots of gin and the same number of ice cubes, I Facebook message Gerda, an ex of his. She might help me make a decision- a final one.

"Aww! I saw you split up! that's a shame!" she replies, almost immediately. "Yeah- he's wiped his whole page all the way back… to…. like 2014!" She sounds almost happy.

He has deleted me from his life in 2 hours. Two years of posts and photos and shares and group chats. He's single now and so am I. The pain of this is unbearable.

"I really thought you were the one he'd finally settle down with. He seemed finally committed!" Gerda goes on.

"What do you mean finally committed?" I type. "Well, he cheated on me with some weird looking woman called Tracy or Tara or Trina in AA and got done for a telecoms offence against me as well! He's cheated on all his partners, multiple times. Didn't you know? There's no love lost with his kids' mothers!"

"Why didn't you tell me all this before?" I rave "I needed to know all this fucking months ago!"

"I didn't want to pop your bubble. It all looked so great on Facebook, I honestly thought he had finally been tamed. It's not my place to say anything." She's defensive in her shame of letting me get fucked over. "He'd only say I'm a crackpot or psycho. It's what he does to cover up his shite. He's evil."

Two more drinks later, I message his friend K who I really like, "K, I've dumped Jonny. He's a cheating, lying cunt. There's been a granny at the pool he's been cracking on to and the daughter wants to make a complaint. It's all so out of control! I need to speak to Sinead because I think he's going to try for her again now I've ended it. He's evil! Can you message her and tell her we need to talk? She hates me, but I don't know why- please, I need answers!"

"Lucy, Sinead is a psycho. You're best staying away from her. You're the best thing that's ever happened to him!"- pretty useless. Typical K, easy going and unhelpful. "Fuck sakes, K! That's not what I need to hear right now. I need answers! I fucking want answers!" In the end I spend the rest of the evening messaging people I think can make me understand what is happening but no one cares.

Red Flags:

- _Taunting and Testing with Half-Truths._ This helps Narcs ascertain how much they can tell you about their other secrets and behaviours. Plus, telling part of the story truthfully releases a little pressure valve for them and still allows them to protect their own status in your eyes as "honest, fragile and perfect". They dare not tell you the FULL true version, *because then you may tell the world who and what they really are! Oh, and discard them before they can discard you!*

- *Coldness at your pain, I'm referencing the Flying Monkeys and Enablers here. The people around your Narc. Don't expect information or support or even empathy when you are crying out for it. They don't care. It's really that simple. If they do care, they hide it because if they dare "betray" the Narc by showing you any care or helping you work out what's happened, they will be punished by the Narc.*

- *Your decision to leave/end it somehow becomes theirs! Narcs simply can't be "dumped". Its absolute agony for them if you "get in there first". Their reaction will either be extreme hoovering to get you back on side and dump you later, when you are not ready for it, OR they will react with such rage it feels like they have chosen to dump you for their own reasons.*

March into April 2016

I manage to doze a little on the sofa with all the lights on and the television playing back to back repeats of a dreadful Glasgow soap opera.

The sound of a man's deep, Scottish voice has woken me up. In the briefest of seconds, I think it's him. He's changed his mind. He's here and we're going to his doctor for a referral. Then it all floods back and in my empty flat, I wail in distress, writhing in blankets and clutching my face and stomach like I'm sick.

This pain is unbearable. Can I kill myself? Is that the best thing to do? I just want peace. To not feel like this.

I don't understand why I keep swinging between loss and rage, love and hate, grief and murderous thoughts. How can I be missing him, yet feel such disgust? What's wrong with me!?

He has to know what to say and do to fix this. I've fixed him. I've given everything to him. Yes, I'm going to see him and he can explain what the fuck is going on inside me.

Using my keys to open the main door, I stomp up the stairs and put my key in the lock, but his is on the other side. He does this when he wants to be alone…or not disturbed.

I bang on the door, flap the letter-box and hold it open. "It's me- I need to talk to you," I say, not too loudly, into the flat. There's a scuffle behind the door and some mumbling. I've woken him up. I almost fall down the stairs backwards in surprise when he opens the door. He looks dreadful. I feel a pang of regret. My beloved is broken-hearted.

Still dressed in daytime clothes, he smells of sweat and stale alcohol. "Lucy, I'm sorry. Please, baby, don't be angry. Please, I'm sorry. Don't leave me," he is begging and grappling at me as I storm past him into the bedroom. I'm half-pretending to be serious- now I've seen him, I want to see if he might take up my offer of rehab again.

I left a few items here, just in case he would agree to rehab. The idea of totally taking myself out of his flat never felt right. I look around and see cigarette buts, an empty glass by the bed and a bowl of drying noodles on the floor. He's partied in my absence.

"You are a fucking, filthy, lying cunt!" I spit at him. "You've been harassing that old woman AND her daughter since before Christmas!"

"It's not true. She's lying, baby! She's a crackpot. She fancies me!" He can barely make eye contact.

Folding my arms, I step away from him and march towards the kitchen. "I've spoken to her, Jonny," I call over my shoulder.

"She's a liar. They're all liars!" he shouts after me. He's still drunk. "It's you I want. You know that! It's always been you."

In the kitchen now, I grab a carrier bag out of a drawer. "The rest can get tae fuck!" he sweeps his arm around as though his exes are all still here, watching.

Doing this, he nearly loses his balance and grabs at the edge of the kitchen top to steady himself.

I brush past him and hear him follow me back towards the bedroom. "If it's me you want, what the fuck is the deal with Sinead?! Eh? I saw the messages between you! Get a second phone. Heart emojis. Four fucking kisses! What the HELL is that about!?"

Throwing a hairbrush and some pyjama bottoms in a bag, I can't bear to look at him. I hate him and yet I want to hug him. Inhale him. Kiss him. Go to bed. Sleep.

"Sinead's a psycho. She sends these daft messages hoping I will be with her. She lives in a fantasy world! I don't want her. She's a crack-pot. I pretend to be interested cos that's the only time I get to see ma wean!"

It sounds convincing. "Why am I not in on your little plan then?" My face is close to his. "If it's such a great, successful, fucking plan, why are you keeping it from me? Secret conversations. Telling her it's me ruining your contact with the baby? What the hell are you doing!?"

"Because if I slag you off, she's happy. When she hears that, she lets me see the baby. You know that. Every time we fall out, she lets me see it!"

I saw the pattern. He's actually telling the truth for once! "Ok- message her now then. Tell her I'm here and I've given you an ultimatum. It's me or her." I throw the carrier bag on the bed and stand, hands on hips, as solid as I can muster.

"Ok? Fucking call her now!" I screech again. "I gave you an ultimatum yesterday and you lost it at me. I can't do this anymore!"

"Babeeeey," he whines. "She won't let me see the kid if I choose you. Please, baby. Please calm down. We've had 2 years together. It's a long time. Please. I don't want anyone else." He starts to cry. My heart tightens. I want the words to be true more than I have ever wanted anything.

"Look- I asked you yesterday, I repeat yesterday! if you'd get proper help. Proper treatment. It's not about her or your kids. It's about you-you are at the root of all this. Get yourself sorted then everything else will fall into place." I sit down on the bed and look up at him with begging eyes. "Please, Jonny- please do the right thing and get well. For us and for you and for your kids."

Sensing my weakening resolve, his face changes. It twists and turns. His top lip curls back in that familiar snarl. "It's all you! All this is you! Your demands! Your controlling behaviour! It's all you, you, you!" He lunges for me. I rear back and almost fall off the bed. Staring at him, I'm rooted to the spot.

"It's you! You're a cheat and a psycho!" he's shouting in my face. I feel spit hit my top lip. His face is inches from mine and he's leaning over me. "You've ruined my life! I'm going to kill you!" He grabs for my face but I roll away and hit the floor. He's crawling across the bed towards me. I'm terrified.

I skirt round the bed behind him. He's so high and drunk, he can't quite work out how to get at me. I grab the pitiful carrier bag at the same time.

Standing at the door, he's 3 metres away and I throw one last parting shot. "I would never, ever have had a baby with you. You're scum. I'm not like your other exes. I never wanted to own you or keep you with a kid. I loved you for who I thought you actually were. You've lost the best of the lot and I hope you rot in hell!" I start to turn away but want to hurt him badly now. I want my truth to hurt him.

"Oh, and by the way, I went back on the pill 2 weeks after you asked me to come off it. Just before Christmas last year." I smile nastily and enjoy watching his mouth fall open in shock at my betrayal.

He doesn't move, but his face softens again like a scolded child who wants a cuddle. "Please, Lucy- don't leave me," he clasps his hands in front of his chest. It's a good act. "I need you". This time I'm not convinced.

"Go and fuck a granny, Jonny. At least then she won't get pregnant. Save the planet from any more baby-mothers and filthy replicates of you! You're a monster!"

Scrabbling at the door I hear movement behind me- "You fucking cunt!" he's shouting. I manage to get the door open and tear the bag on his keys at the same time. Running down the stairs two at a time, I practically fall out into the street. I run as fast as I can, away from this place.

At home, I unpack my clothes and try to put my head back together. It's the last day of March- irony of all irony's tomorrow is April Fool's day.

Later That Night...

A tiny thought pecks behind my eyes. There it is again...Shona. Peck... The words she used to describe him. Peck...harder now... him friending her on Facebook. Peck, peck...loud now. Painful. Peck, peck, peck...that time she babysat for me. I was working later than usual. Catering an event at the pub. PECK! Her face when I walked in the door. She was white as a sheet and curled up on my sofa, almost sinking into the gap between the arm and backrest. Jonathan on the other sofa...smiling widely. Legs splayed wide. Playing on his phone. Not looking at me but giving off this whiff of satisfaction. She was quiet. I asked if she was hungover or had argued with her wee boyfriend. FUCK! It hits me.

"Shona. Did Jonathan ever try anything on with you? Please tell me the truth. Don't be afraid. He's been at it with everyone. No barriers. None. I'm broken. Please tell me." I send the message through Facebook where we have been active friends since returning from Tunisia. She only babysat once and was often too busy to do it again when I asked her. I would have thought, having just turned 18, the wee thing would have needed the money.

She's online in less than 5 minutes and starts to type. I pray for those dancing blue dots to fucking STOP moving. For the answer to be a long No. As the minutes pass, the blood from every cell in my body rushes not to my feet but out across the carpet. Black and thick and poisoned by the man I adored. 6, 7, 8 minutes pass and I swear to God I want to die.

"Yes. On the holiday he started sending me and Elizabeth, that other girl at the hotel, the thick one? dick pics and once a wanking video. My mum wanted to step in but I was embarrassed and we didn't want to ruin your holiday. I didn't send anything back, I swear. It's why I tried to talk to you in the bar but you clearly were mad for him so I just left it. There's something else... I didn't want to babysit for you anymore because when you were late that time, he came onto me and asked me if I wanted any more videos. Right there in your house sitting right next to me. It was horrible. I was frightened and grossed out. I didn't know what to do. The kids were there and you walked in all happy.

215

I just wanted away and couldn't work out how to tell you. He's been hassling me to go and stay at his flat if I ever go out in Glasgow. He's told me where he lives but I've never stayed and just kept saying no. To be honest, there were times on here when you were upset, I thought you knew what he was doing but just staying with him like some women do. He was just so obviously a letch! You really didn't see it?! Oh, Luce... I'm so sorry, honey xxx"

I pour gin in a glass and tank it in one. I make another. I feel less like I want to kill myself. More like I want to kill him.

I open Facebook- he's unblocked me. Right at the top of his feed is a video. He's posted it within the last few hours. Without thinking, I click play. It's a mistake.

It's him and Sinead in the park. They are taking turns to push the giggling child they share. The toddler swings chubby legs in the air as Jonathan pushes from behind and Sinead howls with laughter in front of the swing, facing their child.

The baby is screeching with joy and Sinead's puffed up with spiteful success. The clothing's from the day before. His favourite black jumper and black denims. I stumble to the bathroom and retch.

After some time, I managed to stand up. Its best I try to message Sinead again- she obviously has no idea about what he's up to with me. She thinks it's over and now she has won. Poor her.

She looks proud as punch. Like I used to look- pink-faced, spitefully in love and emboldened with winning again. Her face like mine was, all excited at the future and adoring of him.

The message goes through. She still hasn't blocked me. Maybe she does want to talk but being a bit shy, doesn't know how to broach it. I try again.

"Sinead, I need to meet with you. You know things I don't and I certainly know things you don't. Please. We can get a coffee. Bring a friend if you would be more comfortable. He's gross. Really gross. Jonathan's has said many awful things about you and I think he has done the same to you, about me. We need to cut him out and talk."

She reads the message. Blue ticks but no response. Suddenly her picture disappears and I realise she's blocked me again.

The Next Day

I'm banging and banging on his door. I want the truth. This is all so fucking vile and confusing. No one is acting normal! I'm going out of my mind! No- I've gone out of my mind!

"What do you want, Lucy?" comes the pathetic, slightly high-pitched voice through Jonathan's letterbox. "I neglected my kids. I loved you. What's gone on!? I deserve the truth. All OF IT! Fucking all of it!" I get louder with each F word. By the time I finish, I sound like an animal roaring.

"I never touched no one!" he squeals. This weakness enrages me further.

I give the door another kick. The hardest yet. I wish it was his stomach. To kick it like he kicked me would feel amazing. It would be bliss to make him feel even 10% of the pain I'm in.

Hearing splintering, I look down to see my effing Converse has half-disappeared into the cheap, council chipboard that lucky for him, is between us. In the silence, I hear him sucking on his fake fag and panting. There's a scuffling sound. He's stumbling off towards the kitchen. "Fuck you then!" I shout into the letterbox. It bangs and I like it. By Jove, its metallic clangs are yummy. I imagine myself slapping the metal off his big, cheating, ugly face.

I stop. Abruptly shocked by damaging the door- this is not my style. I don't like this. I don't like who I am. Violent, aggressive and with nothing to lose.

I close my eyes at the tell-tale pinch that means tears are coming. I'm just like all the others, like Sinead, Gerda & and Cherry-Anne. Like them, I've sat on these stairs crying. I'm just like them. Shame floods through me as my knees turn to jelly.

"She's crazy! She's drunk!" he's shouting. "I dumped her and she's gone mad! She wants me back and I'm saying no!" he lies. My, so fucking easily! He's just the poor guy who wants a good life and to get on with it without me, another psycho ex. He's on the phone to someone. That voice is specially used to talk people round. I guess it's his mum. "Yes. Call the police for me, please. She's still here."

I step back away from the door like it's on fire. The person inside is a stranger. Unsteadily, I just make it to the top stair and sit with my back to the door. I sense him there. He is looking out the spy hole. I rest my head on my knees and wait.

On this occasion (back where my story started), they let me go a few hours later. I was calm and honest and spoke politely about what I'd done and what had me so upset and angry that I caused criminal damage. Luckily, the following Monday, it was thrown out of court citing "no further action".

Within hours of me walking out of the court that day, a friend contacted me to say he had changed his settings to "complicated" and tagged Sinead. Freely boasting about his new-found relationship with his daughter and renewed "special friendship" with our stalker was like a knife to my spine.

Facebook became my only contact with the outside world. Posts about my broken heart, humiliation, need for honesty and support from the man who'd done this to me flowed from my fingers and out into public domains. I hoped he'd see how broken I was, sweep in and rescue me. Wrap me up in a hug and simply hold me. Say sorry, explain it all...... most importantly, fix it all.

Initially, I had a decent volume of support, especially from women he worked with and some males too.

These people had seen Jonathan's partners behave like this before and I think they were sympathetic. I suspect a few of them knew about his cheating and felt a little sorry for me but not sorry enough to intervene months ago!

A few days later, I notice he's unblocked me, so if course I message him. "If I get the truth, I can heal. I can get better. Please talk to me," I beg.

"It's not for me to fix you, Lucy. You're not well... I never touched anyone since I met you. It was just daft messages and you just wouldn't leave it alone. You messed it up" Before I can reply, he blocks me again.

Grieving and half crazy, I started to believe him. No one else with answers would talk to me. It was only his voice I heard. I started to blame myself. Believe I'd got it wrong. That I'd made a huge mistake probing him about his lies. I'd messed up a wonderful relationship. I'd been selfish, greedy and paranoid.

"You are the only woman I have never cheated on- even the lads in the work say that," he crooned a fortnight after I left him.

Long, lonely nights. Too much alcohol. Too much pain. I wanted him back. I wanted to go back. "You made me want to be a better person but I couldn't handle the pressure of our love," comes a message 3 weeks after I left him.

By week 4, I was shaking most of the day and crying all of the night. I could hardly string a sentence together. Sitting in the bath or a chair hurt because my bones were protruding. People were telling me to "get a grip and sort myself out", and several messaged me to say they no longer wanted to be my friend because I was acting "crazy".

I wasn't looking after myself on any level and simply staggering to ASDA to buy gin would make me breathless and dizzy. My family refused to intervene or visit. This debacle was all my fault because I "dropped down a class" by dating him and subsequently got what I deserved.

"He's scum. You should have dated someone like a doctor or lawyer like we told you," my father said when I asked for them to visit and help.

Last Week April 2016

"I'm coming to Glasgow. I'm on shore for a bit. I'm seeing my kids then going home to visit pals, then back on the rig again. I can come see you. We can go out." My old friend from school has been in touch. Paul- my first sexual encounter. We've remained friends ever since.

I'm not ready but I don't want to hurt his feelings. "Ok. I need the distraction, to be honest. I think I'm going crazy. I don't even know what the date is today."

"I'll cheer you up and take you out when I visit then." I think he's the only person I would spend time with. I trust him.

Dozens of other men have been messaging me. Some complete strangers and some exes, even people who confess to having crushes on me and waiting for me to be single. I don't reply. All I want is the man I met 2 and a half years ago.

I'm so thin, my face looks stretched downwards and I've a strange grey complexion. My eyes are sunken and even size 6 leggings hang off me.

I took a selfie and put it on Facebook. A cry for help. Paul's commented on the picture, saying he's going to take me to dinner and fatten me up. I've replied with laughing emojis "it's going to take a while. Bring your credit card. I'm about 7 stone". I would be nice to sit with someone kind and talk about the old days. I need to get out and do something normal; even if it's going to take everything I have, I will do it.

Later

"I miss you, baby- look how thin I got." The message comes in and my mouth goes dry. "I cried when I found your red trainers in the cupboard," he types next and my chest thuds. "I need to see you." The last sentence makes my eyes sting. "Look. I'm lost without you." A picture of himself stood in his bathroom in a small white towel. I see that indeed he has lost weight. He follows it up with a picture of his erect penis. He's won. It was only 2 hours ago Paul posted on my Facebook feed.

"I'm working tomorrow. Backshift. I'll be there about 10 am," he goes offline before I can say any more. He's busy and I'm exhausted.

It's a troubled sleep. The dreams are sexual. In the worst one I'm being chased, but the monster has already caught me once. I'm naked & dragging my wounded leg behind me. Whimpering, I try to limp along a long moonlit empty motorway but I can't move fast enough. There is a car behind me and I know without a doubt I am going to die. Trees loom overhead and I can smell damp grass and hear women's venomous laughter.

I wake myself up as the car reaches me. Its 5.15 am. With a whoosh, I remember he's coming back to me today. He is going to fix this. We will be us again. The pain will stop.

"I've not been near anyone since you left me. I need you," he messages at 9 am. He is on his way. Eager. Hungry. Familiar. "Be there soon, baby," all green hearts and laughing emojis.

I've dressed in one of the few things that still fits me- an ethnic-style summer dress. All my form-fitting ones, and even my shorts hang off my gaunt frame. I feel disgusting. I look terminally ill.

I give up putting mascara on. My hands are shaking and I just want to sleep. Wake up in a month, clean of all of this and ready to start again. I just want to be skin on skin with him. Be held close so I can cry.

Answering the buzzer, I open the door and stand on the landing to wait for him. He always liked it when I greeted him personally.

He bounds up the stairs full of bravado- tanned and recently shaved, with what also looks like a fresh haircut. He looks well and not the frantic, lonely, broken soul who texted me last night.

Wandering after him into the living room, I can't help but hesitate in the doorway as I hear her name, yet again. "Hey, baby. I missed you," he kisses me full on the mouth. "Sinead's stopped me seeing the baby again. She's a fucking bitch". I wince. It's been a month since we broke up and already, she's at it.

"Make me a coffee, would you?" He throws himself into his usual place on the sofa, gets out his phone, puts it on charge and starts sucking on his fake fag.

I make the coffee and practice a smile in the glass door of the microwave next to the kettle. It hurts. My face feels numb & unnatural. He hasn't asked me how I am. He hasn't offered me any comfort. "There you go," I mutter and hand him the steaming cup. He looks up at me a bit confused. What's wrong with her? Why is she not all over me? Laughing and smiling and giggling like usual. "Sit with me, baby. Chill out for, fuck sakes," he pats the sofa next to him and his eyes glitter. I know what he wants and I feel a little sick.

Too tired to do anything or say anything when he starts to talk about his "big swollen balls" and how he's "missed me" so much, I stare right through him, frozen. He's here to have sex with me. He's here to make sure I know he owns me. He's here to stop my recovery and my growing friendship with a nice safe kind man I dated 20 years ago.

He grabs my hand and makes me cup his balls- in less than 5 seconds he's pulled his shorts down and is displaying an erect penis faster than it took me to smooth my dress on my lap. "See how much I missed you. My balls are huge. It's all waiting for you. There's been no one since you," he forces a kiss. I am still holding his balls. He is still holding my hand. I give in.

He has sex with me- and changes slightly half-way through and takes anal without my consent. I play along, my dress up around my waist. This feels wrong.

A stronger woman would have said no early on. I didn't say no. I didn't stop it but I didn't want it. The coffee goes cold as he mutters about how hot I am and how much he has wanted me while I've been away from him. I fake an orgasm just so he cums. He always did when he thought he got me there. The power was such a turn on for him.

He pulls out and sits back on the sofa. He doesn't pull up his shorts. He smiles to himself and starts to look for his e-cig. I pull my dress down and sit slightly away from him, looking at my hands.

He takes a slug of coffee and pulls a face because it's cold. "I'm sorry," I say before I can stop myself. "I can heat it up if you want." He tugs his shorts up and puffs out his chest and stands looking out of my bay window as though expecting an audience.

"No, baby. I'm off to the gym before my shift starts." He's putting his phone in his pocket. He wants out of here. Away from me. Back to his mates in the gym. Back to the life he enjoys without his females there. The manly jokes. The porn. The filthy stories about us all. The arms in an X shape to signify a good-looking target has entered the spa.

"No problem" I whisper and stand up. I feel a drip of his cum slide down my thigh. I need to wash. "Enjoy the gym." I offer a short, sharp smile. It doesn't reach my eyes but he doesn't notice. He's playing with his fake fag- twisting it in his hand to get it to optimum strength.

I pick up the coffee cup and imagine myself throwing it at him square in the face. He stands up and walks past me to the door. This feels all wrong. Dark and twisted and wrong.

"Call you later," he says, with a flip of the hand and steps out onto the landing. The stairwell window is open and the sudden draught makes me shiver. I watch as he bounds down my stairs and stops to look up at me on my half landing. I freeze.

His eyes are dark, predatory, successful. He has been fed. He smiles a soulless, satisfied, vampirical smile that says "I fucked you. I fucked you again".

I recoil. I see the monster and predator he is. The hairs on my arms stand on end and I'm taken back to the last time I saw that look. A 40 something woman in the pool with big jiggly boobs tossing her toddler into the water in the shallows. A black swimming costume covering her ample frame. Plain and in her 40s, she didn't see him staring at her and taking her in. I saw him with that look that day. Standing in the café, I watched him watching her. It had been only a couple of months before. The same predatory, well-fed look.

To my shame, my eyes fill with tears so I back away into the warm safety of my flat. Jauntily jogging down the stairs not looking at me he calls. "Bye, baby! Message you later!" There's an echo and I slam the door to shut him out.

I understand now he thinks this is the beginning of keeping me a filthy secret while he sees Sinead or someone else.

Running into the bathroom, I start to run a hot, soapy sink of water. A bath will take too long. I need him out of me. Off me.

I pull my dress off and throw my knickers in the bin. Naked, I stand in the bathroom and rub at my bony body with a flannel covered in soap. I sob and cry and rant as I wash myself. "Filthy bastard!" "I hate him!" "He's evil!" "You stupid bitch, Lucy." When I look in the mirror, my eyes look almost black with rage and hate. "You have lovely eyes," I hear his voice and smash the mirror.

Shivering and shocked at the mess. I towel myself off in the bedroom. Pyjama bottoms and a jumper. God, I wish it was bedtime.

I strip the sofa cushions and wash them. I hoover, again. I strip my bed even though we didn't even get there. I clean my fridge out. I need to be busy. Turning a talk show on the radio up full blast so I can't hear anything in my head, I get on my hands and knees I scrub the bathroom floor. I use bleach and enjoy my fingers stinging as I scrub and scrub. My nails haven't grown properly for ages & the fingertips have dozens of tiny cuts.

I want every trace of him out of my house. I storm back to my bedroom and go through the washing basket. I throw clothes all over the floor and find a few T-shirts and some underpants as well as one of his work shirts. I put the T-shirts in the bin and push them down into rotting food waste and empty milk cartons. Tearing the underwear up, I grunt and scream with the thrill of it. Hot and sweaty, I wipe round the toilet bowl with the rags I just made. The last time I was on my knees with his underpants in my hands I was blowing him off.

God, I hate him. I hate him with such dark violence he's lucky he bolted. It was necrophilia. I am dead inside and he fucked away on top of me anyway.

Several hours pass and I don't hear from him. I might be a bag of bones and completely out of my mind with grief, but I know him. I know how he operates.

Around 3 pm I receive a message. "Are you OK?" How dare I not chase him after the incredible 12 minutes we shared this morning.

"Yes. Fine, thank you," I manage.

"It was good to see you today x." He's probing for a reaction. My tech silence has shaken him. He doesn't know how to handle me (or anyone) who isn't all over him. I don't reply.

The willpower it takes to turn my phone off is ridiculous but I manage it all the same.

At 7, drink in hand and TV on far too loud, I open my phone and with shaking hands, check my WhatsApp. He's blocked me. Of course he has.

Again, I fall apart on social media. Accusations about what he has done to me and begging to be heard and believed, along with almost suicidal-level grief and posts about how broken-hearted I am.

"If he's so awful, why are you so upset?" reads one message from someone I used to work with. I give up to cry on the sofa. Eventually, I drag myself to bed to simply lie there and stare out of the window.

Listen to: The Carpenters: "Mr Postman"

Red Flags:

- *It's the worst break-up ever. When you split from a Narc you are absolutely in the worst ever ending of any relationship… ever! It's confusing and stressful and bizarrely complex. You have mixed feelings, questions and doubts over your own sanity and decision-making. This is just an exacerbated version of the discards you have experienced and yet you know for sure it's over, so your pain is ten-fold.*

- *Truths suddenly coming out. Once the Narc is apparently out of your life truths of what has REALLY been going on start to float to the surface. In some instances, people who always knew what your Narc was really like, come forward with their stories of what he did to them or people they know. I most other instances "The Mind Fog" is lifting and as they say, "the penny drops" on loads of different things as your memories and instincts and little irregularities all fall into place. It is torture but you can't stop it happening. You won't ever get all your answers, but at the discard stage and for a long time after it, you will certainly get a lot of them!*

- *Other females or friends seem to celebrate your demise and the ending. These supplies and flying monkeys are signalling to you that the Narc has already found your replacement and has been slagging you off for a long time.*

- *The Narc coldly moves on/seems to not be suffering. People with NPD don't feel anything akin to hurt or grief and while you are slowly rotting away in shame and pain, they just… get on with life often with a genuine aura of pride and enjoyment.*

The only way to "hurt" a Narc is to either act like them and move on with another supply yourself or IGNORE them. Although...I know both of these can feel impossible at the time!

May 2016

What happened last week shocked me. I don't like how weak I am so I've made a decision. I've texted Jonathan. "I need closure. One last face to face conversation. Some answers. Then a proper goodbye. It's making me ill." I press send. He blue ticks. He's unblocked me. It's the first Friday of May & a few days after the encounter in my flat.

"I'm on day shift. Home around 5," he replies. Relieved and calm, I feel that tomorrow is the beginning of a new chapter. An opportunity to learn and then, most importantly, heal.

At exactly 5 pm the next day, I press his buzzer. He doesn't buzz me in. Pressing it again, I see him walking towards the security door. Why ask me here to not let me in?

"What's going on, Jonny?" I ask as he opens the door a crack. "I don't want any trouble, Lucy." I pull a face. "What trouble? You had sex with me the other day. You were happy enough then!" He sighs, pulls the door shut behind himself and gestures for me to sit on the step, in the street.

Beside each other now, this feels awkward. He takes the cigarettes from my hand and lights one with my lighter.

"I'm no well, Lucy. I need to be single and to sort my head out," he looks away from me, across the street to the school in front of us. I place a hand on his knee. "It's what I want as well. I'm ill with all the lies and gaps and strange stories going about. That's why I'm here. Just to get closure."

"You imagined most of it for fuck sakes. You're not well. I've told you everything."

A fat tear falls on my skirt. This has been a wasted trip. "Besides, you have cheated on me with that... that Paul guy," he says. He is staring at me now. Angry and jealous. I see a flash of the creature who kicked and burned me. The monster who frightened me and cheated.

"Are you kidding me? You dare say I cheated on you when we are not even together?!" I say this quietly and slowly, sickened by his hypocrisy.

"You moved on too quick. I love you," he says, not crying now. Then a flash of anger. "Oh my God. I can't believe you. I adored you. You fucked with every part of me. I never, ever wanted anyone else. I left you because of the lies- not because of the cheating! How sick is that!? You changed me!" I sob the last few words. He's picking at what looks like a hash hole in his work shorts.

"Fuck it, Jonny. Just you be yourself then. But promise me, you won't keep cheating on women and lying to them. It's not right. Please fix yourself." I can't help but wipe my nose on my sleeve.

Sensing I'm about to leave, he starts to cry. "I had sex with you the other day because I missed you. I haven't been with anyone since you, I swear on the weans' lives." Yes, YOU'RE reading this and you know he was lying.

"I need to go." Standing up, I put my sunglasses back on just as 2 of his neighbours come around the corner and I look down to hide my red, blotchy face. "Alright, mate?" the guy neighbour says to Jonathan, then looks at me.

"Yeah, man. All good." Jonathan treats him to a smile. They step between us and open the door. I envy them- this happy couple walking past us to go upstairs for a Saturday evening together, just like we used to. I swallow a lump in my throat and run my hands through what hair I have left.

"I don't know why you had to do this, Jonny. I never asked for anything except fidelity, sobriety from drugs and basic honesty. I don't understand why you did what you did and won't fix it?" I try and get him to look at me but he's looking down at his feet.

"I love you, Lucy, but I can't be with you. If we are meant to be together, we will find each other again. It will be fate." I feel sick at the crap he wants me to swallow.

"Just sort yourself out. Be a better person and please don't let Sinead do this to another girl who cares for you. She broke us and she's breaking you." He nods and looks down at his lap again, before taking another one of my cigarettes and stands up, putting it in his pocket. He kisses me on the forehead. "You're right, baby. I will do that."

I walk away before he has a chance to say any more. I can't be here anymore.

He shuts his front door. I don't care it sounded like a slam. This was the right thing to do and I feel oddly comforted now.

At home, I eat a meal for the first time in over a month. I even manage a few hours' sleep. This feels like the end of us and the beginning of me again. Thank God.

I'm sitting in the park in the sunshine, reading. I used to read a book every week before I met Jonathan. Desperately trying to find myself again, I'm lathered up in tan oil. With tiny little pigtails, I sit back in the sun and post a selfie of myself. Sunglasses, little skirt and chunky thriller on my lap.

It's about a week since we had the doorstep chat & I've grabbed a few hours to myself while the kids are at school. I'm calm and not unhappy, occasionally checking Facebook and reading a chapter of my book here and there. My concentration is horrendous and I keep forgetting the bits I've read. I'm still not really sleeping or eating, but I feel now he is my past and it's helpful.

My phone buzzes about an hour after I posted the park selfie on Facebook. Number withheld- odd. Maybe it's the school.

"Hello, Lucy speaking," I say cheerfully. "Mrs Hawksby, it's the police. I need to speak with you about an allegation of breach of the peace and harassment," a male voice says.

My heart stops. I look around the park, frantic and confused. "What do you mean?" My book falls to the ground. At the clapping sound, a family nearby enjoying a picnic turn and look at me.

"Your ex-partner has contacted us with a complaint today. I got off the phone with him a few minutes ago. We assured him we would speak to you.

He says you turned up at his property unannounced last Saturday, around 2 pm, and that you were drunk and abusive. You were shouting and threatening, ranting through the letterbox.

The officer's words are like bullets- the lies so extreme. And yet, true... it's like he's mixed up recent history & added bits in to humiliate and criminalise me even more!

He's still talking. That monotone, emotionless labelling, I admit, yes, I'm mortified "you need to cease contact with him or we'll have to arrest you and charge you with a domestic and a breach of the peace."

A cloud goes over the sun and I feel shivery all of a sudden. Pulling my pretty linen skirt over my knees pointlessly and shivering, I try to make peace with this person who has never even met me "This makes no sense. We agreed to talk and have a last chat as part of our break up. We sat outside and I didn't even go in his close to get 3 floors up to his letterbox. He smoked my fags. We were both upset, but I swear no one shouted and no one was threatening- not even him!" My voice has gone up several octaves in panic. I'm afraid now and because of this, true to form, I sound rather irate.

"In light of the damage to his door in the month prior, we believe his version of events," the officer is cold and dislikes me. I can feel it.

"Wait. wait. wait! The neighbours saw us. Have you spoken to the neighbours?! Oh, hang on! He was working that day and the pool doesn't shut until late afternoon! How could he have seen me shouting when he was still at work 6 miles away? Speak to his boss too- ask for his shift timetable! He's lying... look please listen to me. I don't know why but he's lying!" Loud and panicked, my words are like a firing a tommy gun.

I need to calm the fuck down. People are looking, yet I can't stop talking. "Why's he doing this? I don't get it. We left it on good terms and that's the last contact I've had! I've moved on. He cheated. He harmed me. He took drugs. I dumped him!"

"Calm down Mrs Hawksby. Just take my advice and leave him alone," the hostile, practised voice of someone who's never been where I am.

"I've left him alone! It's him who wanted sex with me 2 weeks ago, and a month before that! Look....yes, it's been messy, but whatever he's told you is just not true." I hate miserable, desperate, high-pitched me right now and in panic, I start to cry.

"Listen to my advice or you'll really be in trouble, Mrs Hawksby." He's is firm and unsympathetic, then the phone goes dead. I want to scream across the park! I don't deserve this!

10 minutes ago, this mascara-streaked, pale, crazy girl was quietly reading a book in the sun. Now she's a mess and looks scary.

Later That Evening

In my desperation to talk, I've sent too many WhatsApp's to Sinead. Freaking out at this new turn of toxicity, I'm obsessed with telling her Jonathan is so toxic that he's even lied to police! Maybe if I can explain, she will realise he's the liar and not me.

She's reading them and not blocking me, so I supposed she just needs time to think. Hours go by and she comes online then disappears over and over again. It becomes weird and unsettling.... tipsy, no, drunk, I don't click what's happening. The truth will fix me and help her. I just know it.

Ping! That familiar Facebook sound; it's a friend request and message. Accepting without hesitation, I open it. Let's face it, things can't get much worse.

"Listen, you fucking psycho home-wrecker! Leave Sinead alone. She doesn't want to talk to you!" Maybe I read it wrong. Nope- it definitely says Home-wrecker. That's odd. What home? Wrecked? I don't get it. I'm struck dumb with surprise and I'm also quite drunk.

"Don't fucking speak to me like that!" I retort. Fuelled with shock, I type again. "I never wrecked any fucking home. Sinead created the whole illusion that he proposed! She bought her own fucking ring. He never wanted a relationship with her and that baby was her last try to capture him!"

"Are you kidding me?! She bought her own ring because he had no money. They planned that baby. He was obsessed with having another kid! They were engaged, a couple, and you waded in and ruined it for my friend. She's a wonderful person who never deserved all this! You're a slut!" I'm not quite with it. This is just a strange barrage of abuse from a lunatic.

"What? That's lies. He told me the complete opposite. That's not true. He told me he was single. He claimed he was "looking for love"- he chased me round the works spa for like 6 months! We met in late November 2013! Got together in June 2014!"

As I type it, I feel the horror of her truth wash over me like a tidal wave. I'm drowning. Oh, God. More hurt, just as I'm staggering to my feet, more pain.

"They were still together in Easter 2014," says the next message. Thank God I'm drunk. Oh my God. I'm a home-wrecker?!

If there was such a thing as mind-whiplash, I've got it. The force of what this woman, this random neighbour, says, hits me full force. "He left her in April, I think. Around Easter 2014. He'd been painting the nursery for the baby and then one day just didn't come back. Blocked her and that was that. She was devastated. Broken-hearted, you bitch!" The words blur together.

"Look. I don't know about any of this! I swear to God I believed until a moment ago he hadn't had anyone since he met me in Nov 2013! I honestly believed him that Sinead was what he claimed she was, a casual bed partner who was desperate to trap him any way she could. I had no reason to mistrust it because she acted so mental this whole time! Not one person stepped in to mess with his version of events. It's not my fault!"

She's relentless: "Oh, and the baby was planned! Sinead had some fertility problems so they planned it properly." My heart stops "You're the slut who broke them up!" It's all too much. I crawl to the bathroom and sit on the floor holding my phone.

Oh, fuck! My strange obsession with asking him if he'd "touched" anyone else since Sinead that November 2013 now is starting to make sense. Fuck! I must have probed him on that timing and gap of alleged celibacy a dozen times. I couldn't help myself. My innate intuition just didn't like his answer "no, no one in months, Luce. No one since her that night".

Oh my God, this is why! My instincts were trying to help me! I ignored my own fucking instincts!

I slowly rock back and forth, watching the little blue dots on the screen as she types. What now? Oh God, what now?

I start to cry. I'm a home-wrecker. All the time he wooed me and drew me away from my marriage, he had been having sex with her. Planning a life with her. Fooling her and fucking with me.

"I am so sorry! Please tell her I didn't know! I type frantically. "I'm begging you please tell Sinead now! No one told me. He lied the whole time to us both. He's set us up to hate each other and harm each other. I see that now!"

I look nuts. I look like I'm trying to harass her but I don't stop. I can't stop.

"Is she with him now? Are they together now? It looks like they are in his posts! I don't know. He came to my house on the last Monday of April and had sex with me. We talked for a wee bit after, but now the cops are saying he's wanting to get me arrested! Please tell her. I need to speak to her!"

"I'm on holiday. I'm busy. I'll tell her when I see fit." the neighbour replies. I stop. What?! What the actual fuck? "You're playing God with our lives! You can't do that! She needs to know. If she is with him, she needs the truth!" I type, fast.

"I told you, I'm busy. Now leave me alone!" she replies. Shocked, upset and freaked out, I admit I lose it. I can't help myself. "Listen, you interfering bitch. You've called me all names under the sun and it's clear you have the influence to at least explain I'm not what that bastard says I am, and maybe Sinead isn't what he says she is!"

She's enjoying this. Quickly it degrades into a bitch fight with us just being horrible to each other. It's late at night, I'm a little drunk and very, very fucked up. The lies! Those dreadful lies. All this time!!!! Eventually, she blocks me and I go to bed, to drink and cry. Of course.

A Few Days After the Police "Warned Me Off" ...

My phone has a few records of missed private calls- I don't answer these. I suspect it's something bad- it always is these days. Now I'm not working, I rarely have need to check my emails, but bored and listless, I've started to do it every other day, in the vain hope someone might offer me a job based on LinkedIn again, or maybe some sort of win on one of the daft recipe comps I like to enter.

"Would it be possible for you to call me on the number at the footer of this email, Mrs Hawksby?" the email from Jonathan's workplace reads. I recognise the logo. Why would the hotel, or someone working there, want to speak to me? Puzzled and slightly uneasy, I call the number. As he talks, dread pools inside my chest and wafts upwards to behind my eyes... I can hear the words but I can't make sense of them. It's just too shocking.

"There have been some complaints...in regards to...your partner."

"Ex-partner," I interrupt him and wince at how nasty I sound. "Sorry-he's my ex-partner. I ended it about a month ago now, no, longer-almost 2 months, but we have seen each other a few times since."

"Women have made complaints," there's that word again. What does he mean "complaints"? Then of course, it hits me. Hard. I gasp. He hears me. "I understand this is a shock and I also understand you've not had a good time of it. Can you help us in our formal investigation? I head up the HR team and we would like to interview you about his conduct in the hotel, particularly the gym and spa... we have been told that you may have insight into how he behaves with women on the premises."

"I'm more than happy to help." My voice is different now. Firm, decisive and lacking in any emotion. "He needs stopped, Mr Miller. When do you want me in to speak to you?"

"Tomorrow is best. The sooner the better. We've had concerns for a while now...but it's only recently that I've come into the post and I'm making it my mission to clean up our teams. He's only the beginning."

"Can I ask when the women have made these complaints... the recent ones?" I murmur. I don't want to know, but I need to know."

"One a few months ago and another one in the last few days." The words are like slaps to my skull. "Please try and stay calm. We've spoken to him already and he has denied it 100%. In fact, he's saying you hacked his computer and has already armed himself with a union rep. It's you we need to speak to because you were his partner through some of the complaints and we understand he met you here, at the spa also.

Do I care about Jonathan's job? His hunting grounds? No. Do I care about my own reputation and loyalty to him and his colleagues? Yes. There's no way he's going to blame me for his own creeping, filthy behaviours. No fucking way! "No problem. When do you want me to come in?"

Humiliated and disgusted, I lit Facebook up with post after post of his behaviours- details, sickening details that people found offensive and shocking. Online, I was frantic and looked absolutely bonkers. Just like Sinead had called me. Back then she was wrong. Now she was right.

I made stupid memes up referring to Jonathan and Sinead that someone actually reported as offensive. I posted names, dates and times of his behaviours. Slowly, my friends list dwindled. My version of events was disgusting- how could we have appeared so happy and in love while he did all this?! I must be a liar. I must be a psycho like he said I was. How dare both of us con them... because let's face it, in a strange way, I lied to them too, just like I lied to myself. People liked us, cared about us and congratulated us on announcements, great pictures and soppy chats in open threads. We seduced them.

A couple of people did dare to message me offering support. A few precious ones gave me more information proving I was not the first of his victims. I tried to contact his older children's mothers to explain he had conned me, fed me poison about them. I tried to communicate that I was sorry that I had believed him over them. They didn't reply.

Someone anonymously messaged me threatening to anally rape me, set my kids on fire and tell people I had sex with my father. I reported this believing it was Jonathan. The police said they would visit him and disclosed I was his 4th domestic violence conviction. By this point, I was so far gone I wasn't even shocked.

His ex-girlfriend Gerda and I messaged often, discussing Jonathan and the patterns of behaviour and it was the only thing that soothed me. When she mentioned Narcissistic Personality Disorder, I googled it immediately.

I started to understand I wasn't a lone victim. I was one of thousands and thousands all over the world. This was a revelation. A tiny light at the end of a long tunnel.

I joined Narc awareness clubs and discussion groups and shared my advice and my experiences, but I still wasn't really well enough to. I came across as manic and rather aggressive at times. I was desperate to join the dots and get answers, and yet was still filled with hate and rage. This complex display of emotions unsettled people and I was called names. I was accused of simply being on some sort of 'seek and destroy' mission. I struggled to communicate properly. I couldn't calm the pictures and voices in my head and the only way was for it to pour out, and often it appeared toxic.

I didn't know how to explain how I felt or what he did to me and the others I now knew about, because it was all so fresh and harsh and agonising. I was drinking far too much and this was beautifully blurring the lines and drowning my inhibitions. Ranting and raving on my private Facebook page, I vented everything I felt and tried to get people to understand. I went too far but I just couldn't see it.

Around mid to late May, I started seeing someone. I had to. Now I loathed Jonathan rather than missed him, I'd started to crave sexual contact.

A local guy named Richard with bad tatts, addictions and a crazy ex, he landed right at my feet.

100% on the rebound and part-fucked up and part-faking it, I threw myself and the kids into twisted Happy Families and allowed him to move in the day after we first had sex. I was trying to replace Jonathan, comfort myself and do anything but think. It was a ridiculously stupid, immature and inappropriate decision, so of course I went with it. I was way past making good decisions in pretty much most parts of my life by now.

Yesterday, I made a new friend. We got chatting on the phone FINALLY! after talking online the last few weeks. She's a woman about my age from AA (Natalie). She's helping me navigate where

235

AA itself played a part in what's happened. It's incredibly culty and seems to have no responsibility for any members hurting either each other or "outsiders" like me.

Natalie told me a horrible story and the shock of it has made me feel like I'm going crazy.

Crying and only half listening, I take a slurp of wine and light a cigarette "Did you not hear about this woman in his group? She killed herself, Lucy!" Natalie blurts out suddenly. We had been talking about me changing my phone number, but this grabs my attention like an iron fist.

"No. What do you mean? Killed herself? He used to say all alcoholics are killing themselves without AA. Arrogant prick," Natalie snorts and I take another glug. "No, no. She actually died," Natalie says more gently now. Something prickles and then starts to stab at my memory. Then the truck full of horror hits me. "Natalie, did the woman go on a mad binge and relapse because she slept with one of the people in AA and he dumped her and showed people personal pics and stuff"? The wine has gone to my head and I feel violently sick even saying the words. I know what she's going to say next. "Yeah. How do you know?!" she replies sharply. "Don't tell me he admitted it to you? Oh, my God. Honest for the first time ever. Creepy bastard. Could that be more evil? Never mind. Don't answer that." I hear her take a suck on her spliff. She must be sitting in the garden. It's hot today- the midges will be hellish.

Fuck, I'm numbing out. The shock of this has just made me go cold. I put my glass down before I drop it. I can't feel my hands. My mouth is dry and everything's going black. "Natalie, I have to go. I think that's my buzzer." Before I even hear her say goodbye, I've hung up and I'm retching, running to the toilet.

It's nearly midnight and yet the air is still warm from today's late May sun. My phone's buzzing in my pocket. We've been out for the evening and Richard is just ahead of me, smoking a joint. I don't like it. It makes me feel sick.

Instinctively, I know it's Jonathan. This is a booty call. He's going to try to do this monthly. Like a period, he will turn up, expected and unwanted.

A solid growl- "what the fuck do you want?" is all I can manage. Loudly enough for Richard, 5 yards ahead of me, to spin round and look at me.

"I mish you, baby. Can I come shee you? ... I'm shorry. I love yoush" he slurs. My gut clenches at his familiar voice then hardens in pain at the memories. A cackle escapes me, a hard, jagged spurt of laughter at his arrogance and daring. "Away and take a fuck to yourself instead of me this time, you cunt!" I hiss and hit the screen hard to cut him off. I almost throw it onto the road with fury.

About 20 past midnight, my phone rings again. Richard and I are in the bath by this time, so with a wink, I put it on speaker. I put a finger to my mouth to shush Richard and settle back for the shite I know is coming. My expectations were met, then exceeded.

"Baby, I love you. Come on. I'm sorry"- he sounds a little more sober now.

"Are you actually kidding, Jonny? Are you actually fucking serious?" I can't believe I am actually shocked that he has resurfaced again. A month ago, he fucked me. Two weeks ago, he made a false report to the police that I caused some sort of breach of the peace and traumatised him. What is wrong with this guy?!

"You fucking lied to the police to fuck me over! You told a complete pack of lies to them about when I came to yours a month ago! Why would you do that?!"

"Oh, baby. I don't know. I've not been well. I don't remember anything. Those pigs lie and twist things. Come on, you can't just sweep away 2 years together. We're soulmates. I need you."

He's pleading now. I like it. If I was a guy, I'd get a hard-on. Richard is watching from the tap end and drawing on his spliff. He knows I can handle this.

"Look, I'm a bit busy for your shit now, Jonny. I'm in the bath with my boyfriend. We've things to do. Things like fuck. Fuck and probably fuck again. Oh, and he's taller than you and younger than you. So, jog on!" I smile as Richard splutters a laugh and desperately tries to cover his mouth without getting his joint wet.

"You cunt. You whore, slut, cunt, bitch. I'm fucking going to come to your door and fucking batter him. He's a junkie. I've seen him. He's a fucking ugly junkie bastard!" He is shouting and

237

ranting and I feel a warm glow. This means I have got to him. I have hit him where it hurts and I have hit him hard.

"Oh, you've seen him, have you? How's that, babe? Have you unblocked me to watch me move on? For once in your life, Jonny, you aren't getting what you want. I'm not like the others. I'm not giving in. You're pure evil and you can fuck off back to an ex. Again!" I can't help but shout. I want to reach into the phone and tear his retinas out.

"Listen, mate. You heard her. Just leave it" Richard has intervened. "I'm going to kill you!" Jonathan shouts. I take pleasure knowing he's seething.

He was expecting a repeat of last month. A wan, pale me, silent and sad underneath him while he satisfies himself. "You're a fucking bitch and your kids are ugly and stupid." I hear the words but it takes me a second to realise he HAS actually said that. My beautiful kids who adored and worst of all, trusted him with their mummy. I see red.

"Come on, father of the year! Where are your 3 kids by three different idiots, eh?" How dare he mention my children!

"The baby's here actually!" he declares. My blood runs cold. He has a toddler in his house now? Alone? And he's drunk and almost certainly high, screaming and shouting at us at midnight? "Your high and delusional. If Sinead has let you have that little one on your own, she's as fucking insane as you are. You belong together, the pair of you, and I feel sorry for that kid, the other kids and the fucking future kids you will drag out of poor cows for the rest of your miserable, disgusting life."

I hit end call and glare at Richard. He looks a little afraid. He hasn't seen this side of me. "Make me a drink. Let's go to bed." I'm shaking with rage and I grit my teeth to try and stop juddering in shock.

While Richard's in the kitchen, my phone buzzes again- it's him. I ignore it. I hear it again 10 minutes later and eventually when we go to bed, I put it on silent.

Waking up the next morning, of course I check my phone. A series of WhatsApp's are waiting for me. It's him. "Rich, do me a favour, go make me a coffee before you go, will you?" I kiss him and gently push him out of bed. He groans, but of course he does as I ask. "No bother- I need a smoke anyway." I watch him stand up. He has a hot body. It's better than Jonathan's. A more natural, rangy, muscular shape. I fancy him for sure. It's just a shame he's a waster with nothing to offer. He'll do for now though.

I hear the front door open and then shut. Waiting for that green smell to waft in, I can't help but feel nervous. I get a sniff and realise Richard's safely out of the way.

There are 5 messages, all in the early hours of this morning. There are pictures too. It takes me a few seconds to work out what they're of. As I realise, my heart quickens. I sit up straight and hold the phone tighter. He's sent me pictures of his wrists. Slit wrists. "I'm in hospital, baby. Look what you did to me," he's even put crying emojis and broken hearts. I feel an odd urge to go to him and help him and it's followed up by self-disgust and shame. "I can't live without you" the most recent message, sent just after 10am reads.

"You brought this all on yourself Jonathan." I need to sound strong. I can't let him suck me back in. I can't. I want to, but I can't.

He blue ticks my messages and comes online immediately. He's been waiting for me. "I can't be without you, baby," he whinges.

"I can see your red shorts and your skanky grey carpet- you're not in hospital at all! I don't want you near me. You can't even slit your wrists properly."

"You whore prostitute whore bitch!" he replies. Ah. The real Jonny! The rage and hate and spite because I dare to say NO. "I've got someone too!" he declares.

"Well stop begging me back then, you rat! I'm sure she's great! Your taste is impeccable!"

"Yeah well, you ruined my life!"- that old chestnut again. "Oh, Jonny. Come on! What's this all about? Why do you want to hurt me? Have you not done enough? Why are you lying all the time? To anyone who will listen?" I'm stupid enough to try to reason with him. Dig a little for hidden honesty.

"I'm not lying. You're a whore. You're a cheat. You are a psycho!" he rants. "I wish you well, Jonathan. Go and sort your life out," is my last message before I block him.

Opening the pictures and enlarging them with a slide of my fingers, I can see the cuts are quite deep, although not life-threatening on any level. Superficial and desperate attempts at emotional blackmail.

A tiny part of me wants to go to him. Make sure he's ok. I squash it like a fly and slide in the shower behind Richard. I spin him around by the hips & get on my knees. I forget all about Jonathan as Richard holds my head in his hands and the water rushes over us.

I didn't hear from Jonathan again but I did hear from the police.

Listen to: Queen: "I Want to Break Free"

Red Flags:

- *Reputational Damage.* This is a well-known term to describe how toxic people create credibility for themselves and manage how to discard and humiliate you and still seem "perfect" to others around you. It is during the devaluation stage you will start to make noise on social media, to the Narc's friends and family and anywhere you have previously been seen to be happy. Once you are discarded and blocked, you can't help but try to reach out to your beloved and get answers. Yes, you look like a nutter. A psycho. A stalker even. The Narc has successfully again made one of his/her partners look bonkers while they still look normal.

- *Setting you up as a supply.* This ending the relationship as it was and creating a pattern where they get in touch, hoover a little and have sex with you. With Jonathan, it looks like he was going for a monthly routine and certainly each time I was ever seeing someone else.

- *Using services/agencies as weapons.* This would be threatening you with reports to social services or the police or actually going through with it. It can be making false allegations or setting you up to fail and then reporting your mistake. The mistake can be you going to their property believing it was a *mutual agreement, having friends hiding somewhere to bear false witness and say you were drunk/irate/shouting. Narcs believe that services like the police (for example) are tools to harm your sense of safety and reputation. They love making these "set ups" and will use any means possible. Watch out for these "punishments" after you have rejected them or found them out.*

- *Ruining newness. Narcs can't bear to see you not just happy but being with someone. In other words, they don't want you but they don't want you with anyone else. They will stalk not just you, but any new partner. They will sabotage new jobs, new partners and maybe even new friendships where they can. They will watch you on social media to gain info to help them do this, so watch for bad things happening when you appear to be doing well.*

June 2016

The buzzer has been going late at night this last few days. My phone's also been receiving even more withheld calls. I assumed it was Jonathan or someone connected to him- an angry female or maybe some pissed-off boyfriend of a new victim. Ignoring them all, I tried to carry on with my recovery. Half-hanging out of my tree, but with no contact to Jonathan and now Sinead, I knew I'd get there in the end.

On the first Friday in June 2016, I had another call from the police. They wanted a chat about another allegation of harassment, they said. Surprised, but unperturbed, I toddled off to the station the next day, straight after the school run. It was a lovely sunny day and I had plans for the weekend with Richard and the children. I'd never been interviewed by the police so assumed that if you are invited for a chat, it was simply that- a chat.

"We're going to tape this interview, Ms Hawksby. Would you like a solicitor present?" the officer says to me while his partner sits silent and watching me. My heart flutters a little. This is a lot more formal than I expected. "I don't have one. I don't really know what this is about, to be honest." I smile at the silent officer

and then at the one clearly in charge. I am hopeful that they will
see I am not the sort of person who belongs here. I've tried to dress
smartly in summer trousers, a vest top and sandals. I have plans to
take Richards dog for a walk later before I pick the children up
from school. I really need to get some shopping in at some point.
I hope this won't take long. I look at the clock behind the officers'
heads. 9.35 am.

"We've an allegation of harassment here, Ms Hawksby. Your
ex-partner, a Jonathan Kergan." Something painful spreads across
my chest and up into my throat. Fuck, I can't breathe.

"I don't understand. What do you mean?! How have I
harassed him?"

"He claims that you went to his house a month ago, erm...
early May I believe, and caused him fear and alarm by being under
the influence of alcohol, shouting through his letterbox and
threatening him. He claims you've constantly harassed him since
he ended his relationship with you in late March and that you've
stalked him since. He further claims that you have been so intense
with this demanding behaviour that he was pushed into self-
harming and attempting suicide recently." Both male officers look
disgusted.

My stomach tightens. This can't be happening. I don't
understand. "Look, that's his version of events, but he hasn't told
you that he's the one who has contacted me. That he came to my
home and had barely-consensual sex with me a month ago and that
he tried to do it again only a few days, maybe a week ago. The night
before he hurt himself, he called me 4 times wanting to come and
sleep with me! Is that someone who is being stalked or is that a
stalker?!" My voice has gone up in pitch and I sound as freaked out
as I feel. I try to take a breath and calm down. They won't believe
me if I don't calm the fuck down.

"Look. I have witnesses. I have the messages of him inviting me
to his house that time he says I was at fault, so I can prove he
wanted me there. There was no shouting. Even he didn't shout! I
swear on my life that's all wrong," my voice catches and I look
down. I notice little half-moons on the palms of both hands from
where I've clenched my fists too tight. "I don't know why he is

doing this!" I start to cry. "Please just let me show you in my phone," I reach across the table for it but the silent officer takes my phone swiftly, and puts it between himself and his colleague, face down. It lies on top of the statement Jonathan has signed and swore as the truth.

"We are seizing your phone. Any evidence you have is for court." The quieter officer has the cheek to smile at me. A self-satisfied (won on a scratch card, had a blow job this morning) smile. I want to scrabble across the table and poke him in the eye.

"What?! Court?! If you just let me show you, then there is no need for court. It's all lies! Yes, I've sent texts and stuff, but the things he did to me have been evil. He's made me ill. He's still wanted to see me, have sex with me, talk to me since those messages so how is it effin' fear and alarm?!"

"Watch your language miss. I can see you are quite aggressive, which proves our point of why you are being charged today." Both chairs screech as they stand up. "It's best we put you in a cell while we wait for your solicitor. I suggest you get one quickly as we have more questions for you later. There have been other allegations from other witnesses." The room blurs and tilts. Looking up at them, I realise I can't blink. It's the strangest feeling. Like I'm frozen in a nightmare but with my eyes open.

Before I can say a word, he's beside me and clicking handcuffs on my wrists, and I smell stale sweat and coffee breath. He has to turn the cuffs to the smallest setting because I'm so thin. "Please let me prove it's lies. I can't stay here. I've a dog and 3 kids at home. Wriggling and pointlessly tugging my arms to pull away from him, I'm absolutely panicking. This is all new. A horrible scary mistake. How is this happening?

When I walked into the station 25 minutes ago, a big, round, jolly officer called Jo had welcomed me with a smile and "take a seat, someone will be out shortly". Now no one is jolly. Other idiots like me are sitting sullen and hungover, on grubby wooden benches lining the glass-walled holding area. I can smell stale alcohol and fear.

At the booking-in desk, 2 stern, well upholstered female officers and a steely-haired desk sergeant start to ask me questions.

Do I have any sharp objects on me? Yes, I like to carry scissors around just in case anyone fancies a sudden fringe. Have I been drinking? Yes. I had vodka on my cereal and a shot of tequila with the school lollipop lady. Do I take drugs? No, because I can't afford them. Am I feeling suicidal? I don't want to kill myself, but I do have a list of potential murder victims in my pocket. Do I require a doctor? Yes, for free drugs.

"Undo your trousers, I need to take the cord out of them so you can't harm yourself," an officer says, waving some small scissors at me. "You're not cutting the cord on these! They're River island!" I explain and hear a snort behind me from a junkie wearing trousers with the cord cut out.

She smiles nastily and says "Procedure. For your own safety". Snip- the trousers are ruined. It's a relatively silly thing but it tips me over the edge and I start to cry quietly. This is mental. I don't belong here! Wiping my nose on my sleeve, I watch as she has the cheek to put the cord in the plastic bag now sitting on the desk with the rest of my belongings in.

Every question and every move are designed to remind you that this is a place for people who have a habit of making mistakes.

Shoe-less, all hairpins removed and tearful, I'm marched to the cell nearest the fire exit at the end of a long, cold corridor. The officers walked either side of me, each holding a wrist as though I had been arrested for fucking murder, not some daft messages to my ex.

I'm taken aback to see there's no bed of any description in the cell, just a long, blue, plastic mat. I never have liked Yoga.

The cell is plushly decked out with all you could ever need- the mat, a scratchy blanket, and a leaflet on your rights as an arrested person. In the corner (right by the fucking door), is a lid-less, seat-less, aluminium toilet staring at me with its one eye. "All yer own fault hen," comes her tinny judgemental voice.

To add insult to injury, you have to press the buzzer for the turnkey to flush Long Joan Silver from the outside- lovely. "Hi! I've done a jobby! I'm not allowed the dignity of flushing it myself and have to announce any bodily function through the wee hatch in the door! Winning at life.

12 hours ago, I'd naively trotted down to the police station. The sun on my back, shoes and bag matching, looking like I was off for a day shopping at a cute seaside market, not getting booked for a telecommunications offence because of a pack of lunatics out for my blood.

It's now late morning, and my fury at being arrested for an inflated crock of shit has cooled to sub-zero. The cold pock-marked stone walls around me aren't helping. I'm now just frightened and confused.

I've been assured my solicitor is on his way and then, and only then should I give a statement. That's fine- we can get this all cleared up.

"Hey! I'm the victim here and this is all a mistake," I want to shout. Surely the cops can simply look at my phone and see all his calls to his "psycho ex who's caused him fear and alarm". It's me who should be reporting him- that call, the texts and the pictures from last week were horrendous. I should have reported it but I just wanted to get on with my life.

Not to mention the dick pics and messages about how "thin" he's got and the agreement we made to meet, not just at the end of April but early May too?!

Every half an hour, a turnkey loudly checks each resident in each cell. This is to make sure we haven't managed to commit suicide, apparently. Yeah, by eating the yoga mat or drowning ourselves in the toilet. In fact, jeez...I really wish I had a hairpin so I could French-plait myself to death.

As soon as you start to drift off into a more comforting state of numbness, simmering fear and silence under the blanket, the door rattles and the turnkey shouts "Ok? Hello! I need to see your face to see you're ok!" They only stop shouting Ok (ffs!) and leave you alone once you wave a hand or poke your face out from under the charming, piss-scented blanket. It's a cruel and unusual torture... I'm pretty sure it was used in concentration camps, shouting at people who try to sleep when sleep is all they have and all they want...

The only thing I wanted to do was sleep until I could go home. Walking round a sunshiny, pebbly yard, whistling Flight of the

Concord wasn't an option and apparently, you don't get cigarette breaks either. It's not like it is on the telly. I'm disappointed.

Around lunchtime, the metal window slides open again and a new face peers in. I see flashes of neon green and black and hear their radios crackling. I get a sudden flash- 2 other police officers had come to speak to me. This is where it gets nasty.

"We have an allegation that you sent a picture of a penis to an associate of your ex-partner. A K Burnley. We are arresting you for this as we have seen the picture in question and can identify the Facebook account as yours. We also have messages of an abusive nature to other family members of Mr Keegan, his cousin and wife."

Apparently, Jonathan's cousin and wife had now (coincidentally, on the same day) made an allegation that I harassed and traumatised them. I was being charged with it to run alongside what Jonathan had accused me of. All I had done was demand (too many times) that they get him to pay back money he owed me. I got myself in a state then. I really did. And as usual, I started to cry in sheer frustration. The last time I had any contact with any of them had been a few weeks before!

The police again said matter-of-factly, that detail was for the courts and essentially, I just had to live with it.

K had been my friend. I had only sent him the picture to say if Jonathan didn't give me back the £400 he owed me, I would post it online. This was pre-revenge porn laws and I never meant it at all. I sent it to K and laughing emojis came back from him with "send me another one. Lol"- We had never argued. I liked him. Jonathan had got to him too.

The officers swiftly left and I was alone again. It started to sink in; Jonathan was on the warpath. He wasn't satisfied with me just lying in my own puddle of despair and misery after his cheating and abuse of me. Oh no- he wanted to do as much as possible to humiliate me even further, many weeks after I managed to leave him. He was going to destroy me and use any weapon possible.

Freezing cold, and getting colder as time passed, I pressed the bell for someone to come and bring me a second blanket- I was given a long, purple, corduroy curtain. What did they want me to do? Pull myself together? I allowed myself a giggle then- this was bizarre. More than cruel and unusual.

The curtain was big enough, though, that I managed to wrap myself up in it like a big magenta caterpillar and it was vaguely comforting, especially if I covered my eyes- until turnkey tapped the door to make sure I wasn't dead again.

About 5 pm, I had more visitors- oh joy! Again, 2 more officers, different ones this time. Again, I was read my rights for a 3rd time. I felt like fucking Scrooge.

This 3rd time, lo and behold (play on words there) Sinead had decided I had caused her fear and alarm and apparently, I had "stalked and harassed" her for 11 months.

She left out all the bits where she had made contact with me, Niall or my work and where she had repeatedly blocked and unblocked me and wound Jonathan up at the same time to set me up to lose my temper. Yeah- she forgot to tell the cops that bit.

This is how Narcs work, but no one sent the memo to the police. Shame that.

Stevie Wonder himself would have realised I was a victim- that I had been manipulated, set up and victimised by these people. Not one professional person mentioned Coercive Control to me, nor that I was a classic victim of it.

The police were not interested in the truth or new laws to protect people like me. That was not for arrest or interview, that was for court, apparently. No one cares about the truth when there are targets to meet.

I lay on that slippery blue mat and sobbed for the unfairness of it all and fell asleep. Woken up yet again to make sure I hadn't found some genius way to kill myself with the curtain, I started to slip again. A numbness settled over me. I needed that.

Over the next few hours, more and more women and girls were brought in and placed in cells around mine- drunk, rowdy and angry, the whole place got really noisy, so sleep was not an option.

I began to feel at home. I hadn't slept properly for years now- I knew I was there for the next 3 nights and now I was a criminal, I might as well behave like one.

Most of the other cellmates were in on domestics too. Arguing with partners outside the pub or fighting in the street. Unlike me, they were broad Glaswegian and drunk (or high) and very, very aggressive, shouting at each other through the cell doors and demanding water, the doctor or food.

The three days in the cells dragged on, but in the end, at 5 am on the Monday morning, I was showered and ready for court. Not even nervous, handcuffed and seat belt fastened in my little booth on the Rim-Bus, I sang along under my breath to Clyde radio and looked out of the window at the sunrise as we headed towards the city.

In time, 2 of the 3 allegations were dropped due to lack of sufficient evidence and witnesses not bothering to show up, but the one regarding Sinead stuck and stuck like gum to a shoe. They wanted to make an example of me. Warned that if I dared demand a trial rather than plead guilty instead, I would be more likely to face a jail term, notwithstanding the complete lack of offences prior. I sensed something off with it and still suspect some sort of back-stage bargaining. The Judge was incredibly harsh considering I had never threatened Sinead or even met her or attended anywhere I knew I could meet her. She clearly didn't understand that all of the nasty wording mentioned in the witness statements was actually not illegal as it is not unlawful to rant and rave on a private Facebook page. She hadn't clicked that it was odd many of my messages and posts were demanding WE or I be "left alone" nor that Sinead could only see my page if she was proactively looking for dirt. The judge didn't understand that a stalked person feeling "traumatised" by my contact would simply block me or even change her number… However, indeed I had sent messages and sent too many, so facing up to what I did, I pled guilty. The 3-month tag actually rather suited me- people thought it was a pedometer and by the time I received the conviction, my mental health was so bad I barely left the house anyway.

Richard and I have had another week together but it's not working for me now- he's got lazy and selfish. The love eyes I liked a month ago are blank, red-rimmed and stoned. His mad ex is still calling and texting, demanding he "go to the shops" for her or meet her to "talk".

Only this morning I laid down the law; "watching you pander to your ex and falling asleep in the afternoon, off your nut on whatever your taking, is just a bit too fucking familiar to me, Richard. Man up, or do one." He stared at me blankly so I made the decision for him. I bought myself my own dog that very same day. I called her Chance because quite frankly I was sick of giving other people chances and thought it was about time I gave myself one.

At some point over the next few days, Richard's mad ex and a friend started to send me abusive messages and threats.

Enraged by the content of these badly-spelt and rather vicious unwarranted messages, I fought back. Relentlessly, I mocked their spelling, lack of vocabulary and the rather vile profile picture attached to the Facebook account the abuse and threats are coming from.

"Come to the park. You're getting it, you old bag," comes another message. It's now 4 am. This has gone on for the last 3 hours.

I reply "No bitches, you're coming here. I'll put the kettle on skanks- see you soon!" I send a follow-up message with my full address including postcode in case their junkie bikes have a satnav. Fifteen minutes later, my buzzer went. Dressed in denims, a hoodie and my trusty green Converse, I waited in the dark of my flat for them. I knew they had come to attack me at my own home so felt it was fair enough I gave them a fight. I heard whispering and decided it was about time I defended myself to animals, like an animal. "Let's get her" one voice said "aye. I'm going to mess her face up" the other voice said.

Before she could even bang on the door and wake my children up, I swept the door open and I high kicked her twice in the face. As she screamed for help and her friend ran away, I tried to drag her into the darkness of my flat. Just to talk, of course. Sadly, I tore her sleeve off her bright yellow hoody so she escaped. Just for good measure I threw my son's bike at the pair of them as murder plot against me foiled, they scuttled away.

I heard the next day I heard that they told Richard a gang attacked them in the park. I kept the grubby yellow sleeve and stuffed it with socks for Chance to chew.

In the spiral of self-destruction and the Narc infection, I added yet more dark behaviours in. As soon as I found out that Richard had cheated on me with crazy big-burd, I slipped deeper into bad behaviours.

I became extremely promiscuous and not particularly fussy. A jump from one dark place, well, to frankly another.

Mid-June 2016

Social services just left. They made a flying visit last September after Jonathan was arrested, and knowing I had children, darkened my door again today, as it's now a few days since I was charged with my first offence regarding Sinead. Slamming the door behind them, I realised the workers were completely untrained in emotional abuse and certainly narcissistic abuse. No one asked me why or how my life suddenly seemed to get so messed up.

Social workers should have spent more time with me, probing why suddenly I was an offender for the first time, at not yet 36 years old. Why out of nowhere in June 2016, I was arrested for committing a "horrendous crime against another woman I hadn't even met".

Why I was so thin. Why I had so little confidence that I had allowed him back into my bed, my home, my life. Why I kept saying over and over it was "just a blip" and he "needed help"? The social workers should have looked at me, my lovely home, my long professional career and wondered why now I suddenly had a rubbish job cooking part time in a pub & adored a wild, addicted, abusive, criminal partner.

They should have spoken to the school and they would have been told this previously bubbly nicely-presented mum often looked tearful, drawn, distracted and traumatised. They should have dug deeper into Jonathan's background of criminality, especially regarding women and addictions.

I should've been told that he had several other domestic abuse convictions and that many other convictions featured violence and relapses in addictions.

That first social services visit in September 2015 had been a possible open door for me to escape him many months before he finally sent me over the edge. I would suggest social workers should have a tick list for emotional abuse and ideally narcissistic abuse to go through when they visit domestic abuse victims. They don't do anything like this, and it's letting people like me fall through the cracks.

Note: Domestic Abuse is still a criminal act, even if you are no longer with your Narc- you must report it.

For me the "The 22 Question Toxicity Test" would read:

1. Do you find yourself making your partner a priority over your own needs?
2. Do you find yourself making your partner a priority over your child/rens needs?
3. Have you missed appointments or occasions when your partner has upset you or hurt you?
4. Have you struggled to eat or sleep more than once a month due to your partner s behaviours?
5. Would you say the relationship is equal in that your partner looks after you and shows you he/she cares as much as you care for them?
6. Has your income and/or expenditure been affected by your partner's behaviours?
7. Do you find that your life is up and down with emotional upsets more than it is quiet and calm?
8. Does your partner have a series of broken relationships (and children) behind him/her that are negative with a lot of difficulty in the present affecting your relationship?
9. Do you find yourself questioning your own perception and reality because your partner tells you that one thing is true but you feel or KNOW it's not?
10. Do you find that you have to make excuses for your partner and that he/she says everyone is to blame rather than they are?

11. Does your partner take responsibility for situations and make efforts to amend them? Do his actions speak louder than words, for example?
12. Does your partner regularly go in moods or abandon you then return to the home or the relationship making promises that it won't happen again, but it does? A lot.
13. Does your partner have addictions to any of these- sex, drugs, alcohol, gambling, shopping or anything that creates a rush or distraction for them from "real life"?
14. Do you often feel as though this person has different personalities for different situations and that perhaps only you and his/her exes have seen the worst of those personalities over and above the other people in his/her life?
15. Do you find yourself doing things sexually and/or socially that you haven't done before? For example, are you a different person for your partner and have you overstepped boundaries or personal rules you had in place before you met them? Extreme sexual acts, drugs etc.
16. Does this person sometimes behave cold, detached and as though you are not of value to them? You can cry or beg but they simply refuse to budge until THEY are ready.
17. Is life a hamster wheel... a pattern of ways in which you are treated good and bad that seems like it has gone on for more than 3 months?
18. Do you find you're constantly analysing your partner's behaviours and language and trying to make sense of things in an obsessive way-googling mental illnesses, seeking ways to keep your partner happier and calm for longer periods?
19. Do you find that yourself (or other people) are targets for inappropriate levels of bile and rage when they dare cross the Narc, reject them or challenge their ego in some way?
20. Do you watch your ex and see them become totally different people (tailored to suit the new partner) in each relationship and is each person "the one" and "better" than you?
21. Does your partner still cling to past hurts or shame from being with you and cast it up to hurt/humiliate you- even

though you are not together they are still "going on" about 2,3,4 years ago?

22. Does your ex seem to stay in contact (or make contact out of the blue) regularly to gain fuel from you? Random invitations to coffee, his/her place or simply to have sex?

Throughout my time with Niall, I would've answered yes to several of these questions. Narcissism manifests in many ways depending on the "recipe" of toxic ingredients, for example, the person's upbringing, intellect and family/lifestyle situation.

I would say he would score highly on the Narcissist scale, but I have to admit, one trait he lacks is apathy towards our 8-year-old son- he is extremely focused and generous with him, although he hasn't had so much as a conversation with his 2step-sons (who took his name) since the day he left our home.

Niall also cares very much about his work and doing a good job for his clients. I don't know for sure if he is a Narcissist but the abuse he has exposed me to fits the NPD Abuse red flags in far too many ways to have been omitted from this book.

However, of course with Jonathan, I would've answered vehemently yes to many of these questions probably as soon as 6 months in. Maybe sooner.

Today

Today, life is far improved! In the spirit of honesty, I am not yet completely healed and feel perhaps I never will be. That is the power and danger of relationships with Narcs; they change you forever. Accepting this fact is empowering though!

Accepting you are forever different and scarred is very important in the overall healing process. Accepting your dark and sometimes, embarrassing actions when you were dealing with a Narcissist is very important. We all have light and shade in our personalities and understanding them, self-evaluating yourself is very enlightening! Knowing your demons helps you manage them. Denial and fear are both emotions that stop personal growth and can hinder positive outcomes.

So, what happened to me after I realised, I'd dated the Devil? To try and organise what had happened to me, I started writing this book. A book I would have bought myself!

Yeah, I admit it... I did start it as a sort of "fuck you" to him and his cohorts, but that sense of revenge quickly dissipated when I realised, I was still letting my disgust towards my haters rule my thoughts and affect my ambitions.

Once I batted away the "Vengeful Jiminy Cricket" on my left shoulder, the book bloomed into something not beautiful, but gutsy, honest and helpful, instead of blame-full and angry.

As I wrote (and listened to 80s rock ballads, guzzling either gin or black coffee), I started to purge the feelings and thoughts that made me fall for such dangerous people and act like one myself!

As I edited (over and over and over again!), I realised that this book is not even really about me; it's about all Narc victims. Because he (and the other harmful people mentioned) has acted out this terrible play so consistently, they label themselves without realising it. They have become teachers on their own toxic behaviours and I can use this, and so can you!

As my true personality & hope, started to gradually grow back around Summer (2018), little tendrils of the "old, good me" and buds of a new, strong and resilient me tickled my consciousness and I gradually woke up. I still made some mistakes, oh boy yes! But I own them and I do try my best to be honest and open about these where I can.

Then this year (2019) started to see a much wider project than this book. It struck me like a scalding hot metal spoon to the back of my neck, (d'ya get what I did there!?) I could use my professional skills, contacts and knowledge in community development and health improvement, as vessels to spread the messages in this book.

So what next?

I'm going to make sure the judicial system is fairer for victims, harsher on perpetrators (especially repeat offenders like my Jonathan), more open-minded and ready to listen to the "Why's" of criminality like mine. I'm want to make my (22-question Narc Abuse) checklist standard procedure when a social worker comes out to see you and your children when bad behaviours or criminality starts to play a part in a person's life.

A project running alongside this book (and future ones!) would educate, inform and support people who are struggling with a psychologically toxic person in their life, and also train the professionals here to help us. I'm prolific on LinkedIn and gradually getting my other social media back, although I shall never use Facebook again! Well, I'm 90% sure I won't!

As a first stage, I have already created a series of learning modules on the red flags in this book and put myself out there to speak at events like conferences and training days. I'm working on delivering training to companies interested in the well-being and mental health of their staff, to enable them to have at least 1 person in the building every day to sit and discuss their concerns around toxic relationships.

I even had a (controversial!) epiphany about what bits are useful about Narcs! I've created some training sessions and consultation services around personality-mapping in large private companies to help them manage toxic bits and the good bits of a Narcissistic Person. You know the bad bits now, but the good or "handy" personality traits can be harnessed and used skilfully by a manager. These would be; the selfish drive to exceed expectations and show off, the determination to succeed and the undoubted ability to charm clients or buyers for example.

Book number two is germinating in my new, metallic, pink laptop right now! This time a part- fictional book (again to educate) on catfishing, online dating, spousal rape/spiking and strong women with dark secrets. The best bit is when the Narc gets murdered, but I won't tell you whodunnit.... I've called it "The Monster in the Bed"- Catchy huh!?

Full of drive, passion and determination, I'm going to make good of my bad experiences and awful mistakes and make no apologies for holding my head high and wearing my heart on my sleeve.

Oh! Wait...don't go! One last thing... remember the phone number I noted down that awful night in September 2015? The one with no name attached to it and he called it twice but was ignored? Well... I typed it into WhatsApp 15 months later and messaged the person. Would you believe, I wasn't even shocked or upset to discover it was another "me"?! She was a (well-hidden) 3rd girl he was seeing right through 2013 and well into 2014. Yeah, I know... gross. She too had gone on to work through his damage and learn about Narcissistic Abuse because like me, and like all other victims, her journey with him followed ALL my red flags you've read about here.

We've remained friends and shared many sad, triggering conversations and although sometimes we get upset by each other's stories, we still find strength in the knowledge we were the ones who "escaped".

Listen to: Taylor Swift: "Look what you made me do"

Lightning Source UK Ltd.
Milton Keynes UK
UKHW010636300421
382900UK00001B/94